BECKETT, TECHNOLOGY AN

Critics have often focused on interiority in Beckett's works, privileging the mind over the body. In this new approach, the first sustained analysis of embodiment in Beckett's prose, drama and media works, Ulrika Maude argues that physical and sensory experiences are in fact central to the understanding of Beckett's writing. In innovative readings of sight, hearing, touch and movement in the full range of Beckett's works, Ulrika Maude uncovers the author's effort to shed light on embodied experience, paying attention to Beckett's interests in medicine and body-altering technologies such as prostheses. Through these material, bodily concerns Beckett explores wider themes of subjectivity and experience, interiority and exteriority, foregrounding the inextricable relationship between the body, the senses and the self. This important new study offers a novel approach to Beckett, one in which the body takes its rightful place alongside the mind.

ULRIKA MAUDE is a lecturer in English Literature at the University of Durham, UK.

BECKETT, TECHNOLOGY AND THE BODY

ULRIKA MAUDE

University of Durham

CAMBRIDGE UNIVERSITY PRESS

CAMBRIDGE UNIVERSITY PRESS
Cambridge, New York, Melbourne, Madrid, Cape Town, Singapore,
São Paulo, Delhi, Dubai, Tokyo, Mexico City

Cambridge University Press
The Edinburgh Building, Cambridge CB2 8RU, UK

Published in the United States of America by Cambridge University Press, New York

www.cambridge.org
Information on this title: www.cambridge.org/9780521181501

First published 2009
First paperback edition 2010

A catalogue record for this publication is available from the British Library

Library of Congress Cataloguing in Publication data
Maude, Ulrika.
Beckett, technology, and the body / Ulrika Maude.
p.   cm.
Includes bibliographical references and index.
ISBN 978-0-521-51537-5
1. Beckett, Samuel, 1906–1989—Criticism and interpretation.   2. Body, Human,
in literature.   3. Literature and technology.   4. Body, Human (Philosophy)
5. Literature and medicine.   1. Title.
PR6003.E282Z7736 2009
848'.91409–dc22
2008041172

ISBN 978-0-521-51537-5 Hardback
ISBN 978-0-521-18150-1 Paperback

For Shamus

Contents

Illustrations

Acknowledgements

This book has benefited from the support and encouragement of a number of people. My greatest intellectual debt is to Steven Connor and Lawrence Rainey, who read and commented on early versions of this work. Derek Attridge and Andrew Gibson have also offered valuable feedback, as have the anonymous readers at Cambridge University Press. I have discussed several of the ideas here with my dear friend Gerald Doherty, who first taught me as an undergraduate, and continues to be inspirational. My gratitude and thanks also go to Ray Ryan at Cambridge University Press. His encouragement and guidance have been invaluable. I am lucky, also, to have benefited from the friendly expertise and help of Maartje Scheltens and Christopher Feeney.

The Beckett community has provided much support. In particular, I would like to thank Chris Ackerley, Garin Dowd, Matthew Feldman, Stan Gontarski, James Knowlson, Mark Nixon, John Pilling, Laura Salisbury and Shane Weller, who have all directly contributed to this project in various ways. Many others have offered incisive feedback at conferences and various gatherings, and Rónán McDonald, Elizabeth Barry, Louis Armand, Matthew Feldman and Erik Tonning invited me to give papers and participate in discussions that helped shape the project.

Jörg Hucklenbroich and Stephan Spering at Südwestrundfunk in Stuttgart offered me exceptionally generous and friendly research support, which opened up new areas of thought. Both have also tirelessly answered queries. I am immensely grateful to them for their help. Warm thanks are also due to Jane Maxwell at Trinity College Library Dublin, and, as ever, to Mark Nixon at the Beckett International Foundation at Reading. Edward Beckett kindly granted me permission to quote from unpublished manuscripts, and Stan Gontarski generously allowed me to reproduce an image of his direction of *What Where*. Thanks are also due to Südwestrundfunk, Stuttgart for permission to reproduce an image from *Nacht und Träume*. Extracts from Samuel Beckett's letters to

Thomas MacGreevy and from his manuscripts and notebooks held at Trinity College Dublin, the University of Reading and Südwestrundfunk Stuttgart are reproduced by kind permission of the Estate of Samuel Beckett, care of Rosica Colin Limited, London.

Early versions of parts of chapters 1, 4 and 6 have previously appeared in *Journal of Beckett Studies*, *Samuel Beckett Today/Aujourd'hui*, *European Joyce Studies* and Richard Lane's edited collection, *Beckett and Philosophy* (Palgrave, 2002). The publishers are gratefully acknowledged.

I also owe a debt of gratitude to my colleagues at the University of Durham, especially to my close, wonderful friend Corinne Saunders, who has encouraged me in every possible way, and proved an excellent collaborator on projects that span the medieval to the modern. I would also like to thank the brilliant Patricia Waugh for her friendship and support. The Department of English Studies and the Faculty Research Fund at the University of Durham have financed several trips to archives and conferences, as well as assisted with costs for permissions.

My parents, Helena and George Maude, have shown enthusiasm and interest in the project, and offered good-humoured encouragement in its completion. My greatest debt of gratitude is to Shamus Smith. This book is dedicated to him.

Introduction

Samuel Beckett's writing foregrounds the body in both representational and textual ways. This can be evidenced in the careful attention his work devotes to sensory perception, most notably the experiences of seeing, hearing and touching. Equally striking is Beckett's emphasis on different forms of movement in his work, whether voluntary, such as walking, limping and crawling, or involuntary, such as shaking and trembling. Beckett's work also problematises the neat distinction between these two types of movement, introducing others, such as tics, that reside in the more indeterminate space between the two. Everyday bodily functions, furthermore, seldom appear normal or unconditioned in Beckett's writing. Frequent, too, is the maiming and fragmentation of the body. These effects are paired and further intensified by textual ones, such as the broken syntax and rhythm of Beckett's performative prose.

This book assays the manifestations of embodiment in Beckett's prose, drama and media plays. It parts company with early readings of Beckett's work, in which the body is largely reduced to an impediment. It also acknowledges that in poststructuralist approaches, the significance of the body often mutates into signification. Instead, this book negotiates a third stance, a materialist one, located at the intersection of textual, phenomenological and cultural concerns.

Although the body in Beckett's writing has received critical attention, crucial aspects of its pronounced status in Beckett's work have remained unaddressed. The first wave of Beckett scholarship, characterised by the work of critics such as Hugh Kenner and Martin Esslin, read Beckett as a transcendental writer who subscribed to a Cartesian dualism. The prominence of the body and its decrepitude was accredited to the body's inherent otherness; what truly mattered in Beckett was the mind and its capacity to move beyond matter. One of the most famous examples of this view is Hugh Kenner's discussion of 'The Cartesian Centaur' in *Molloy*.[1] Kenner argues that the body in *Molloy* is likened to the man-made machine, namely the bicycle which, like the body, enables the characters' arduous motility. Locomotion, however, is a painful and laboured process because of the imperfection of the body, which pales in the light of the superiority of the rationally constructed bicycle. The body and its surroundings, in this view, are read as little more than obstacles. To subject the abundance of bodily experiences in Beckett's work to such a one-dimensional reading, however, is to offer a reductive analysis of Beckett's writing. Such a reading leaves unanswered the striking instances in the *oeuvre* that invest value in embodied experience. It similarly ignores Beckett's repeated, albeit often reluctant, realization of the unsustainable nature of transcendental thought. Nor does Kenner's reading respond to the centrality of sensory perception in Beckett's work; rather, it fails to take account of those instances in the *oeuvre* that evoke a sense of wonder amidst an austere world view.

The last two decades have seen a shift away from purely metaphysical concerns, to what could broadly be characterised as poststructuralist approaches to Beckett's work. This second wave of Beckett criticism has been better equipped to tackle the complexity and duplicity of Beckett's writing. It has inaugurated brilliant new ways of approaching the question of subjectivity in Beckett's work. In addressing the author's textual foregrounding of the body, poststructuralist critics have brought attention to its prominence in Beckett's *oeuvre*. However, these readings have often shared a poststructuralist bias, which has emphasized the discursively produced body at the expense of the material, fleshly one. Yet the prominence of the maimed and visceral body in Beckett's work clearly signals the author's attempt to move beyond the confines of discourse.

What has been written about less, is the persistence with which Beckett explores the very basics of bodily existence, those conditions that are already in swing before culture lays its mark on embodied identity, and that are thereafter modified and reshaped by its effects. If, as is sometimes suggested, it is the material body that forms the ultimate foundation of identity, by constituting that self that is both singular and, in its perpetual complexity and mutability, always plural and indecipherable, then it is Beckett more than any other writer who deals with this predicament in his work.

The last two decades have seen a proliferation of theoretical approaches to the body. Whether the focus has been on gender, sexuality, textuality or any other bodily construct, books on different aspects of the topic have flooded the market. The prominence of theories that challenge rationality has played a crucial part in the heightened interest in the body. Some

critics even believe these theories have reversed the early humanist privileging of the mind. Poststructuralist thinkers, Michel Foucault at the
forefront, can indeed be said to have inaugurated the contemporary
interest in embodiment, by stressing the significance of the body in their
discussion of knowledge, power and the regulation of physical difference
and desire.

Although Foucault can be said to have initiated the current interest
in embodiment, the body in his work emerges as a discursively ordered
product of institutionalised knowledge and power.[2] The emphasis, rather
than being on the body itself, lies on discourse.[3] Similarly, post-Lacanian
feminism, in its anti-essentialist drive, has stressed the discursively produced nature of gender, exemplified in the work of theorists such as
Hélène Cixous and Luce Irigaray.[4] While my aim is not to refute the
importance or value of either of these influential theoretical standpoints,
one could argue that the body is often curiously neglected, if not absent,
in both. In what could broadly be characterised as poststructuralist
thought, the discursively produced body takes precedence over, if not ecli-
pses, the flesh. Put another way, the problem of representation is privileged
over experience. One of the salient characteristics of poststructuralist
accounts of embodiment, therefore, is the curious mutation of the significance of the body into the problem of the body as signification.

Foucault, however, inheriting the nineteenth-century stance of the
dandy, posits the individual body as the site of resistance to the regu-
larisation of disciplinary powers. As Anthony Giddens has suggested,
the body, in modernity, becomes a 'visible carrier of self-identity'.[5] It is
precisely the contemporary belief in embodied experience as the locus of
identity that also generates a proliferation of identity politics that stem
from different carnal standpoints, determined by considerations such as
gender, sexuality, ethnicity or social class.

In cultural-materialist theory, the body becomes a site of construction
that responds to the 'demands of rapidly changing cultural norms and
values'.[6] One dimension of this approach to embodiment is the emphasis
on cultural practices, and their significance to the construction of identity. Theorists such as Jameson and Baudrillard have stressed the shaping
force of culture on the body, but in their thinking, 'it is the image of the
body rather than the body as such that is central to identity. The body is
seen as being saturated with cultural signs or as becoming merely a series
of cultural quotations.'[7] Pierre Bourdieu is one of the few theorists to
have discussed the influence of cultural practices on the body itself. He
argues that the consumption habits of different social classes produce

bodies that differ in shape, size, weight, posture and health, as well as in mannerisms and gestures.[8] While Bourdieu's meditations on the body are compelling, little consideration is given to prereflective physicality. Cultural-materialist approaches, therefore, court the risk of presenting an 'over-socialized conception' of embodiment: the phenomenology of the body and its sensuous potentiality are too lightly overlooked.[9]

In Beckett's writing, prereflective physicality becomes progressively more prominent.[10] This coincides with a gradual stripping down of cultural codes, in what can be seen as a form of phenomenological reduction or bracketing, evidenced, for instance, in the austerity of Beckett's settings. Through a discussion of the manifestations of physical suffering and pleasure, different forms of perception and the significance of motility and technology in Beckett's writing, this book will question three critical myths about Beckett's work: namely, that it tends towards disembodiment, silence and stasis, none of which, in this reading, is ultimately advocated in Beckett's work.

Although the question of gender in Beckett's *oeuvre* is a pertinent one, it remains beyond the scope of this study. I have chosen not to address the topic, because a cursory discussion would not do justice to its complexity. In my reading, Beckett moves from an initial misogyny, particularly prominent in *Dream of Fair to Middling Women* (1932; published 1992) and *Murphy* (1938), and still overtly present in *Molloy* (1951) and *Malone Dies* (1951), to a more universalist, albeit not gender-indifferent view.[11] This shift can be detected in *All That Fall* (1956), a play which sports Beckett's first female protagonist, Maddy Rooney. It can be evidenced most clearly in such late works as the stage play, *Rockaby* (1980), and the novel, *Ill Seen Ill Said* (1982), with their sympathetic portrayal of female protagonists.[12] The question of masculinity in Beckett's work is an underresearched area, which merits substantial and sustained analysis of its own.[13]

In order to address the basic modalities of embodiment manifest in Beckett's writing, I begin by turning to phenomenology and, more specifically, to Maurice Merleau-Ponty (1908–61). *Phenomenology of Perception*, Merleau-Ponty's major work, constitutes a unique consideration of embodiment, and one that has not been surpassed by subsequent thinkers.[14] Published in 1945, in the aftermath of the Second World War, *Phenomenology of Perception* argues that, instead of being an object in the world, the body, by constituting not only the subject's point of view, but subjectivity itself, forms the foundation of all forms of human experience. Merleau-Ponty stressed what he called the 'primacy' of perception, foregrounding the importance of prereflective experience to our encounter with the world.

My discussion of embodiment in Beckett's work hence opens with an overview of Merleau-Ponty's theory of the incarnate subject. Merleau-Ponty not only worked in Paris contemporaneously with Samuel Beckett; he was also situated at the École Normale Supérieure when Beckett was working there as *lecteur* from 1928 to 1930.[15] According to Mme Merleau-Ponty and Beckett's publisher, John Calder, Merleau-Ponty's library contained several of Beckett's works.[16] Lois Oppenheim also points out that Beckett's friend, Georges Duthuit, was a close acquaintance of Merleau-Ponty's, and may have functioned as 'a conduit' between the two men.[17] It is, furthermore, possible that Beckett's pupil at the École Normale Supérieure, Jean Beaufret (1907–82), a philosophy student and future expert on Heidegger, was familiar with the young Merleau-Ponty.[18] Both, after all, were to become advocates of phenomenology.[19] During this time, the young Beckett often discussed philosophy with 'the Beausprit', as the author called him in his letters to Thomas MacGreevy.[20] Alberto Giacometti, whom both Beckett and Merleau-Ponty knew, is yet another possible 'conduit' between the two men.[21] Most crucially, however, Beckett and Merleau-Ponty shared the intellectual climate of inter-war and post-war Paris. Although, therefore, we do not know whether Beckett read Merleau-Ponty's work and do know that Merleau-Ponty read Beckett's, my aim here is not to suggest that the one was influenced by the other, as much as to use Merleau-Ponty's work as an index or backdrop against which to illuminate central concerns in Beckett's writing. Merleau-Ponty's work, as we shall see, has at least this much in common with Beckett's writing: whereas Merleau-Ponty's *oeuvre* signals the first conscious effort in philosophy to bring the body to the forefront, Beckett's work can be read as one of the most serious inquiries of this kind in literature. The common denominator between the two writers is the concept of the phantom limb, which in the work of both authors is based on an idea of corporeal memory. I shall argue, therefore, that the work of Beckett and Merleau-Ponty shares several fundamental characteristics but, simultaneously, other crucial and profound discrepancies. Whilst, therefore, this book is not constructed around Beckett and Merleau-Ponty *per se*, the topic forms the focus of the first chapter; Merleau-Ponty's ideas will also be returned to in several subsequent chapters of this book.

The primary texts discussed in the first chapter are Beckett's extended essay on Proust, written in 1930, and his stage play *Krapp's Last Tape*, from 1958. Throughout this book, I will discuss works that have been considered central to the author's *oeuvre*, as well as others that have received less critical attention. The corpus includes Beckett's correspondence, manuscripts and notebooks, as well as his stage plays, novellas, film, prose fragments, radio plays, novels and television plays. I also discuss Beckett's critical writings as an index of his aesthetic preoccupations. With the exception of the early correspondence, notebooks and critical writings, the common denominator is the focus on Beckett's mature works, here understood to begin with the novellas, *First Love, The Expelled, The Calmative* and *The End*, written in 1946. In this reading, Beckett moves away from an initial Cartesianism, especially prominent in the novel *Murphy* (1938), albeit in the form of parody, to a more complex, yet at times reluctant, abandonment of dualism.[22] The mature and late works, in short, form Beckett's most intricate and intense investigation into issues of embodiment.

Much of Beckett's interest in the body manifests itself through an emphasis on different forms of sensory perception; this theme will form the topic of chapters 2, 3 and 4. Chapter 2 focuses on the importance of the visual dimension in Beckett's prose and *Film* (1964).[23] It begins with an overview of received Western notions of vision and rationality, followed by a discussion of Beckett's correspondence with his close friend, the poet and critic Thomas MacGreevy. The chapter also briefly addresses Beckett's critical writings. In both the letters and the critical works, Beckett reveals his preoccupation with the reorganization of perception in modern art which, in turn, is intricately connected with a re-evaluation of subjectivity. This discussion will be followed by a reading of two of Beckett's novellas, *The Calmative* and *The End* (1946), in which Beckett re-imagines the experience of seeing anew, in embodied and fallible terms, and further develops his investigation into the status of subjectivity. I close the chapter with a discussion of Beckett's *Film*, in which he explores the question of self-perception and stages his conclusions about sovereign subjectivity.

A number of early critics have discussed the importance of hearing in Beckett's work, arguing that sound functions as a marker of interiority in Beckett's writing. The focus of these readings, in other words, has been on the inner ear of the mind, rather than the embodied ear of flesh in Beckett's work. Beckett's writing, and modernist literature more generally, none the less, dedicates extraordinary attention to hearing and listening. This is no doubt at least partly due to the rapid development of various auditory technologies in the second half of the nineteenth century and the early decades of the twentieth, particularly in the period between 1875 and 1925. The telephone and the phonograph, for instance, were both invented in 1876. Although magnetic recorders, too, date from this period, tape recorders did not reach popular consumption until the mid 1950s; Beckett's work is the first to bring one on stage. Sound technologies, such as radio, gramophone, telephone and audiotape, in fact reconfigure our received notions of time and space. They hence have an important impact on the body and our understanding of its boundaries.

What has been overlooked, the third chapter will argue, is the special relevance the acoustic has to issues of embodiment in Beckett's writing. Unlike the proximity senses – namely touch, taste and, to some degree, smell – that ground the Beckettian subject in the body, hearing promises a certain expansion of corporeal boundaries. Sound, furthermore, is not only more expansive than the proximity senses; it also traverses obstacles that vision cannot overcome, transporting the subject across spatial and temporal confines. The transporting quality of sound in Beckett, however, does not free the subject from the grasp of its material, situated condition. On the contrary, through an analysis of four of Beckett's radio and stage plays, namely *All That Fall* (1956), *Embers* (1959), *Krapp's Last Tape* (1958) and *That Time* (1975), all of which make use of various auditory technologies, I argue that Beckett, showing an acute awareness of the complex phenomenology of sound, ultimately grounds the acoustic in an austere materialism. By virtue of its multispatiality and multi-temporality, made possible by various sound technologies, the acoustic, by doubling and remaking the subject, in fact serves only to augment and intensify the predicament of the body: Beckett's characters transgress spatial and temporal confines only to be rooted ever more firmly in the physical conditions of existence.

Chapter 4 focuses on the shorter prose fictions that Beckett wrote in the 1960s, namely *All Strange Away, Imagination Dead Imagine, Ping* and *The Lost Ones*. Critics have tended to view these texts, which are linked not only in imagery but also through their textual genetics, as allegories of the human condition or as parables of the authorial process. Closer scrutiny of them, however, reveals that they engage in a probing examination of the contradictory nature of perception and the embodied state of subjectivity. Through a systematic set of negations, marked by the abandonment of the first-person narrator, the privileging of gesture and posture over language and hearing and, most prominently, the priori-tising of the sense of touch over that of vision, these works question and undermine the primacy of the conceptual order, foregrounding exteriority and surface over interiority and depth. The narrating voice itself, through its application of conflicting and ultimately self-negating registers, becomes the locus merely of further doubt and uncertainty. The same can even be said of the persistently failing mathematics of the narrator. In short, the systematic interrogations and negations in the texts set in motion a vacillating dynamic between subjectivity and its dissolution.

The fifth chapter is dedicated to the prominence of different forms of motility in Beckett's work. The primary texts discussed figure amongst the most canonised in Beckett's *oeuvre*, namely the three novels of the Trilogy, *Molloy, Malone Dies* and *The Unnamable*, written in the late 1940s, and the stage play, *Waiting for Godot*, written between *Malone Dies* and *The Unnamable*. I shall focus on different modes of motion prominent in these works, whether voluntary, such as walking, rolling or crawling, or involuntary, such as twitching, convulsing and trembling. The chapter will also contain a consideration of the abject body, and the impact of the grotesque tradition on Beckett's writing. The bodies in Beckett, as a result of their abject and unruly nature, threaten the subject's autonomy, but for the very same reason, they remain stubbornly individuated.

The focus of the sixth and final chapter is on the impact of perceptual technologies on Beckett's work. New technologies are often conceptualized in relation to the human body, as prosthetic devices that function either as instances of organ- or sensory extension, or as forms of organ replacement, to make up for an individual deficiency or lack. Beckett, whose work foregrounds technology both in its media and as an actual presence, examines the manner in which new technologies change the way in which we see, hear and more generally perceive the world, producing in us a double-perception that differs from earlier modes of perceiving. Inventions such as Étienne-Jules Marey's chronophotography (1880s) and Wilhelm Röntgen's X-rays (1895) enhanced the human eye and appropriated scopic ideas of knowledge, whilst simultaneously underscoring the limitations and lack in human, embodied vision. In a number of his works, this chapter argues, Beckett stages the manner in which perceptual technologies, by being more objective, stark and 'reliable' than the human eye and ear, not only differ from but perhaps also liberate human perception from its association with rationality and objectivity, freeing it for sensuous, subjective and aestheticised perceptual experience. If technology, Beckett seems to suggest, does the quantifiable seeing and hearing for us, human perception is freed for qualitative sensory experience. Beckett's television plays, *Ghost Trio* and *... but the clouds ...*, the chapter argues, centre on the subjective, embodied, yearning human eye and ear.

Medical technologies form an important subcategory of perceptual technologies. The sixth chapter will close with a consideration of the impact of medical imaging techniques on Beckett's work. Beckett himself had first-hand experience of these techniques, having, for instance, undergone a series of X-rays and gruelling bronchoscopies in 1968. These technologies transgress the boundaries of interior and exterior, turning the body inside out, making us strange to ourselves. They also digitise and replicate the body, reproducing it as code or pixellated image. These two-dimensional and fragmented images that give the subject or physician an understanding of anatomy and physiological processes, 'frantic with corporeality', also virtualise the body, suggesting, often in problematic ways, its reconfiguration.[24] They hence participate in what Hal Foster has called 'the double logic of the prosthesis'.[25] I conclude with a consideration of instances of this tension in Beckett's late television plays, *Nacht und Träume* and *What Where*.

CHAPTER I

The body of memory

In recent years, several fine works on different aspects of embodiment have appeared in print. What many critical accounts of the body have had in common, however, has been a tendency to analyse the various facets of embodiment as effects of discourse. At its most extreme, this trend has not only eclipsed the material dimension of embodiment, but diminished the body itself to the status of a concept. As Bryan Turner has argued, 'despite all the references to pleasure and desire, a structuralist analysis of the body...ignores the phenomenology of embodiment.'[1] This trend has also had an impact on Beckett studies. While a number of critics have addressed Beckett's textual foregrounding of the body in striking and compelling ways, the role of the body as the complex and perpetually mutable basis of subjectivity in Beckett's writing has received less critical attention.

Despite the transcendentalist claims of early humanist readings of Beckett's work, critics now widely concur that the Beckettian characters' experience of the world is a markedly physical, bodily experience. Whether we are dealing with the prose or the drama, it is the body, rather than the *cogito*, that gives the characters assurance of their existence. In *Company* (1980), the narrated character is lying on his back in the dark, listening to a voice. He is aware of this 'by the pressure on his hind parts and by how the dark changes when he shuts his eyes and again when he opens them again'.[2] His existence, in other words, is determined and even brought about by tactile, visual and acoustic sensations. In *Footfalls*, we learn, through the female voice that narrates May's childhood conversation with her mother, that it is not enough for May merely to feel her existence through motion; May also needs to *hear* she exists, however faint the feet fall. When May, a moment earlier in the play, addresses her mother, the conversation, not surprisingly, centres around the mother's bodily needs: 'Would you like me to inject you again?...Would you like me to change your position again?...Straighten your pillows? Change your drawsheet?

Pass you the bedpan? The warmingpan? Dress your sores? Sponge you down?'[3] Much of the dramatic tension in Beckett's drama, as Pierre Chabert has pointed out, stems less from the psychological conflicts of conventional theatre than from the starkly physical conflicts of bodily existence.[4]

In literature, as in our own private experience, we notice the body – which in day-to-day life can acquire a peculiar transparency – more acutely when it troubles or delights us. The bodily experiences in Beckett's work, especially before the late prose, are often brought to the reader's or spectator's attention through the characters' difficulties in moving, in the falling, rolling, limping and crawling that recur in Beckett's writing. Similarly, Beckett foregrounds the body by making normal bodily functions, such as eating or excreting – Malone's '[d]ish and pot, dish and pot' – seldom appear normal or unconditioned in his work.[5] This said, however, we should not see Beckett's *oeuvre* as 'a portrait gallery of cripples', but rather as one of the most serious efforts in literature to bring the body to the forefront.[6]

There is, in other words, a distinction between being merely aware of the body and being compelled to pay conscious attention to it. Virginia Woolf argued in 1930 that 'literature does its best to maintain that its concern is with the mind; that the body is a sheet of plain glass through which the soul looks straight and clear, and, save for one or two passions such as desire and greed, is null, and negligible and non-existent.'[7] Woolf goes on to list an array of bodily experiences, such as 'heat and cold, comfort and discomfort, hunger and satisfaction, health and illness', and laments that 'of all this daily drama of the body there is no record'.[8] Beckett's work, along with the writing of his modernist peers, such as Joyce, however, forms an exception, and Beckett's interest in Proust, in whose works bodily experiences also play a significant role, may in part stem from this factor. Deirdre Bair, in her biography of Beckett, discusses Beckett's interest in the French author Jules Renard (1864–1910), whose ability to study himself and in particular whose approach to 'natural functions' Beckett admired: '"He always speaks so well about chewing and pissing and that kind of thing"', Bair reports Beckett to have said to his friend Georges Pelorson, and points out the similarities between Renard's diaries, in which Beckett was particularly interested, and *Malone Dies*.[9] In *How It Is* (1964), first published in French as *Comment c'est* in 1961, Beckett's concern for the body is summed up in his narrator's mention of the great needs that will eventually fail him: 'the need to move on the need to shit and vomit and the other great needs all my great categories of being'.[10]

In theory, Beckett's interest in the body and the physical world in general coincides with the trend in phenomenology, represented more by Heidegger and Merleau-Ponty than by Husserl and Sartre, that called for a reorientation from the transcendental to the phenomenology of everydayness.[11] Although Heidegger acknowledged the corporeality of our existence, together with the important point of the body's temporality, it was Merleau-Ponty who, with his theory of the incarnate subject, brought the body to the centre of philosophical interrogation.

In order to shed light on his theory of the incarnate subject, Merleau-Ponty, in *Phenomenology of Perception*, first published in 1945 and written during the Second World War, introduces the phenomenon of the phantom limb. If the amputee is consciously aware of the loss of one of his limbs, Merleau-Ponty asks, why, as is well known, does he still feel pain in the missing limb, or even occasionally attempt to use it.[12] More baffling still is the fact that an emotion or a circumstance similar to the one that caused the loss of the limb habitually creates a phantom limb in subjects who previously had no sensation of one.[13]

In order to find a solution to this paradox, and simultaneously expose the inadequacy of both rational and empirical philosophy to address the problems of embodiment, Merleau-Ponty introduces the concept of the habitual body or body image, his idea of 'an organic thought through which the relation of the "psychic" to the "physiological" becomes conceivable'.[14] For although psychology, at first glance, would appear to offer the most obvious solution to the phantom limb, at least in the cases in which the personal emotions, history and memories of the patient function as the triggering element, it fails to explain the disappearance of the phantom limb when the nerves of the former limb leading to the brain are severed. Instead, then, an explanation is needed of how psychic factors and physiological conditions merge into one. For the phenomenon, as these factors indicate, is neither the result of a mere *cogitatio* nor the simple consequence of objective causality.

The phantom limb appears to be connected to a refusal of mutilation, but bodily deficiency can only continue to be evaded if the subject is aware of the situations in which he faces a risk of having to encounter the disability, just as the subject of psychoanalysis, Merleau-Ponty adds, knows precisely what he does not want to face. Otherwise the repressed issue could not be avoided with such success. We refuse mutilation, says Merleau-Ponty, because a part of us remains 'committed to a certain physical and inter-human world', and continues to tend towards this world despite disablement and handicaps.'[15]

To have a phantom arm is to remain open to all the actions of which the arm alone is capable; it is to retain the practical field which one enjoyed before mutilation. The body is the vehicle of being in the world, and having a body is, for a living creature, to be intervolved in a definite environment, to identify oneself with certain projects and be continually committed to them.[16]

The world however, not only conceals but also reveals to the subject his or her deficiency, for we are conscious of the world through our bodies. When our habitual world arouses in us intentions that we can no longer fulfill, by presenting to us objects which appear as utilisable to limbs that we no longer have, we become aware of our disability precisely to the degree that we are ignorant of it. We bury our intentions in objects which, however, exist externally to our intentions, although they may exist for us only to the extent that they arouse in us volitions or thoughts.[17] Beckett shows an awareness of this issue in many of his works, although the relationship his characters have to intentionality is less affirmative and more complex than Merleau-Ponty's account of the matter.[18] In *Malone Dies*, for instance, Malone's inventory of possessions includes '[o]ne boot, originally yellow, I forget for which foot'.[19] Malone, of course, is incapable of walking. The recurring bicycles that the characters are unable to ride and the chairs that they can no longer sit on or the food their bodies no longer digest, function in a similar manner, accentuating the bodily disabilities of the characters. It is precisely through the contradiction between our intention on the one hand, and our actual ability on the other, that Merleau-Ponty comes to the conclusion that our bodies consist of two distinct layers: that of our habit-body and that of our actual, present body. A similar bodily layering or non-coincidence, as we shall later see, also figures prominently in Beckett's writing.

A phantom limb, therefore, is not a mere recollection but is, in fact, the same arm that has been lost to the subject, 'that same arm, lacerated by shell splinters, its visible substance burned or rotted somewhere, which appears to haunt the present body without being absorbed into it. The imaginary arm is, then, like repressed experience, a former present which cannot decide to recede into the past.'[20] We are dealing with a bodily memory, an organic intelligence, whose applicability reaches far beyond the experiences of mutilation. We are faced with a phenomenon akin to repression, in which a traumatic occurrence leaves the subject forever trapped in a past future which is no longer accessible to him. Merleau-Ponty says,

One present among all presents...acquires an exceptional value; it displaces the others and deprives them of their value as authentic presents. We continue to be the person who once entered on this adolescent affair, or the one who once lived in this parental universe. New perceptions, new emotions even, replace the old ones, but this process of renewal touches only the content of our experience and not its structure. Impersonal time continues its course, but personal time is arrested.[21]

Through the two bodily layers, the habitual and the present body, the body is, in fact, the meeting place of the past, the present and the future, because it extends the past into the bodily present, simultaneously containing the outlines of the future that the body anticipates.[22] Bodily experience therefore cannot be reduced to introception occurring at a particular moment of the present. Neither is bodily temporality reducible to the order of objective time, as the experience of the phantom limb shows us.

According to Merleau-Ponty, the subject, 'at the dawn of perception', begins to outline the '"indeterminate horizons" which signal the emergence of a world for us'.[23] The temporal structure of our body enables us to 'carry this primitive acquisition of horizons along, so that a more determinate world of objects can begin to exist'.[24] The world is therefore not ready-made but rather built up in a dialectical movement between the incarnate subject and the world. A case in point are habits: to learn to ride a bicycle or to play an instrument or to become accustomed to a particular item of clothing, 'is to be transplanted into them, or conversely, to incorporate them into the bulk of our own body'.[25] We are not dealing with intellectual analysis or with a mechanical recording of impressions but rather with the 'bodily comprehension of a motor significance', a bodily knowledge which reveals the body as an expressive space, with a language of kinds of its own.[26] The body, says Merleau-Ponty, 'is our general medium for having a world'.[27] Through its different operations, whether they be merely life-sustaining, expressive in themselves, or whether 'the meaning aimed at cannot be achieved by the body's natural means' and acquires an instrument, our bodily experiences force us to 'acknowledge an imposition of meaning which is not the work of a universal constituting consciousness'.[28] This is what Merleau-Ponty refers to as 'a new meaning of the word "meaning"'.[29]

The notion of the habitual body or body image, then, is our intuitive sense of our bodies, which makes everyday functioning possible. It is the body's own sense of occupying space, without which the most simple actions would become impossible.[30] Put in phenomenological terms, the present body functions as an object in an intentional act of consciousness, whereas the body image or the habitual body involves the idea of pre-intentionality.[31]

The bodily memory, habits and motor capacity that Merleau-Ponty discusses seem exceptionally relevant if we consider not only one particular work by Beckett but the whole Beckettian canon. Indeed, in trying to recall individual features and events, especially in the different prose works by Beckett, the reader easily becomes uncertain and muddled up about characters, character-traits and events and their correspondence to particular works. Certain character-traits, such as old age and decrepitude, repeat themselves throughout Beckett's works. Moreover, other identifying markers such as greatcoats, hats, boots, crutches, bicycles and stones (to mention but a few Beckettian props) are endemic to the works. Frequent, too, is the maiming of the body, which varies in degree from work to work. It is almost as if the whole Beckettian *oeuvre* had its own body image, into which certain articles of clothing and certain orthopaedic accessories were as a rule incorporated.

Merleau-Ponty's discussion of the body image and of bodily memory seems both strangely to coincide with and problematically to differ from Beckett's discussion of involuntary memory in his book on Proust, written in 1930 and published a year later.[32] The stance Beckett takes towards habit forms the first problem, for the notion of habit has profoundly negative connotations in Beckett's *Proust*, as a result of the numbing effect habit has on perception. Habit, Beckett says, goes hand in hand with voluntary memory in Proust's work, which is an inadequate instrument of evocation, for it is a construct of the intellect; uniform, colourless, distanced; devoid of feelings of anxiety.[33] Voluntary memory, in its bluntness, fails miserably to evoke the past, for we can only truly remember 'what has been registered by our extreme inattention'.[34] By this, Beckett is referring to experiences that occur outside the realm of habit and conscious attention, those experiences 'accumulated slyly and painfully and patiently', that form 'the essence of ourselves'.[35] Merleau-Ponty's habitual body or body image, however, in spite of the body's association with habit, is both constituted and functions on a prereflective realm, before the separation of subject and object; before, that is, the subject's entry into an objective, or what later theorists would call symbolic, realm. It is the present body for Merleau-Ponty, instead of the habitual one, that pertains to the realm of the objective world governed by the intellect. In phenomenological terms, it is the present body that functions as an intentional object, thereby rendering the difference between Merleau-Ponty and Beckett terminological rather than ideological.

Involuntary memory, says Beckett, cannot be evoked at will, but is 'provided by the physical world, by some immediate and fortuitous act of perception'.[36] For Proust as for Beckett, it seems, this kind of memory alone can bring back the past in full. Here, however, we are faced with a second problem, for Beckett's account of the subject's relation to involuntary memory is itself contradictory. On the one hand, Beckett seems to find in Proust's involuntary memory proof of the non-repeatability of the subject; on the other, involuntary memory seems to provide the very possibility of 'retrieving the past self as it was'.[37] The conflict here seems to be between a continuous and in some sense unified self and a deeper belief in the discontinuous nature of subjectivity, in the individual seen, as Beckett puts it, as 'a succession of individuals'.[38]

If we return, once more, to Merleau-Ponty's discussion of the phantom limb, we find the conflict between the continuity and discontinuity of individuality in the very phenomenon of the phantom limb itself. The body, in Merleau-Ponty, functions as a register of experiences, carrying the past within it, and therefore providing the subject with a sense of continuity, while simultaneously, in its dynamic aspect, differing from that past. The phantom limb, therefore, functions as an involuntary memory of kinds, one that cannot be consciously willed away, but rather forms part of the incarnate subject's identity, while yet being lost on an objective, intentional level.

Merleau-Ponty himself discusses Proust's ideas of intellectual or voluntary memory, the mere description of the past, consisting only of characteristics rather than full structures of experience. Authentic memory, Merleau-Ponty says, involves our bodies in a past experience, evokes in us emotions and sensations which we have difficulty facing and yet are not willing to leave behind.[39] In Beckett's *Proust*, bodily perception, instead of isolated thought, is indeed the triggering factor of involuntary memory, for the first occurrence of it is brought about by the 'long-forgotten taste of a madeleine steeped in an infusion of tea'.[40] Further examples given by Beckett include smells, noises, visual perceptions and even the action of stooping, a motor activity that the body is aware of essentially through the sense of touch.[41] Beckett's treatment of involuntary memory is synaesthetic, for it is triggered by one form of sensory perception, but involves them all.[42]

Beckett's work itself abounds in examples of embodied memory, in characters caught in past experiences that keep re-emerging like phantoms throughout the canon. Memories in Beckett, just as in Proust, furthermore, are evoked through the whole gamut of the senses. *Krapp's Last Tape*, essentially a memory play, written in English in 1958, will here serve as an example of the much wider functioning of embodied memory throughout Beckett's writing.

Krapp's Last Tape is the story of an old man who, once a year, on his birthday, records a tape in which he narrates the events of the past year. When we encounter Krapp, it is his sixty-ninth birthday, and he is about to record another tape. Instead, however, Krapp ends up listening to a recording made on his thirty-ninth birthday: 'Just been listening to that stupid bastard I took myself for thirty years ago, hard to believe I was ever as bad as that.'[43] As Beckett explained to Alan Schneider, the American director of his plays: 'Krapp has nothing to talk to but his dying self and nothing to talk to him but his dead one.'[44] When Krapp returns to recording the new tape, there is little left for him to say. The spooling tape recorder on stage brings to mind Beckett's observation on time in *Proust*: 'The individual is the seat of a constant process of decantation, decantation from the vessel containing the fluid of future time, sluggish, pale and monochrome, to the vessel containing the fluid of past time, agitated and multicoloured by the phenomena of its hours.'[45]

If, as has been suggested, the principal activity in *Krapp's Last Tape* is the act of listening, then we should begin by noting that two different kinds of sound figure in the play. On the one hand we have the sounds that originate in the actual physical and temporal location of the stage, such as the clatter of the metal tins in which the tapes are kept; the thump of the dictionary and the ledger when they are banged on the table; 'the clink of the glass against the bottle' when Krapp goes backstage for a drink; and last but not least 'the noises of the body itself: Krapp's breath, panting slightly, . . . his shivers, the sounds of mastication, of throwing up, his sighs of satisfaction or coughing when he drinks; the sounds of Krapp moving on the stage'.[46] The noises and sounds that have their origin in stage activities, in other words, function as markers of the present tense in the play. Krapp's past, on the other hand, is signalled by the voices and other sounds, such as the laughter, that we hear on the tapes. A sonorous tension is thus created between the present and the past, bringing not only Krapp, but the audience, too, to a close perceptual awareness of the different tenses in operation.[47] This temporal effect is further intensified by the stage direction, '*looks at his watch*', which is repeated three times in the course of the one-hour play.[48]

The different acoustic 'scenes' in *Krapp's Last Tape*, as Beckett acknowledged, engage both Krapp and the audience with varying degrees of intensity. In 'Suggestions for T.V. Krapp', a list of notes for a then prospective television version of the play, Beckett refers to the episodes as having different 'listening values' that he grades 'Low', 'Intermediate' and 'High', the first being of little impact: 'All references to health and work.'[49] These, it would be fair to say, belong to the realm of Beckett's own variant of 'voluntary memory'. In the case of the other two categories, however, the playing, pausing, winding and changing of the tapes make not only Krapp re-experience his past, with all of the senses re-activated by the triggering effect of the voice; they also make it clear that if Beckett's audience is brought to the theatre as much to hear as to see, the missing visual imagery, notwithstanding, is provided by the act of listening. The oscillation of the different audio-temporal levels, in other words, serves not only to make Krapp relive his past in a peculiar form of time travel; the tapes also enable the audience, because of the visualising quality of sound, to see the phantom of the younger Krapp on stage, side by side with the now decrepit Krapp.[50] At times the audience is even presented with a *mise-en-abyme* effect, as when Krapp is listening to a passage in which a younger version of himself recites his experiences of listening to 'an old year': 'Hard to believe I was ever that young whelp. The voice! Jesus! And the aspirations! [*Brief laugh in which* KRAPP *joins.*] And the resolutions! [*Brief laugh in which* KRAPP *joins.*] To drink less, in particular. [*Brief laugh of* KRAPP *alone.*]'[51] Not only, in other words, do we have Krapp joining his middle-aged version in laughter over his younger self; we also have the young Krapp laughed at by the middle-aged Krapp, who in turn is laughed at by the old Krapp. The audience is thus faced with three protagonists, two of them phantoms.

The voice on tape functions much like a conductor of perception, evoking the particular sensory experiences that prevail in each recollected memory. The famous scene in the hospital garden is a case in point: although Krapp does not initially remember the 'black ball' when he is reading the ledger, rather, as the stage directions have it, '*He raises his head, stares blankly front. Puzzled*', once he has listened to the tape, Krapp can again feel the ball in his hand, just as he vows on the tape he always will.[52] The full impact of the memory of the mother's death is hence truly activated not by the written note on the ledger which does not result even in voluntary memory, nor by the sound of Krapp's voice, but by the tactile sensation of the 'small, old, black, hard, solid rubber ball' that Krapp once clutched, and is thereafter left clutching, 'until [his] dying day'.[53] It is almost as if it were the past body that summoned Krapp from the spaces and places he once occupied.

One of the most moving examples of embodied memory in Beckett is the lake scene in *Krapp's Last Tape*, which is repeated, with slight variations, three times in the play. The first time Krapp comes upon the recollection it is narrated in explicitly tactile terms: '– my face in her breasts and my hand on her. We lay there without moving. But under us all

moved, and moved us, gently, up and down, and from side to side.'[54] The
fact that Krapp is hard of hearing emphasises the intensity with which
he listens to the tape, his hand cupping his ear, his body 'bent or twisted
over the machine'.[55] The different effects the voice has on the present
Krapp can be read across his face in a succession of expressions, almost as
if it were the body that became 'the sensitive receptacle upon which the
voice engraves itself'.[56] Krapp's face is a blank of annoyance, but when
the memories evoked by the voice cause a change in Krapp's level of
attention, the mask of his face ruptures, 'his body unbends, unfolds,
moves away from his listening posture, the trunk and face slowly lift, a
relaxation is produced of hand and face'.[57] The recorded voice transports
Krapp through time and space to locations beyond the scope of the other
senses, only to thrust these senses into action. Through the voice on tape,
in other words, Krapp grows a phantom body. When Krapp relistens to
the tape, the scene is experienced in terms of sight, sound, tactile sensations, the body in motion, rocked by the undulating water:

– gooseberries, she said. I said again I thought it was hopeless and no good going
on and she agreed, without opening her eyes... I asked her to look at me and
after a few moments... after a few moments she did, but the eyes just slits,
because of the glare. I bent over to get them in the shadow and they opened...
Let me in... We drifted among the flags and stuck. The way they went down,
sighing, before the stem!... I lay down across her with my face in her breasts and
my hand on her. We lay there without moving. But under us all moved, and
moved us, gently, up and down, and from side to side.[58]

The distinction between the present Krapp and the past one collapses, yet
it is also made more acute by the sense of loss that accompanies Krapp's
recollections. The doubling of the body that the voice effects, in other
words, far from freeing Krapp from the constraints of embodiment, serves
only to make the predicament more severe. The boat scene ends the play,
leaving the protagonist '*motionless staring before him*'.[59] The tape winds
on, establishing an uncanny continuity of movement between the rocking
boat and the austere stage. Through the voiced bodies and the spooling
tape recorder Krapp is irrevocably linked to his losses.

    In the section of *Phenomenology of Perception* dedicated to sexuality,
Merleau-Ponty writes about a girl who, when forbidden to see her lover,
suffers from insomnia and a loss of appetite, eventually losing her voice,
much as if it had been severed from her body like a limb lost in an
accident. The voice is not reawakened until the girl is left free to
encounter her lover. Merleau-Ponty explains the loss of voice, which he

compares to the manner in which 'certain insects sever one of their own legs', by the fact that the significance of the interhuman world has been lost to the girl once the most fundamental of interhuman relationships is denied her.[60] The voice, devoid of its interhuman function, has lost its meaning: 'The memory of the voice is recovered when the body once more opens itself to others or to the past, when it opens the way to co-existence and once more . . . acquires significance beyond itself.'[61]

Something similar is at stake in *Krapp's Last Tape*, in which damage is registered in the voice itself. Krapp's present voice is described as 'cracked'; the importance of this detail is disclosed by the fact that Beckett wrote the play with Patrick Magee's voice in mind, after he had heard Magee reading passages of his prose on the BBC Third Programme in December 1957. James Knowlson recounts how moved Beckett was 'by the cracked quality of Magee's distinctively Irish voice which seemed to capture a sense of deep world-weariness, sadness, ruination and regret'.[62] Steven Connor discusses the manner in which our voices can function as 'a persona, a mask or a sounding screen' through which we project ourselves to the world, and adds,

At the same time, my voice is the advancement of a part of me, an uncovering by which I am exposed, exposed to the possibility of exposure. I am able to shelter behind my voice, only if my voice can be me. But it can be me only if it has something of my own ductility and sensitivity: only if it is subject to erosion and to harm. My voice can bray and buffet only because it can also flinch and wince. My voice can be a glove, or a wall, or a bruise, a patch of inflammation, a scar, or a wound.[63]

When Krapp's younger voice is heard on tape, it is a '*Strong voice, rather pompous*', achingly different from the broken, at times raucous voice of the decrepit man on stage.[64] The play of continuity, discontinuity and loss is acted out in the voices, distinctly other while irreducibly connected.

The theme of memory in *Krapp's Last Tape*, the temporal sedimentation of body upon body, other and yet same, that our existence in its discontinuous unity consists of, keeps recurring throughout the Beckettian canon, with slight, phantasmagorically fading and reappearing variations that verge on the boundary of existence and non-existence, much like the phantom limb experiences in Merleau-Ponty's work. The scene at the lake in *Krapp's Last Tape*, which first occurs in *Dream of Fair to Middling Women*, is one of the fundamental memories in Beckett's work, like the recurring scene in Beckett's prose of an old man and child plodding along a narrow country road: 'Nothing from pelves down. From napes up. Topless baseless hindtrunks. Legless plodding on. Left right unreceding on.'[65] Once the narratee has walked down the country road in his youth, he is left walking down it for ever, 'Sole sound in the silence your footfalls . . . So many since dawn to add to yesterday's. To yesteryear's. To yesteryears'.'[66] Recollections like these keep emerging and waning like phantom limbs throughout the body of Beckett's writing.

It is in the nature of memories, in the flow between past and present, to be incomplete, phantomlike, fragile. Memories in Beckett, however, have their own special air, which gives them their idiosyncratic quality. In *Not I*, Mouth has a sudden flash of feeling coming back, 'imagine! . . . feeling coming back! . . . starting at the top . . . then working down . . . the whole machine'.[67] The unnamable, in the final part of the novel, experiences itself as an ear that grows itself a body. If we are, in the case of Mouth and the unnamable, dealing with actual phantom limb experiences, what is distinctly Beckettian about the memories is the plainly corporeal nature of the recollections. Triggered not by mere intellectual memory but by the body's own recollection of sensory experience, the strange time and place sequences in works such as *Company*, the four novellas, *That Time* or any other Beckettian haunting of the present by the past, become explicable in so far as the past is sedimented in the body itself, in a perpetual present continuous tense that leaves what has once been experienced and what can never truly be left behind irreversibly echoing in the characters' bodies. The bodies in Beckett seem not only to exist in several tenses, but to have both a time-arresting stative aspect and an active, dynamic one that is almost time itself. It is as if the contradictions present in Beckett's account of involuntary memory were in fact aspects of continuity and discontinuity embedded in the very notion of bodily existence.

The clash between the stative and the active corporeal aspects is one of the triggering factors of the negative bodily experiences that form such an important part of the Beckettian canon.[68] Our awareness of what we have been physically capable of in the past and of what we can no longer achieve makes our bodies the focal point of our anxieties, causing us, at times, not to coincide with ourselves. In *Molloy*, the narrator, while lying in his mother's bed and narrating his quest for his mother, experiences his limbs as alien: 'when I see my hands, on the sheet, which they love to floccillate already, they are not mine, less than ever mine, I have no arms . . . And with my feet it's the same, sometimes, when I see them at the foot of the bed, one with toes, the other without.'[69] The incapacitated limbs in their present aspect are no longer recognised as the same limbs that once enabled the riding of the bicycle that the body, in its habitual,

stative aspect, still continues to consider within its reach. In the second
act of *Happy Days* a reversal of this experience occurs, for Winnie, who
is now buried up to her neck in the mound, mentions her arms and her
breasts, and goes on to add, 'What arms? – What breasts?', as if the current
loss of these body parts rendered their existence in the past suspect,
reducing them in effect to hallucinations, turning the habitual body itself
in *Happy Days* into yet another example of phantom bodily experiences
in the Beckettian canon.[70] Steven Connor has drawn attention to the
'careful, sometimes even tender attention to awkwardness' in Beckett.[71]
He makes special mention of clumsiness, and goes on to add,

The English word 'clumsy' is derived from a Northern dialect word *klumse*,
which means benumbed by cold. The clumsy one is weighed down by his cold or
numb body, by a body that he does not fill or coincide with sufficiently to
command. His body is faster and slower than itself at once. His body is of a piece
with the ground, but has not yet acquired the grace of the ground.[72]

When the body, in contrast, is at one with itself, on a day on which we
happen to play a musical instrument or to run or to dance or to perform
any other motor activity particularly well, Gabriel Josipovici observes, 'we
feel ourselves to be *more ourselves* than is normally the case, more actively
part of the world'.[73] In the negative bodily experiences we so frequently
encounter in Beckett, the habitual body, the body in its stative aspect,
functions as a signifier that is out of sync with its signified.

   In short, Beckett grounds subjectivity, its enigmatic play of continuity
and discontinuity, firmly in the body. Beckett's work coincides with
Merleau-Ponty's precisely in its insistence on the body's irreducibility.
Where Beckett differs from Merleau-Ponty, however, is in the avidity
with which the philosopher finds in the body a new locus of meaning.
While Beckett's work insists on grounding subjectivity in materiality, it
radically departs from Merleau-Ponty's work in its stern refusal of all
forms of transcendence. The affirmative nature of Merleau-Ponty's thinking is lost in Beckett. The points of convergence are matched by a fundamental divergence. In this respect, the connection between Beckett and
Merleau-Ponty remains shimmering and fragile, not unlike the flickering
phantoms we encounter in their works.

CHAPTER 2

The place of vision

The critical interest in embodiment has coincided with a reassessment of theories of vision. In the last two decades, countless studies on the topic have appeared in print. Amongst the most prominent figure Jonathan Crary's fine *Techniques of the Observer*, on the role of vision in modernity, and Martin Jay's book, *Downcast Eyes*, which maps the denigration of vision in twentieth-century French thought.[1] Similarly, the gaze has occupied a central position in feminist and cinematic theory. Although these accounts have problematised the dissociation of sight from the body, relatively little has been written about the embodied, fleshly nature of vision. David Michael Levin, Jonathan Crary and Laura Danius figure amongst the few critics to have addressed the incarnate nature of sight.[2]

Early discussions of the visual dimension in Beckett's writing took a comparative form: critics focused on the influence of the visual arts on Beckett's work. Enoch Brater has written extensively on the topic; other critics who have offered fascinating insight into the significance of the visual arts on Beckett's work include James Knowlson, Ruby Cohn and Dougald McMillan.[3] More recently, Jessica Prinz has written on the influence of expressionism on Beckett's drama.[4]

In recent years, the theoretical interest in vision has generated some compelling readings of the role of sight in Beckett's work. Steven Connor, for instance, has written of the gaze of the Shower/Cooker couple ('German, *schauen* and *gucken*, "staring", "gawping"') in *Happy Days*, while Anna McMullan has focused on the gaze in Beckett's late drama.[5] Jane Alison Hale, for her part, has written about the use of perspective in Beckett's dramatic work, arguing that Beckett dissociates vision and reason, which have been intricately intertwined since the Renaissance invention of perspective.[6] More recently, Lois Oppenheim has offered a phenomenological reading of the role of vision and the visual arts in Beckett's critical writings.[7] With the exception of Steven Connor's essay 'Between

Theatre and Theory: *Long Observation of the Ray*' however, the material, embodied nature of vision in Beckett's work has been largely overlooked.[8]

In order to demonstrate the manner in which Beckett parts company with received notions of vision, I shall begin with a brief overview of Western, disembodied notions of sight. In this brief survey, I shall focus, in particular, on the question of subjectivity, with which the history of vision is intricately bound. This will be followed by some observations on Beckett's early correspondence with the poet and critic Thomas MacGreevy, and his critical writings, which attest to Beckett's keen interest in the reorganization of perception in modern art. In order to demonstrate the manner in which these ideas are reflected in Beckett's own creative writing, I shall then offer a reading of two of Beckett's novellas, *The Calmative* and *The End*, written in 1946. Both texts foreground the embodied nature of sight in Beckett's work, but also expose the attitudes inherent in the identification of vision, rationality and subjectivity. The chapter will close with a discussion of Beckett's *Film* (1964), which thematises self-perception and stages Beckett's conclusions about the relationship between vision and autonomous subjectivity.

Vision has played a constitutive role in theories of subjectivity, for the apparent detachment of the spectating subject has consolidated belief in the subject's independence of the object, as the by now notorious links drawn between the 'eye' and the 'I' indicate. While the proximity senses, most emphatically touch, involve the subject's interaction with the object, visual sensations have been believed to stem from a realm in which subject and object remain distinct. Seeing, after all, requires little perceptible activity on the part of the subject.[9] Although the same can be said about hearing, it does demand action on the part of the object, for sound is not emitted from objects as easily as light. Vision seems therefore to exist effortlessly in its own right, elevating it to the status of theory or of that which is consistently valid, while hearing and touch, partly by being more explicitly temporal, pertain to the field of practice and fleeting instances. Vision also endows the perceiver with an air of immunity and detachment, for not only does vision benefit from physical distance in that we get a better view of our focus of interest from afar than we do closer up; the perceiver also remains at a remove from the potentially corrupting aggressiveness and raw power of lived experience.[10]

A brief summary of the history of vision reveals that, at least since Plato, reason has been conceived and imagined in terms of sight.[11] For Aristotle, for instance, sight was the supreme sense because it resembled the intellect most closely, 'by virtue of the relative immateriality of its knowing'.[12] The association of sight with reason only became heightened in Cartesian thought. As Paul Ricoeur has observed, Cartesian philosophy 'is contemporaneous with a vision of the world in which the whole of objectivity is spread out like a spectacle on which the cogito casts its sovereign gaze'.[13] Ricoeur's observation coincides with, if not originates in Heidegger's essay 'The Age of the World Picture' (1938), in which Heidegger finds the essence of modernity in the idea of a world picture, which should not be understood as an image of the world but as the world itself 'conceived and grasped as picture'.[14] Neither should we think that some fundamental change has occurred in the world picture itself, thus drawing a dividing line between the medieval and the modern; on the contrary, Heidegger argues, 'the fact that the world becomes picture at all' is the distinguishing essence of modernity.[15]

Heidegger, like Ricoeur, traces the origins of the world picture back to Descartes, in whose metaphysics truth first became 'transformed into the certainty of representation'. The emergence of the world as picture is historically contemporaneous and interwoven with the idea of man as subject, 'that being upon which all that is, is grounded as regards the manner of its Being and its truth'. Man, Heidegger continues, 'becomes the relational centre of that which is as such'.[16] Anything that is, in other words, is now only in being in so far as it is at man's disposal, before him, as an object in relation to the viewing subject. Man becomes the setting in which whatever is presents itself; simultaneously, the stance man takes towards his surroundings depends, for the first time in history, on man alone. The attitude becomes one of mastery, and the world is given order through the process of enframing. Heidegger calls to mind the definition of *vorstellen*, 'to represent': 'to set out before oneself and to set forth in relation to oneself. Through this, whatever is comes to a stand as object and in that way alone receives the seal of Being. That the world becomes picture is one and the same event with the event of man's becoming *subiectum* in the midst of that which is.'[17] The separation of the self from the picture, in other words, is the precondition for grasping the enframed totality, just as the mind, in Cartesian thought, 'is said to be set apart from the material world it observes'.[18]

* * *

Beckett's interest in a new experience of seeing can be detected in his early correspondence with Thomas MacGreevy, held at Trinity College Dublin. In a letter dated Cooldrinagh, 18 October 1932, when Beckett was 26 years old, he wrote to Thomas MacGreevy of 'mourning for' what he found in 'Homer Dante & Racine & sometimes Rimbaud the integrity of the eyelids coming down before the brain knows of grit in the wind'.[19] Like so much of Beckett's early correspondence, this letter seems to suggest an aesthetic in the making, by signalling the kinds of formative influences and aesthetic qualities Beckett admired. The MacGreevy correspondence is revealing precisely for containing so many references to Beckett's reading, whether in prose (e.g. Melville), poetry (e.g. Keats), philosophy (e.g. Schopenhauer), psychology (e.g. Alfred Adler: 'Another one track mind'),[20] science (e.g. Darwin) or critical works (e.g. MacGreevy himself on Eliot and Yeats). The correspondence also, crucially, provides us with a document of Beckett's passion for painting, and the various visual artists and aesthetic qualities in their work that inspired or moved him.

Like so many of his contemporaries, such as D. H. Lawrence and Virginia Woolf, for instance, Beckett was particularly taken by the work of Paul Cézanne. In 1934, whilst visiting the Tate Gallery in London, Beckett saw one of Cézanne's many paintings of the Mont Sainte-Victoire, which prompted him to write one of his most famous and often-quoted letters to MacGreevy, dated 8 September 1934: 'Cézanne seems to have been the first to see landscape and state it as material of a strictly peculiar order, incommensurable with all human expressions whatsoever.'[21] What Beckett particularly admired in Cézanne, as he put it in another, undated letter, written according to James Knowlson's detective work on 16 September 1934, was the 'sense of his incommensurability not only with life of such a different order as landscape, but even with life of his own order, even with the life... operative in himself'.[22] Beckett also famously admired Jack B. Yeats's canvases for similar reasons. He detected in them an 'ultimate hard inorganic singleness', and a 'perception & dispassion' which was 'beyond tragedy'.[23]

Beckett's interest in the visual dimension and the broader question of subjectivity becomes explicitly manifest in his critical writings on the visual arts, and in his more general fascination with the nature of the aesthetic. There is, furthermore, a discernible shift in interest in Beckett's critical writings from an initial concentration on literature, as 'Dante... Bruno. Vico .. Joyce' (1929) and *Proust* (1930) prove, to a post-war focus on painting, evidenced in reviews and texts such as 'MacGreevy on Yeats' (1945); 'La Peinture des van Velde ou le monde et le pantalon' (1946); 'Peintres de l'empêchement' (1948) and *Three Dialogues with Georges Duthuit* (1949), to mention but the best-known pieces.[24]

Beckett himself did not think highly of his critical writings and, for a good while, resisted their republication. The critical texts, however, are more astute than Beckett gave them credit for, revealing the author's early interest in an art that aims to move 'outside of systems of relations assumed requisite to philosophical understanding'.[25] This interest could be evidenced as early as 1934, when Beckett wrote his pseudonymously published 'Recent Irish Poetry', where he discussed 'the new thing that has happened, or the old thing that has happened again, namely the breakdown of the object' equated in the text with 'the breakdown of the subject'.[26] In 'Peintres de l'empêchement', first published in *Derrière le miroir* in June 1948, Beckett situates the van Velde brothers, Bram and Geer, within a history of art interpreted as 'painting's changing relationship to the object'.[27] In the essay, Beckett states that 'the essence of the object is to elude representation', and the role of art to represent 'the conditions of that elusion'.[28] In 'La Peinture des van Velde ou le monde et le pantalon', written two years earlier, Beckett proposed that Bram van Velde's paintings are 'held in suspense, suggesting not just an unfinished quality, but an unfinishable situation'.[29]

The manner in which Beckett sustains and develops his interest in the subject–object relationship is manifest in the most famous of his writings on the visual arts, *Three Dialogues with Georges Duthuit*, first published in *transition* in 1949.[30] In the dialogues, Beckett and Duthuit discuss the work of three painters: Pierre Tal Coat, André Masson and Bram van Velde.[31] Beckett is critical of Tal Coat precisely for remaining within the constraints of 'a composite of perceiver and perceived'.[32] Although André Masson, according to Beckett, explores the subject–object relationship in his work, Masson, too, still 'continues to wriggle': 'it seems to me impossible that he should ever do anything different from that which the best, including himself, have done already'.[33] For Beckett, as we have seen, the object of representation resists representation, something that he finds Bram van Velde to acknowledge, and a view that Beckett shares with Maurice Merleau-Ponty, who, in *Phenomenology of Perception*, writes that it is

of the essence of the world and of the thing to present themselves as 'open', to send us beyond their determinate manifestations, to promise us always 'something else to see'. This is what is sometimes expressed by saying that the thing and the world are mysterious. They are indeed, when we do not limit ourselves to their objective aspect, but put them back into the setting of subjectivity. They are even an absolute mystery, not amenable to elucidation, and this through no provisional gap in our knowledge, for in that case it would fall back to the status of a mere problem, but because it is not of the order of objective thought in which there are solutions.[34]

In a letter to Duthuit of March 1949, Beckett writes in approbation of Bram van Velde's art: 'Ce n'est pas le rapport avec tel ou tel ordre de vis-à-vis qu'il refuse, mais l'état d'être en rapport tout court et sans plus, l'état d'être devant.'[35] [It is not the relation with such and such an order vis-à-vis that he refuses, but the state of just being in relation and, purely and simply, the state of being in front of.][36] Apart from making reference to the frontality of vision, as opposed to the more engulfing and hence less 'objective' nature of the acoustic and the tactile, Beckett is also seriously questioning the very plausibility of a subject–object divide:

Quoi que je dise, j'aurai l'air de l'enfermer à nouveau dans une relation. Si je dis qu'il peint l'impossibilité de peindre, la privation de rapport, d'object, de sujet, j'ai l'air de le mettre en rapport avec cette impossibilité, avec cette privation, devant elles. Il est dedans, est-ce la même chose? Il les est, plutôt, et elles sont lui, d'une façon pleine, et peut-il y avoir des rapports dans l'indivisible? Pleine? Indivisible? Evidemment pas.[37]

[Whatever I say, I will appear to be enclosing [van Velde] again in a relation. If I say he paints the impossibility of painting, the denial of relation, of object, of subject, I appear to be putting him in relation to this impossibility, this denial, in front of it. He is within, is this the same thing? He is them, rather, and they are him, in a full way, and can there be relations within the indivisible? Full? Indivisible? Obviously not.][38]

Apart from simply making reference to van Velde's art, Beckett is also here making a self-referential remark about the nature of his own medium of expression, namely language: the difficulty of addressing the dilemma at hand in isolation from a preconceived relationship between categories, on which language as a medium, any language, is by definition based.[39] Beckett is hence questioning not only the more general problem of representation, but the entire stance of opposition and relationship that this entails. For the birth of the world as picture identified in Heidegger's essay also heralds the birth of humanism or what Heidegger terms anthropology, 'that philosophical interpretation of man which explains and evaluates whatever is, in its entirety, from the standpoint of man and in relation to man'.[40] From this moment onwards, the position of man becomes conceived of as a world *view*, and whatever is is in existence only to the extent that it can be referred back to man's life-experience. The world becomes reduced to a structured picture produced by man. Through 'such producing, man contends for the position in which he can be that particular being who gives the measure and draws up the guidelines for everything that is'.[41] This is why Heidegger also writes about the death of gods but of the very birth of religious experience through the 'transformation of the Christian doctrine into a world view'.[42] The struggle between world views leads to 'the calculating, planning, and moulding of all things. Science as research', Heidegger adds, 'is an absolutely necessary form of this establishing of self in the world.'[43]

Seen from this point of view, Beckett's early comments about Cézanne's painting, made on 8 September 1934, in a letter to Thomas MacGreevy, are more than revealing:

> What a relief the Mont Ste. Victoire after all the anthropomorphized landscape... or paranthropomorphised... or hyperanthropomorphized by Rubens... after all the landscape 'promoted' to the emotions of the hiker, postulated as *concerned* with the hiker (what an impertinence, worse than Aesop and the animals), alive the way a lap or a *fist* is alive.[44]

Beckett is protesting precisely against the falsifying view of 'landscape', depicted as if it existed *in relation* to the viewing subject. Beckett, after all, had stressed that Cézanne 'seems to have been the first to see landscape and state it as material of a strictly peculiar order, incommensurable with all human expressions whatsoever. Atomistic landscape with no velleities of vitalism, landscape with personality à la rigueur, but personality in its own terms, not in Pelman's *landscapality*.'[45] What Beckett appears to be suggesting, in other words, is that Cézanne manages the unmanageable: namely to paint, at least to some extent, past and beyond preconceived categories of representation.[46]

In 1945, eleven years after Beckett had written his letters on Cézanne to Thomas MacGreevy, Maurice Merleau-Ponty published his own essay on Cézanne, entitled 'Cézanne's Doubt'. The essay first appeared in the December issue of *Fontaine*, a monthly periodical dedicated to poetry and French literature, and was subsequently reprinted in Merleau-Ponty's collection of essays, *Sense and Non-Sense* (1948), as the collection's lead piece.[47] This is how Merleau-Ponty characterises the work of Cézanne:

> His painting was paradoxical: he was pursuing reality without giving up the sensuous surface, without following the contours, with no other guide than the immediate impression of nature, with no outline to enclose the color, with no perspectival or pictorial arrangement. This is what Bernard called Cézanne's suicide: aiming for reality while denying himself the means to attain it. This is the reason for his difficulties and the distortions one finds in his pictures between 1870 and 1890. Cups and saucers on a table seen from the side should be elliptical, but Cézanne paints the two ends of the ellipse swollen and expanded... In giving up the outline Cézanne was abandoning himself to the chaos of sensation, which

would upset the objects and constantly suggest illusions, as, for example, the illusion we have when we move our heads that the objects themselves are moving.[48]

It is interesting to note that as early as *Proust*, Beckett himself makes mention of the manner in which the 'observer infects the observed with his own mobility'.[49]

What was striking for Merleau-Ponty was the manner in which Cézanne seemed to abandon himself to sensation.[50] Cézanne, who was of the opinion that one should paint faces as objects, 'wanted to depict matter as it takes on form', to portray 'the lived perspective, that which we actually perceive', rather than the ordered and rationalised compositions of Renaissance perspective and geometry.[51] As Cézanne himself observed to Émile Bernard: 'You have to create a perspective of your own, to see nature as though no one had ever seen it before.'[52] What is remarkable and simultaneously terrifying about Cézanne's work, Merleau-Ponty argues, is precisely that 'he painted as if no one had ever painted before.'[53] Cézanne bracketed, to use a phenomenological term, scientific, preconceived assumptions of how the 'world *should* look', and emphasized instead, in all its strangeness, 'the lived perspective as the visible world arises in relation to [the] living body'.[54] In this way, Merleau-Ponty argues, Cézanne revealed 'the base of inhuman nature upon which man has installed himself'.[55] Like Beckett, who had emphasised the relief of encountering Cézanne's canvases after 'all the anthropomorphised landscape – van Goyen, Avercamp, the Ruysdaels', Merleau-Ponty stresses the 'inhuman character' of Cézanne's work which, he added, 'penetrates right to the root of things beneath the imposed order of humanity'.[56]

Cézanne's aesthetic, for Merleau-Ponty, grew not out of a preconceived idea or concept; rather, Merleau-Ponty writes, the 'meaning of what the artist is going to say *does not exist* anywhere...It summons one away from the already constituted reason.' For Cézanne, ' "[c]onception" cannot precede "execution" ' – this would only anthropomorphise the landscape anew.[57] Beckett himself, as early as 1937, had made a similar observation, condemning the German painter Max Klinger 'for projecting concepts on the canvas, rendering "the optical experience post rem, a hideous inversion of the visual process, the eye waiving its privilege" '.[58] For Cézanne, in contrast, there is nothing before expression 'but a vague fever, and only the work itself, completed and understood, will prove that there was *something* rather than *nothing* to be found there'.[59] This something or nothing, which has an odd reverberation with Beckett's 1937 letter to Axel Kaun – in which he wants to 'bore one hole after another' in language, 'until what lurks behind it – be it something or nothing – begins to seep through'[60] – is the very source of Cézanne's doubt – a doubt which prompted the elderly painter to wonder 'whether the novelty of his painting might not come from trouble with his eyes, whether his whole life had not been based upon an accident of his body'.[61]

* * *

In his letter of 8 September 1934, Beckett complains to MacGreevy of 'the Impressionists darting about & whining that the scene wouldn't rest easy.' He goes on to say:

How far Cézanne had moved from the snapshot puerilities of Manet & Cie when he could understand the dynamic intrusion to be himself & so landscape to be something by definition unapproachably alien, unintelligible arrangement of atoms, not so much as ruffled by the kind attentions of the Reliability Joneses.[62]

In Cézanne's mature pictures of the Mont Sainte-Victoire, the lines no longer converge in the manner we expect. The mountain appears stark and barren rather than sheltered, and the land open, lacking the boundaries that in pastoral images would frame the view. The art critic Meyer Shapiro describes the 1904–6 version of the Mont Sainte-Victoire in the following manner: 'The earth approaches chaos, yet is formed of clear vertical and horizontal strokes in sharp contrast to the diagonal strokes of the mountain and the many curving strokes of the sky.'[63] Cézanne has done away with the rules of perspective. He has given in, as Merleau-Ponty suggests, to 'the chaos of sensation', and is recording the experience on his canvas.[64]

Beckett, one could argue, had his own Mont Sainte-Victoire, a landscape he, like Cézanne, compulsively returned to in his various writings. For Beckett's letters to Thomas MacGreevy contain numerous references to the Dublin mountains that keep recurring in unexpected configurations throughout Beckett's *oeuvre*, much as the Mont Sainte-Victoire, Cézanne's native landscape, keeps reappearing on the painter's canvases. In one of his earliest letters to MacGreevy, written at his family home, Cooldrinagh, on 5 January 1930, when Beckett had returned to Ireland after his period at the École Normale Supérieure from 1928 to 1930, he observers to MacGreevy, in a question that is more rhetorical than actual, 'How do you work with these hills behind you.'[65] In another letter, written two years later, and dated Cooldrinagh, 18 October 1932, Beckett writes,

I walk unmeasurably & unrestrainedly, hills and dales, all day, and back with a couple of pints from the Powerscourt Arms under my [?] belt . . . I disagree with

Figure 1. Cézanne's *Montagne Sainte-Victoire*, 1904–6

you about the gardenish landscape. The lowest mountains here terrify me far more than anything I saw in Connemara & Achill. Or is it that a garden is more frightening than a waste? I walked across Prince William's Seat, a low mountain... and was reduced almost to incontinence in the calm secret hostility.[66]

In his letter of 8 September 1934, Beckett recalls, in low spirits, having been 'exhausted of meaning by the mountains'.[67] He found in the Irish landscape 'a nature almost as inhumanly inorganic as a stage set'.[68] The echoes of these sentiments later find their way into a number of Beckett's works.

* * *

In his creative writing, then, Beckett is faced with the following dilemma: how to overcome the preconceived categories on which language and our received thought-patterns are based, in something of the manner in which he had seen Cézanne break away from received modes of representation.[69] The challenge for Beckett's writing would not only be to re-imagine the relationship between subject and world, and hence to outline a new phenomenology of perception, but to create a mode of expression in which these re-imaginings could be represented.

In the *Four Novellas*, which inaugurate Beckett's mature style, one can detect a striking emphasis on verbs of vision. Beckett wrote his four novellas, *First Love, The Expelled, The Calmative* and *The End*, in the final months of 1946. They are the first texts he originally composed in French and later translated into English.[70] *The Calmative*, the penultimate novella in the collection, is the story of the first-person narrator, who leaves his den to traverse a strange town he has not seen before, but one that he, oddly, none the less, appears to recognize. *The Calmative* has an extraordinary emphasis on vision, as can be evidenced in the recurrence of the verb 'to see', which, in its different declinations, is mentioned seventeen times in the novella. In addition, the verb 'to look' appears five times and the verbs 'to gaze', 'to eye' and 'to focus' are each mentioned twice. Amongst further vision-related verbs in the novella figure 'to appear', 'to loom' and 'to shine'. There are also a number of visual adjectives, such as 'blind' and 'glittering'.[71] The man who, towards the end of the novella, gives the narrator a phial, is said to have a 'radiant smile'.[72]

The novella's emphasis on vision is heightened by references to a peculiar silence, and to the recurrent failure of vocal articulation. When the narrator reaches the town, he observes that '[t]he trams were running, the buses too, but few, slow, empty, noiseless, as if under water.'[73] The young boy the narrator encounters on the quayside is similarly described as 'silent'; when the narrator attempts to address the boy, he himself fails: 'I marshalled the words and opened my mouth, thinking I would hear them. But all I heard was a kind of rattle, unintelligible even to me who knew what was intended.'[74] Back in town again, the narrator encounters '[n]ot a single private car, but admittedly from time to time a public vehicle, slow sweep of light silent and empty'.[75] It is as if Beckett were here performing his own variation of bracketing, a peculiar phenomenological reduction into the nature of visual experience. The absence of sound is made all the more prominent by the contrasting presence of a powerful light, for the city is described as 'brighter than usual' and the nave in the cathedral as 'brilliantly lit'.[76] The narrator observes the 'extraordinary radiance' and 'atrocious brightness' of the streets, and makes mention of the fact that he is 'famished for shadow'.[77]

In addition to verbs and adjectives of vision, the novella makes frequent note of eyes. The narrator mentions the young boy's 'guttersnipe's eye', and tells himself not to 'open [his] eyes'.[78] The eye itself is presented not as detached and disembodied, but as fleshly and vulnerable, subject to damage and decay, as the narrator acknowledges at the outset of his journey when he mentions 'the eyes soon sockets'.[79] The man the narrator encounters in the cathedral is described as 'wild-eyed'; when he slides 'out of sight', all that remains is 'the vision of two burning eyes starting out of their sockets', a comment that again highlights the incarnate nature of the eye.[80]

The narrator draws attention to the fallible nature of sight itself, when he comes across the ramparts: 'Cyclopean and crenellated, standing out faintly against a sky scarcely less sombre, they did not seem in ruins, viewed from mine, but were, to my certain knowledge.'[81] Rather than giving the narrator access to an instantaneous comprehension of the scene, vision is from the outset described as prone to miscalculations. A distinction is made between what the eye sees and the narrator knows, problematising the received relationship between vision and rationality. The visual adjective, 'cyclopean', also appears in 'Peintres de l'empêchement'. Bram van Velde's work, Beckett writes in the essay, depicts 'the unshakable masses of a being apart, enclosed and drawn back in itself for ever, trackless, airless, cyclopean, with brief flashes of lightning, with colors from the spectrum of black'.[82] Beckett argues that while for Geer van Velde the object resists representation, in the case of Bram, it is the artist's own eye that poses the resistance ('l'empêchement-oeil').[83] The narrator of *The Calmative* goes on to mention the stars he sees on the horizon, and again distances sight from reason by pointing out that they are 'not to be confused with the fires men light, at night, or that go alight alone', for both fires and stars, seen from the narrator's vantage point, look all too similar.[84]

Vision is also subject to other physical restraints. The narrator, for instance, mentions a flagstone, 'which I was not focussing, for why focus it'; when he watches a boy with a goat recede into the horizon, he remarks, 'soon they were no more than a single blur which if I hadn't known I might have taken for a centaur'.[85] Blurring in Beckett highlights the physiological limitations of sight, and the constraints the eye as an organ lays on our field of vision. One thinks of David Michael Levin's point about the spontaneous and uncontrollable changes that occur in the field of visibility:

What happens when we stare intensely at something? Instead of clear and distinct perception, blurring and confusion; instead of fulfilment, the eyes lose their sight, veiled in tears; instead of stability and fixation at the far end of the gaze, we find a chaos of shifting, jerking forms as the object of focus violently tears itself away from the hold of the gaze.[86]

Blurring is also an ironic comment on the codes of mastery inherent in vision, a theme Beckett revisits in *Film*, as we shall see, and something that was also on Cézanne's mind, as the painter pondered over his failing eyesight.

The objects of vision in *The Calmative* themselves repeatedly resist the narrator's gaze, as when he sees a curious cyclist pedalling by: 'I watched him recede till he was no more than a dot on the horizon.'[87] Something of this nature also happens when the narrator, for the second time, encounters the girl he has seen in the cathedral tower:

I succeeded however in fastening briefly on the little girl, long enough to see her a little more clearly than before, so that she wore a kind of bonnet and clasped in her hand a book, of common prayer perhaps, and to try and have her smile, but she did not smile, but vanished down the staircase without having yielded me her little face.[88]

Beckett is acknowledging that although vision sets the object apart from the viewing subject, and hence posits itself as an 'objective' sense, 'sight also composes that view or scene or perspective by being *a selective interpretation of appearances or visual representations*'.[89] What is more, vision in *The Calmative*, as the verb 'fasten' implies, presents itself as a temporal synthesis that requires intent and effort on the part of the perceiver. As Merleau-Ponty writes:

The act of looking is indivisibly prospective, since the object is the final stage of my process of focusing, and retrospective, since it will present itself as preceding its own appearance, as the 'stimulus', the motive or the prime mover of every process since its beginning. The spatial synthesis and the synthesis of the object are based on this unfolding of time.[90]

Yet, the little girl in the cathedral does not 'yield' her face. The negative form of the archaic 'yield' only further adds to the air of resistance, for the verb means '[t]o surrender, give way [or] submit', which brings to mind Beckett's views of Geer van Velde, for whom, in 'Peintres de l'empêchement', the object of representation resisted representation ('l'empêchement-object'), evidenced, too, in Cézanne's lifelong efforts to capture the Mont Sainte-Victoire on canvas.[91]

The powerful light that surrounds the narrator of *The Calmative* itself functions as an obstacle to vision, for the eye, instead of being empowered, is only blinded by the 'atrocious' light.[92] Beckett is drawing attention to the vulnerable character of sight, for '[t]he eyes are a specialised organ for "reading" the ambient or reflected light'; in the case of radiant light, 'one sees only whiteness and can gain little visual information about the source or the environment'.[93]

Vision in the novella, furthermore, can no longer be associated with *theoria*.[94] When the narrator is in the harbour, he says: 'the quays were deserted and there was no sign or stir of arrival or departure. But all might change from one moment to the next and be transformed like magic before my eyes.'[95] Far from presenting the narrator with the 'immutable essence' of objects, an assumption that has contributed to the primacy of vision in Western culture, the scene is subject to sudden and baffling transformations.[96] In fact, all the landscapes the narrator encounters are prone to incomprehensible shifts: the narrator is in a cathedral tower where he sees an old man and a girl, then on a street where another man gives him a phial in exchange for a kiss, then back again at the top of the tower as in a ghostly succession of dream images that keep fading in and out of focus. The landscapes of *The Calmative* are in constant flux, unlike conventional perspective images that duplicate the spectator's fixed vantage point. Besides drawing attention to the intermittent character of sight, Beckett is making a further comment about the nature of vision. The narrator says: 'suddenly I was descending a wide street, vaguely familiar, but in which I could never have set foot, in my lifetime'.[97] The strange *déjà vu* incident only enhances the complexity of the narrator's experience, in which perception, memory and imagination exchange functions and merge into one. Similarly, in the novel *Watt*, which Beckett completed in 1945, the protagonist experiences what could be described as a series of optical illusions: 'as Watt fixed his eyes on what he thought was perhaps the day again already, the man standing sideways in the kitchen doorway looking at him became two men standing sideways in the kitchen doorway looking at him.'[98]

Vision, in the Western tradition, has been considered the only sense that respects the division between subject and object, for in touch, taste, smell, and even hearing, as we shall later see, the boundaries between self and world become blurred. In *The Calmative*, however, the narrator infects the object of vision with his own experience. A case in point is the remark he makes of the trees he encounters: 'They were the perishing oaks immortalized by d'Aubigné. It was only a grove.'[99] Later, the narrator sees 'a lush pasture', but rushes to add, 'nonsuch perhaps, who cares, drenched in evening dew or recent rain'.[100] If categories such as perception, memory and imagination lose their differentiating characteristics, the neat distinction between subject and object must also become problematic.[101] The sharp division between imagination, perception and memory is also questioned by Merleau-Ponty, who suggests, firstly, that perception is intertwined not only with the rational intellect but also with the artistic imagination, and who, secondly, brings memory into the field of perception, through his exploration of the phantom limb.

The objects the narrator of *The Calmative* perceives refuse to render the instantaneously comprehensible whole that has been considered one of the advantages of vision over the explicitly temporal hearing and touch. On the contrary, in the novella, Beckett brings vision closer to the proximity senses, firstly by stressing the material, embodied nature of sight, and secondly, by emphasising that vision may not, after all, constitute the space that guarantees the subject's detachment from the world, but rather, through the chaos of sensation, makes him part of that world. If the neat distinction between subject and object ceases to be plausible, the spectator's relationship of subjection and mastery towards the object also dissolves. The novella ends with the narrator's impotent, anti-anthropocentric remark, reminiscent of Beckett's observations about Cézanne's landscapes: 'in vain I raised without hope my eyes to the sky to look for the Bears. For the light I stepped in put out the stars, assuming they were there, which I doubted, remembering the clouds.'[102]

In *The End*, the final novella of the series, the narrator is expelled from a charitable institution. He is given some money and a new set of clothing, and compelled to search for shelter elsewhere. After spending time in several different types of enclosures, the narrator finally finds shelter in a boat. The novella ends with the narrator having 'visions' of 'gliding over the waters', where he ultimately waits for the boat to sink.[103]

The unpredictable and disorganised landscapes of *The Calmative* are again present in *The End*:

In the street I was lost. I had not set foot in this part of the city for a long time and it seemed greatly changed. Whole buildings had disappeared, the palings had changed position . . . There were streets where I remembered none, some I did remember had vanished and others had completely changed their names.[104]

Vision is again presented in fleshly and fallible terms: the light is 'blinding'; the eyes 'not completely spent' and the flowers the narrator has gathered form 'a haze of many colours'.[105] When the narrator gazes at the sky, he does so 'without focussing it, for why focus it? Most of the time it was a mixture of white, blue and grey, and then at evening all the evening colours.'[106] From his final abode, the narrator says, 'the eyes rose to a confusion of low houses, wasteland, hoardings, chimneys, steeples and towers'.[107] Again, a coherent whole refuses to present itself; instead, we encounter only 'confusion'. When the narrator sees the river, he retorts: 'Here all seemed at first sight more or less as I had left it. But if I had looked more closely I would doubtless have discovered many changes. And indeed I subsequently did so.'[108]

When the narrator describes the Greek woman's basement, which is his first dwelling place, he says: 'Now I didn't know where I was. I had a vague vision, not a real vision, I didn't see anything, of a big house five or six stories high, one of a block perhaps.'[109] The narrator's observations vacillate between vision and imagination, making the certainty of what is seen precarious and erratic. The most pronounced manifestation of a similar blending occurs at the close of the novella:

the next thing I was having visions, I who never did, except sometimes in my sleep, who never had, real visions, I'd remember, except perhaps as a child, my myth will have it so. I knew they were visions because it was night and I was alone in my boat. What else could they have been?[110]

The collapse of categories encountered in *The Calmative*, in other words, also forms one of the most striking characteristics of *The End*.

What *The End* adds to the treatment of vision in *The Calmative* is the fact that the narrator is from the outset the object of the other's gaze. He says: 'My appearance still made people laugh, with that hearty jovial laugh so good for the health.'[111] Even the horse the narrator encounters stares at him; the same also applies to the driver of the carriage. One day, when the narrator is in his basement room, he receives a visit from a policeman: 'He said I had to be watched, without explaining why.'[112] The presence of other people disturbs the narrator's relationship to his surroundings, which, as Sartre argued, in the presence of another person, will no longer arrange themselves around the viewing subject, but instead, reorganise themselves in relation to *the other*:

There is a total space which is grouped around the Other, and this space is made *with my space;* there is a regrouping in which I take part but which escapes me, a regrouping of all the objects which people my universe . . . suddenly an object has appeared which has stolen the world from me. Everything is in place; everything still exists for me; but everything is traversed by an invisible flight and fixed in the direction of a new object. The appearance of the Other in the world corresponds therefore to a fixed sliding of the whole universe, to a decentralization of the world which undermines the centralization which I am simultaneously effecting.[113]

Beckett is, furthermore, drawing attention to the objectifying gaze of the other that not only serves to establish the spectator's detachment from the object, and is hence crucial to the construction of the viewer's identity but, as Sartre reasoned, also compels the subject that is the object of the gaze to judge *itself* as an object.[114] The most acute example of this occurs when an orator appears at the narrator's street corner: 'All of a sudden he turned and pointed at me, as at an exhibit. Look at this down and out, he vociferated, this leftover. If he doesn't go down on all fours, it's for fear of being impounded. Old, lousy, rotten, ripe for the muckheap.'[115] This is the awareness not only of the for-itself as in-itself, but 'of the for-itself *of* the in-itself' which in *Being and Nothingness* is the trigger of nausea.[116]

  Perception, in *The End*, threatens the boundaries between subject and world, firstly through the narrator's own perceptions, and secondly through the gaze of others. This triggers the narrator's relentless attempt to seek various enclosures, and hence put an end to the onslaught of sensory perception. He does this by succumbing to progressively more secluded enclosures that range from a basement and a cave by the sea to a hut in the mountains. As the narrator observes at the outset of the novella, having made mention of a 'tedious twilight': 'I longed to be under cover again, in an empty place.'[117] Beckett's experiment into detached and autonomous subjectivity through a form of sensory deprivation reaches its height at the end of the novella, when the narrator finds shelter in a boat whose lid 'fitted so well I had to pierce a hole'.[118] Lying on his back in the dark, as so many of Beckett's characters do, contemplating his occasional desire to get up and leave, he observes: 'I felt them hard upon me, the icy, tumultuous streets, the terrifying faces, the noises that slash, pierce, claw, bruise.'[119] Tactile, visual and acoustic perceptions merge into one, in the narrator's synaesthetic memories of perceptual assault. Sensory stimuli, however intrusive the narrator feels them to be, nevertheless cannot be discarded. Even in his state of deprivation, the narrator continues to perceive his surroundings, for not only does the world invade his abode in the form of tactile and acoustic sensations, which range from the cries of gulls, the lapping of the waves, the sound of the rain falling and the 'howling, soughing, moaning, sighing' of the wind, to the feeling of raindrops 'exploding' on the narrator's skin; the narrator even has visual sensations in the dark isolation of the coffin-like enclosure: 'Flat then on my back I saw nothing except, dimly, just above my head, through the tiny chinks, the grey light of the shed.'[120] The narrator, in other words, fails to reach a state of detached subjectivity, and even in the maximum state of isolation he has achieved, the division between subject and object becomes blurred: 'I heard the lapping of water against the slip and against the bank and the other sound, so different, of open wave, I heard it too. I too, when I moved, felt less boat than wave, or so it seemed to me, and my stillness was the stillness of eddies.'[121] It is in the nature of the senses to enable the subject's expansion beyond itself, and, similarly, to allow the world to permeate the self. The senses in Beckett's novellas effect an intermingling with the world that collapses any neat subject–object dichotomy. Even as an experiment, therefore, Beckett's phenomenological reduction stumbles over its own impossibility: there is, in the novellas, finally no escape from the situatedness that is the precondition of embodied subjectivity.

In 'Indirect Language and the Voices of Silence', from 1952, Merleau-Ponty argues that while imagination remains a variant of perception, it allows 'interruptions and discontinuities, mixings, foldings and intertwinings between visible and invisible, real and imaginary'.[122] In 'Eye and Mind', a late essay published in 1961, he observes that painting 'scrambles all our categories'.[123] In a similar vein, Michel Foucault, in *The Order of Things*, discusses what he calls heterotopias, landscapes that 'desiccate speech, stop words in their tracks, contest the very possibility of grammar at its source; they dissolve our myths and sterilise the lyricism of our sentences'.[124] What Foucault means by his heteroclitic spaces are ones in which different categories that cannot occupy the same space seem nonetheless to coexist; in heterotopias, 'fragments of a large number of possible orders glitter separately . . . without law or geometry'.[125] Beckett's disruptive images could be said to function in the manner of hetero-topias, displaced landscapes that lack logical continuity. This is perhaps how Beckett imagined a mode of representation for his prose: the landscapes, at times drawing on the limitations of our perspectival view, and at others, discarding perspective and categorical distinctions altogther, refuse coherent syntax, presenting to us instead a scene of disruptions, and in the process, foregrounding the intermittent, fleshly nature of sight.

'Perhaps', Beckett wrote, in the letter of 8 September 1934, 'it is the one bright spot in a mechanistic age – the deanthropomorphizations of the artist. Even the portrait beginning to be dehumanised as the individual feels himself more & more hermetic & alone & his neighbour a coa-gulum as alien as a protoplast or God.'[126] Beckett's comments bring to mind Cézanne's desire to paint faces as objects, for Beckett detected in his canvases 'the sense of [the painter's] incommensurability not only with life of such a different order as landscape, but even with life of his own order, even with the life . . . operative in himself'.[127]

* * *

In *Film*, written in 1963 and filmed in New York in 1964, Beckett returns explicitly to explore the question of perception.[128] *Film*, shot in 35 mm black and white and directed by Alan Schneider with Buster Keaton as O, is important from two points of view: firstly, because it focuses on the question of the subject as the object of perception and secondly, because the mode of representation is restricted almost purely to the visual.[129] Stan Gontarski points out that although Beckett wanted to exclude dialogue from the start, he did originally plan to include realistic sounds in the film. In his notebook for *Film*, Beckett writes: ' "No cars. One cab drawn by cantering nag, (hooves) driver standing brandishing whip. Bicycles." '[130] Beckett also wished to include the sound of O's panting.[131] The final version, however, is a silent film in which the sole sound is a 'sssh!' whispered once in the first part of the work.[132] Beckett's decision to exclude all sounds except the onomatopoeic 'sssh!' for silence points to another phenomenological reduction in operation. As Ruby Cohn observes, the 'sssh!' functions as the 'signal of silence for the rest of the film. It is also a comment on the medium of film, which is visual in spite of "talking" pictures.'[133] Beckett, at one stage in his youth, had enter-tained ideas of becoming a cameraman and of reviving the genre of silent film. He even wrote to Thomas MacGreevy that 'a backwater may be created for the two-dimensional silent film that had barely emerged from

its rudiments when it was swamped'.[134] Beckett went so far as to contact
Sergei Eisenstein, hoping to become his trainee in Moscow.

Film has two protagonists, O and E or 'object' and 'eye', 'the former in
flight, the latter in pursuit'.[135] The basic, albeit scant storyline consists of
E's persistent pursuit of O and O's progressive attempt to escape perception. *Film* emblematically opens and closes with a close-up of Keaton's
veiny, bloodshot eye and its wrinkled, shiny lid, which emphasise the
physical, fleshly nature of sight.[136] 'The Eye', significantly, was also the
original title Beckett used for *Film*.[137] There is, in keeping with *Film*'s
focus on vision, a striking emphasis on surfaces, whether the texture of
the wall in the opening shot, Buster Keaton's creased and lined skin or
the crumbling plaster of the walls of the room. In the preproduction
discussions which included Alan Schneider, Boris Kaufman (cinema-
tographer) and Barney Rosset (producer), Beckett said, 'we're trying to
find the technical equivalent for visual appetite and visual distaste. A
reluctant, a disgusted vision, and a ferociously voracious one.'[138] The
spectator is therefore confronted with what appear to be two different
focalisers; O's viewpoint, however, is not introduced until the third and
final part of the film.

Film has received a fair deal of critical attention, especially bearing
in mind its limited availability. Early commentators, amongst them
Raymond Federman, read *Film* as a self-referential comment on cinema.
In Federman's view, ' "Film" . . . represents an attempt to expose one of
cinema's most flagrant failings today: the exploitation of sound, action,
plot, and message to the detriment of the visual image.'[139] Hugh Kenner
comes to a similar conclusion about *Film*'s self-referential nature, observing
that it is a 'philosophical film which is in part about the order of escape
we are indulging in when we go film-watching'.[140] Steven Connor, for
his part, has focused on the nature of the gaze in *Film*. *Film*'s emphasis on
vision, Connor writes, 'is no longer a matter of ensuring the confirming
gaze of others, but of escaping a gaze which is now experienced as
oppressive, even though it turns out that the structure of looking is
constitutive of the self, since being consists in observing oneself in consciousness'.[141] Sylvie Henning, in turn, has written about *Film* as a
'dialogue between Beckett and Berkeley', while for Wilma Siccama, *Film*
focuses on the 'interlacing of perceiver/perceived', in what Siccama
emphasises is a '*dynamics* of spectating'.[142] More recently, Yoshiki Tajiri
has argued that *Film* stages the manner in which technology penetrates
self-consciousness in Beckett's work.[143]

Film, like *The Calmative*, is littered with explicit references to spectating or, as is at times more accurate, its eradication. In the opening scene, O rushes through run-down streets, 'hugging the wall on his left, in opposite direction to all the others. Long dark overcoat... with collar up, hat pulled down over eyes, briefcase in left hand, right hand shielding exposed side of face.'[144] O's physical distress can be evidenced in his laborious gait and stumbling, and in the visible panting that results from his walk. In his shrouded attempt to reach the apartment, O bumps into a staring couple whose ogling attitude is emphasised by the 'lorgnon' and 'pince-nez'.[145] When O reaches the stairway leading to the room, he risks running into a flower lady, whose gaze, like that of all others, he is intent on avoiding. When O finally does reach the room, it turns out to be far from the comforting enclosure Beckettian characters endlessly seek. In the notes to the script, Beckett, in effect, describes O 'hastening *blindly* to illusory sanctuary'.[146] Not only does the flat have a window that functions as the 'eye' of the room, and that simultaneously gives access to further potential spectators; to add to O's anxiety, the apartment is filled with a plethora of gawping objects: a cat; a dog; a parrot; a goldfish; a figure of 'God the Father' nailed to the wall with enormous, 'severely' staring eyes; a mirror; a folder with a fastening mechanism that resembles eyes and an ornamental decoration on the back of a rocking chair that brings to mind an eerie face.[147] The problem of self-perception is anticipated in the manner in which O winces each time he is confronted with the mirror, which occurs three times in the course of the twenty-one-minute film. Finally, O takes from his briefcase a set of photographs, seven in all, which are not only themselves objects of vision but in which further spectating takes place. The first photograph is of a male infant and his mother, '[h]er severe eyes devouring him'.[148] The second photo is of the child at the age of four with '[m]other on chair beside him, big hand on knees, head bowed towards him, severe eyes'.[149] The third picture is of the boy at the age of 15, with a dog 'on its hind legs looking up at him'.[150] A later photograph is of the man at the age of 21, with '[a]rm round fiancée. A young man takes a snap of them.'[151] In all but the last photograph, in fact, the man, who turns out to be O himself, is being observed. Even in the final picture, however, an observer is implied, as a result of the fact that someone has taken the photograph. What the photographs anticipate, besides emphasising O's non-coincidence with himself, is precisely O's inability to sidestep the scene: as we shall see, O will time and again find himself part of the picture.

In the first two sections of *Film* E functions as the focaliser. However, once O reaches the apartment, a shift in focalisation occurs, and we see 'two kinds of images – the protagonist's perception of the room, [and] the camera's perception of him perceiving'.[152] The manner in which to communicate the shift between the two viewpoints posed a technical problem for Beckett:

This difference of quality might perhaps be sought in different degrees of development, the passage from the one to the other being from greater to lesser and lesser to greater definition or luminosity. The dissimilarity, however obtained, would have to be flagrant. Having been up till now exclusively in the E quality, we would suddenly pass, with O's first survey of the room, into this quite different O quality. Then back to the E quality when O is shown moving to the window. And so on throughout the sequence, switching from the one to the other as required.[153]

In the preproduction discussions, Beckett said, 'The main thing is that it has to be an absolute difference in quality [between E and O], reinforced by the fact that O pans and E cuts.'[154] In *Film*, the technical problem of making the shift perceptible was ultimately solved through the use of a gauze filter that Beckett had originally considered in his 'Percipi Notes' and that resulted in the blurring of the frames.[155] O's vision, Beckett said, 'is really a different world. Everything becomes slower, softer. That's the quality we're looking for. Not slow motion.'[156] When O views the room, in other words, the objects become indistinct and the hold the spectating subject has over the world becomes problematic. Beckett added that O's is 'not a poor physical vision', which would imply, as Beckett himself said in the preproduction conference, that his gaze is a hesitant, even reluctant one, more concerned with repelling than with grasping the world.[157] As Beckett observed, 'O is not a man who refuses to look at all. He looks very carefully at the room. He wants to get out of all this business, but he does look very carefully at the room.'[158] Feshbach, however, has drawn attention to the fact that from the time Beckett 'wrote the script (April 1963) through the filming (July 1964), and beyond, he suffered from cataracts (coatings like gauze or veils?) in both eyes, an opacity of the lens that strikes down the vision'. Beckett, furthermore, feared blindness, which he had witnessed develop in Joyce.[159] What Feshbach's observations make clear is how acutely aware of the physiological, embodied nature of sight Beckett was at the time of the writing and filming of *Film*.

The script begins with Bishop Berkeley's dictum, '*Esse est percipi.*'[160] Appropriately, Berkeley's writings centre around the question of perception and, most emphatically, that of vision.[161] For Berkeley, objects exist only under the condition that they are perceived: *esse*, in the case of inanimate beings, can be reduced to *percipi*. Perceiving itself, on the other hand, is confined to beings of spirit, for whom *esse* hence means *percipere*. If, however, 'ideas' exist only as perceptions, then the problem of their existence in the absence of a perceiver must be raised.[162] Berkeley solves the dilemma by answering that 'All objects are eternally known by God, or which is the same thing, have an eternal existence in his mind.'[163] In Berkeley's hierarchy of perception, in other words, beings ultimately gain their existence though divine perception.

In his attempt to flee perception, E shrouds the window with a drape, puts out the cat and the dog, covers the goldfish bowl and the parrot's cage with his overcoat, veils the mirror, tears up the figure of 'God the Father', even rips up the photographs he has been carrying in his brief-case.[164] Through this act of obliteration, O not only eradicates ani-mate perception, both human and animal, but also, more poignantly, divine perception, which is destroyed with the picture of God. Jane Alison Hale has suggested that:

The biography recounted by the set of photographs corresponds in many respects to the story recorded by *Film*: a man has successively repressed much extraneous perception in his life – animal (the dog), human (mother, public, young photo-grapher, little girl), and divine (the prayers of the second pose) – yet his self-perception remains.[165]

As Beckett puts it in the script for *Film*: 'Search of non-being in flight from extraneous perception breaking down in inescapibility of self-perception.'[166]

Film, finally, disavows the possibility of a separation of the self from the world. This is brought to O's attention not only through the gaze of the couple and the objects he encounters, but through E, the eye, that at the end of *Film* turns out to be O himself.[167] Although, in other words, O does his utmost to escape all forms of perception, E goes to the same effort to keep O in view. The doubling of the self by means of the camera eye brings to mind *Krapp's Last Tape*, in which a similar effect is achieved by means of the tape recorder. In *Film*, the fact that both O and E wear an eye patch helps to reinforce their association with the 'monocular' view of the camera lens. When we encounter E's face at the end of the film, he is standing next to a 'big nail visible near left temple' that formerly held the picture of God in place.[168] E's face, in other words, replaces the empty patch left on the wall by the torn image of the divinity. Divine perception is replaced by self-perception, which in turn is developed into an ontology.[169]

Because of self-perception, it becomes impossible for O to extricate himself from the picture, whether here understood as the frame, the film or the world. If autonomy is based on the fact that the subject is the *agent* rather than the *object* of perception, by focusing perception on the self, Beckett collapses the categorical distinction and shatters the illusion of autonomous subjectivity, as the names Beckett gives O and E in the script, 'object' and 'eye', the latter a homonym of 'I', so clearly indicate. It follows that there can be no enframed totality for the subject to grasp; no world that exists at a remove from the spectator and guarantees the subject's autonomy. O ultimately acknowledges this at the end of *Film*, when, in a gesture of despair, he hides his face in his wrinkled, veiny hands.

For Beckett, in short, vision no longer guarantees the spectator's detachment from the world. Instead, the eye is embodied, fallible and subject to damage and decay. The aim to become pure subject in Beckett's writing manifests itself in two ways: as the characters' endeavour to cut themselves off from the world of sensory experience, and as their attempt to isolate themselves from the objectifying gaze of the other. Even in the sensory deprivation of the barren spaces they inhabit, however, the characters continue to interact with their surroundings, or to create phantom landscapes with which to interact when actual landscapes are no longer to be found. What *Film* finally adds to Beckett's discoveries is that even after the elimination of extraneous perception, self-perception remains active, not only collapsing the distinction between subject and object, but proving that to be is to perceive, and in the process secularising Berkeley's Christian doctrine.

For Beckett, the subject is of the order of the world, rather than existing in relation to it, a factor Beckett foregrounds throughout his landscapes in which figure is forever threatening to merge into ground. The eye situates the subject in the world rather than detaches it from its surroundings. This somatic immediacy may finally be one of the ways in which Beckett's work achieves that mourned for 'integrity of the eyelids coming down before the brain knows of grit in the wind'.[170]

CHAPTER 3

Hearing Beckett

Early critics have often discussed the importance of hearing in Beckett's work, noting that sound functions as a marker of interiority in Beckett's writing. The centrality of sound and hearing in Beckett's work, however, has received surprisingly little attention in more recent criticism. The puzzling neglect of this central concern may partly be due to misreadings of deconstructive theory that, in its rejection of 'phonocentrism', has led to a form of phonophobia or aversion to all things heard. As Douglas Kahn and Gregory Whitehead have observed, it has remained 'almost unheard of to think about sound'.[1]

Beckett's lifelong interest in sound and hearing, implicit in his second-person narratives and prose fragments and foregrounded in much of the drama, is explicitly manifest in *All That Fall*, the first radio play Beckett wrote (1956).[2] Beckett had been approached by the BBC in the June of 1956 to write a play for the experimental Third Programme. *All That Fall* was most probably prompted by the request, as the first reference Beckett made to the play would suggest: 'Never thought about a radio play technique, but in the dead of t'other night got a nice gruesome idea full of cartwheels and dragging feet and puffing and panting.'[3] What seems to have inspired Beckett to write his first piece for radio, in other words, was the opportunity the radio medium offered to utilise sound, as opposed to purely linguistic expression.

Beckett's interest in sound and hearing has prompted critics to focus on the 'disembodied' nature of voice in Beckett's works.[4] Beckett turned to the radio medium, early critics concluded, because it offered him the most effective means of portraying a character's mind, which humanist critics have considered the author's prime objective. In 1971, in an article on radio drama appropriately entitled 'The Mind as Stage', Martin Esslin wrote: 'it is through the ear that *words* are primarily communicated; and words communicate concepts, thought, information on a more abstract level than the images of the world the eye takes in'.[5] In his influential essay, 'Samuel Beckett and the Art of Broadcasting', first published in 1975, Esslin developed his ideas further:

Through the use of acoustic perspectives the radio writer and director can clearly convey to the listener with whose ears, from which subjective viewpoint, he is witnessing the action, and indeed inside whose mind he is supposed to be. Thus, by the use of stylised and distorted sounds, radio can create a subjective reality halfway between the objective events experienced and their subjective reflection within the mind of the character who experiences them – halfway between waking consciousness and dreamlike states, halfway between fact and fantasy, even hallucination.[6]

Radio, Esslin argued, allowed Beckett to eliminate much that was superfluous in his work, in favour of a privileged interiority. In a similar vein Clas Zilliacus, in a study published a year after Esslin's essay, urged that 'It is characteristic of the radio medium that its means of expression are aural, temporal, nonspatial and uncorporeal.'[7] The last two adjectives provide the key to many readings of Beckett's radio plays: the radio enabled the kind of disembodiment that Beckett had been seeking in his writing.[8] I shall suggest, however, that the special relevance the acoustic has to issues of embodiment in Beckett's work has been overlooked. Beckett's experiments with sound, and in particular sound technologies, though offering his characters some respite from the constraints of embodiment, ultimately bear witness to the persistence with which Beckett grounds subjectivity firmly within a material context. To advance this argument, I shall discuss four works in which sound plays a prominent role: Beckett's first two radio plays, *All That Fall* (1956) and *Embers* (1959), and the stage plays *Krapp's Last Tape* (1958) and *That Time* (1975). In each, one can discern a complex analysis of the phenomenal significance of sound and hearing to the question of embodied subjectivity.

All That Fall begins with Maddy Rooney's journey to the Boghill railway station to meet her husband Dan. During her trek to the station, Maddy encounters a host of friends and acquaintances with whom she discusses ailing relatives and her own ill health. Once Maddy, after much effort, reaches the station, she discovers that her husband's train has been delayed. Eventually, the train arrives, and the couple begin their physically arduous walk back home. Despite repeated questioning by Maddy, Mr Rooney is mysteriously unwilling to disclose the reason for the train's delay. At the end of the play, Jerry, a boy who aids the blind Dan Rooney, reveals to Maddy that the hold-up has been caused by a child falling on the track. Dan Rooney's silence and his possible stake in the incident are left ambiguously unresolved.

The play has attracted a fair amount of critical attention which has been relatively accordant in tone. In 1962, Hugh Kenner argued that the play's theme is transience, and that, ultimately, 'all living is an illusion'.[9] Kenner added, 'What the dramatic medium compels us to do is acquiesce in this indifference of expression to fact; a sound or two, a word or two, we find, has the power to make us believe virtually anything.'[10] Martin Esslin, in turn, inaugurated the view that *All That Fall* functions as a dramatisation of the clash between 'objective reality' and Maddy's mind.[11] Subsequent readings have followed similar lines. For Katharine Worth, for instance, the use of the experience of 'blindness as a radiogenic device', epitomised in *All That Fall* in the figure of Dan Rooney, 'create[s] the atmosphere of an inner landscape'.[12] Linda Ben-Zvi comments on the 'world that exists within the skull of Maddy Rooney', although she also astutely concludes that the play 'explores the possibility of verifying self through physical means'.[13] Robert Wilcher writes of 'Maddy's experience of the impingement of external reality upon the private world in her skull'.[14] Similarly, in Everett Frost's reading, *All That Fall* deals with Maddy's journey 'as it is perceived by Maddy Rooney from within the mind of Maddy Rooney as she is in the process of experiencing it'.[15]

Another, not unrelated strand of criticism has focused on the question of language in *All That Fall*. Ruby Cohn, for whom the 'control of speech' is the play's major achievement, comes to the conclusion that Maddy 'walks and talks past all obstacles. That is her way of saying No to Nothingness.'[16] Thomas van Laan adopts a different stance. Through the structured use of overstatement and understatement, van Laan argues, *All That Fall* dramatises the common Beckettian theme of the failure of language.[17] Clas Zilliacus, in a more recent reading, agrees that *All That Fall* is 'all about language', but concludes that on the thematic level, the play is constructed around the realisation that 'all creation' falls.[18] Whilst astute in their readings of puns and biblical references, these critics pay little attention to Beckett's use of sound in the play. Beckett's prolific use of sound in *All That Fall* goes against the essentially speech-based tradition of radio drama.[19] It also renders problematic the claims about the play's focus on interiority and language. A close reading of the play that takes into consideration the phenomenology of sound and hearing will suggest that *All That Fall* prioritises exteriority and matter over interiority and the problems of conceptual thought.

One might begin such a reading by taking note of a paradox. Though *All That Fall* is a radio play, it is also, as Martin Esslin has pointed out, an intensely visual play.[20] Elissa Guralnick has accurately observed that *All That Fall* may be 'more visually seductive' than most of Beckett's stage plays.[21] Furthermore, it does not rely on the acoustic and the visual alone. As Jonathan Kalb has observed, the play is also littered with tactile references, as in the 'scene', charged with sexual overtones, in which Mr Slocum tries to help Mrs Rooney up into his car: 'Oh!...Lower!...Don't be afraid!...We're past the age when....There!...Now!...Get your shoulder under it....Oh!...[*Giggles*] Oh glory!'[22] Different forms of perception figure strongly in *All That Fall*, to the extent that Maddy Rooney even fears 'perceivedness'; she feels threatened by the gaze of the hinny she encounters on her way to the station, although she is also, significantly, anxious about the extinction that silence threatens to subject her to, as if aware of the fact that all depended on sound.[23] Maddy's anxiety tallies with other features of the play, for it owes much to the peculiar relationship between sound and setting, sonic source and physical world.

As a result, perhaps, of the cultural coding of the sensorium and, more specifically, the predominance of vision in Western culture, it is one of the characteristics of sound to make us see what we hear: 'The ability to do so is part of our psychology; instinctively, we visualize sounds in terms of images. By contrast, we tend not to hear what we see.'[24] More accurately even, if no source for the sonic can be identified, the auditor will construct an origin for the sound, because a sound without a source is not only an empirical impossibility; such a sound would be unbearable.[25] Steven Connor writes:

Sound, and especially the sound of the human voice, is experienced as enigmatic or anxiously incomplete until its source can be identified, which is usually to say, visualized; visual objects, by contrast, do not appear to us to need complementing or completing. We ask of a sound 'What was that?', meaning 'Who was that?', or 'Where did that come from?', but feel no corresponding impulse to ask of an image 'What sound does this make?'[26]

Closely connected to the way in which sound prompts us to visualise its source is the manner in which the sonic can acquaint us with its setting. We cannot hear the existence of mute objects, but may, at times, distinguish the surroundings of a sound we do capture. Rudolf Arnheim, an early theorist of film and radio, writes: 'Under certain restricted conditions, distances in space can be heard. The size and form of the space as well as the nature of the confining walls are expressed more or less distinctly by the kind of resonance.'[27] Furthermore, the sense of hearing, because sounds 'penetrate us from all directions at all times', places the subject within a world rather than in front of one as vision does.[28] When a sound event cannot be spatially situated, as in the case of transmitted sounds, our psychology is such that the auditor tends to construct a space to accommodate the sounds heard.

Many critics, as Katherine Worth has remarked, have indeed 'been struck by the richer-than usual realism' of *All That Fall*. Worth, who first suggested that the play created 'the atmosphere of an inner landscape', later argues that: 'More of the day-to-day world is allowed into this than into any other of the radio plays... there is a strong sense of real topography.'[29] Similarly, Clas Zilliacus, who stressed the non-spatial nature of Beckett's radio works, observes that *All That Fall* 'hits an odd key in the author's gamut of impotency: it has a verbal concreteness, a defined locale, and a larger cast than any other play of Beckett's save the first, *Éleuthéria*.'[30] There is, in other words, an inconsistency between various critics' emphasis on interiority and their simultaneous stress on the play's realism and day-to-day topography. Not only is the play spatially specific; the material world it constructs is so forceful that it finds its way into the critical commentary.

The 'realistic' setting of the play is achieved by Beckett's abundant use of the sounds of a rural community: cooing ringdoves, rolling cartwheels, a ringing bicycle-bell, squeaking brakes, a rattling motor-van, a hooting car-horn and a thudding train.[31] The play's spatial realm, however, is more complex than critical commentaries have implied. *All That Fall* opens with '*Music faint from house by way. "Death and the Maiden"*.'[32] We hear the sound of several animals, and of Maddy Rooney's tread. The auditors of the play are simultaneously transported, through the sounds they hear, to the house with the music, the location of the animals and the road Maddy Rooney is walking along, whilst also remaining in their own geographical sound space. This implies that the listeners occupy at least three spatial dimensions at once: their own physical location, Maddy's and the spaces that surround her. Even a fourth spatial dimension is implied by the music, for Maddy herself is transported by sound alone into the 'ruinous old house' in which 'Death and the Maiden' is played.[33] At this stage, the music becomes louder, and the stage directions specify '[s]*ilence, but for music playing*'.[34] At no moment, however, does Maddy physically enter the house of the '[p]oor woman'.[35] For the listener of the radio play, the house therefore constitutes a fourth-degree spatial dimension: two removes from the location Maddy herself happens to be in, and one remove from the things Maddy sees as well as hears. The latter belong within the frame of the play's 'sound picture', unlike the interior of the house, which is never actually directly entered by means other than hearing.[36]

The transporting quality of sound that Beckett exploits in *All That Fall* sets hearing apart from the proximity senses, whose functioning requires physical contact between the subject and sense object.[37] Sound, however, also differs from visual stimuli in possessing a peculiar 'strength that light cannot rival: it can penetrate solid walls, boom through the depths of the ocean, go round corners, shatter delicate glasses, or force its way through the earth'.[38] The sense of hearing, in other words, enables the auditor to traverse obstacles the other senses cannot overcome. Hearing, therefore, provides 'a more extended or distant geography, an experience of wider spaces and the relationship between places'.[39] Through hearing, the auditor, furthermore, occupies several spatial dimensions at once, which only serves to perpetuate the peculiar spatialising quality of sound that Beckett puts to use in *All That Fall.*

On a textual level, *All That Fall* foregrounds its acoustic nature by containing a number of wittily self-referential lines of dialogue. The most prominent of these are the 'scenes' in which Maddy questions her own whereabouts or existence. When Maddy, descending from Mr Slocum's car, finds herself ignored by Slocum and young Tommy, she sardonically remarks, 'Don't mind me. Don't take any notice of me. I do not exist. The fact is well known.'[40] The play makes an even more striking reference to its radiophonic status when Maddy comes across Miss Fitt, who, like Tommy, does not greet her but simply keeps on walking: 'Am I then invisible, Miss Fitt?' Maddy provocatively retorts.[41] Through Maddy's self-referential comments and the play's several references to 'people' who are 'not really there at all', the text interrogates the status of the acoustically constructed characters it evokes.[42]

The absent bodies, however, repeatedly find their way into *All That Fall.* Maddy refers to herself as having 'a once female shape'; Miss Fitt remarks that Mrs Rooney looks 'bowed and bent', and Dan Rooney makes mention of the '[t]wo hundred pounds of unhealthy fat' that Maddy carries around.[43] Maddy, furthermore, comes into existence for the audience as an assemblage of the corporeal sounds she makes; not only, in other words, do we hear the sounds of animals, the wind, the rain, Mr Slocum's car, horns and signals, the train; we also hear Maddy's huffing, puffing, moans, groans, her crying, her laughter and the way she blows her nose. This would be impossible on stage, television or screen, where 'the visual perception of her existence would proceed independently of the sonic assemblage of it'.[44] Beckett's almost obsessive insistence on corporeal sounds in the play, rendered in the text as directions such as '*Sobbing*', '*Breathing hard*' and '*Sound of handkerchief loudly applied*', not only goes against a philosophical tradition that has aimed to obscure all signs of the voice's origin in the body; it, together with the repeated references to different forms of perception, contributes to the creation of an embodied character in the absence of a body and a space.[45]

The body has further means of penetrating the world of the play, for everyone's relatives, whether parents, wives or daughters, 'are in constant pain. This is true of Christy, Mr. Tyler, Mr. Slocum, Jerry, Mrs. Tully, and, of course, the Rooneys.'[46] 'The inhabitants of Boghill seem literally bogged down, impeded', as Linda Ben-Zvi remarks.[47] Physical discomfort is so prominent, in fact, that it constitutes the thematic dimension of the play, as its title reference to Psalm 145 indicates. Maddy quotes: '"The Lord upholdeth all that fall and raiseth up all those that be bowed down."'[48] The quotation is followed by the couple joining '*in wild laughter*'.[49] For not only does everything in Boghill take a fall, including the child who is run over by the train; Maddy herself suffers from 'kidney trouble', 'fat and rheumatism and childlessness', and even mentions the fact that she 'may collapse at any moment'.[50] We learn that Maddy has been 'laid up there a long time' by a difficult illness; she also makes repeated mention of the fact that she feels 'very cold and weak'.[51]

Physical suffering and pain, however, trigger a crisis in representation, because they are virtually inexpressible in language. Elaine Scarry has argued that pain differs

from every other bodily and psychic event, by not having an object in the external world. Hearing and touch are of objects outside the boundaries of the body, as desire is desire of x, fear is fear of y, hunger is hunger for z; but pain is not 'of' or 'for' anything – it is itself alone. This objectlessness, the complete absence of referential content, almost prevents it from being rendered in language: objectless, it cannot easily be objectified in any form, material or verbal.[52]

The fact that physical suffering exists within the boundaries of the body, whilst simultaneously having no exterior referent, renders it 'not available to sensory confirmation'.[53] More accurately even, pain, unlike hunger, desire or even fear, seems to lack the directionality or orientedness of intentional acts, which complicates its rendering within the symbolic structures of language. By the introduction of the sounds of the body, however, Beckett overcomes this impediment. The auditor becomes aware of Maddy's physical discomfort not so much through the remarks made about her ill health that constitute little more than abstract concepts, as through the disquietingly explicit moans and groans of physical distress that accompany the sound of Maddy's dragging feet. Similarly, in Dan Rooney's case, it is not the knowledge of his blindness, stiffness or 'coronary' as much as his incessant panting that alarms us.

In Western literature, physical pain and suffering function as tropes designed to put an end to troping: they bring to a halt different forms of metaphoric transformation. A classic example of this occurs in *Don Quijote*.[54] While the protagonist's world is coloured by the excessive reading of romance literature (*libros de caballerías*), which has made Don Quijote dangerously prone to metaphorisation, his companion, Sancho Panza, categorically refuses to metaphorise. For Don Quijote, inns are transformed into castles, innkeepers into kings and travelling monks into highway men, but Sancho Panza's view remains stubbornly down to earth. An early example of this occurs in the famous windmill scene in the novel: where Don Quijote sees giants 'with their long arms', Sancho sees only 'the sails' of the windmills, 'which are whirled round in the wind and make the millstone turn'.[55] Sancho Panza, therefore, more accurately, is associated with metonomy in the novel: a form of troping in which 'mapping occurs within a single domain', rather than across domains as in the case of metaphor.[56] The result of this characteristic of metonyms is that they tend to be employed for real-world effects, but even more significantly that they exclude the transcendental dimension.[57]

The manner in which the novel associates Don Quijote and Sancho Panza with the different types of trope finds its most obvious manifestation in the characters' names. While the word *quijote*, in old Spanish, stands for a type of armour, thus, in a comical way, constituting a leap to the knightly tradition of romance literature, *panza* is the familiar word for stomach, and could be translated as 'belly' or 'paunch'.[58] Don Quijote's name, therefore, constitutes a categorical transformation, while Sancho Panza's functions metonymically, foregrounding the character's association with bodily needs by relying on the combinative axis of language. While Don Quijote forgets to eat and spends sleepless nights in romantic reverie about Dulcinea, Sancho Panza is gluttonous and sleeps soundly, even on muleback. If fatigue and hunger, by pointing to corporeal processes, function as markers of embodiment, the ultimate metonym for carnal contingency in the novel is physical pain. Time and again, in the course of the narrative, Sancho is beaten black and blue.[59] Sancho Panza's character, through its metonymic association with contingency, carries the nascent code of modernity in the novel, while Don Quijote himself stands for the dolorous collapse of the transcendental dimension.

In *All That Fall*, the corporeal sounds of suffering have precisely a metonymic function: they return sound to its material origin whose ultimate marker is the human body. While all sound, by leaving its source, allows for an expansion of physical boundaries, the sounds in *All That Fall*, on account of their metonymic nature, enact matter's crude resistance to metaphoric transformation. The sounds of physical distress, foregrounded in stage directions such as '[*p*]*anting, stumbling, ejaculations*' and '*effort*', point to the decrepit human body that binds the subject to its material context.[60] The visceral quality of the human body is also graphically epitomised in Maddy's cry, when she is confronted with the 'cleg-tormented eyes' of the welted hinny: 'Oh let me just flop down flat on the road like a big fat jelly out of a bowl and never move again! A great big slop thick with grit and dust and flies, they would have to scoop me up with a shovel.'[61] The distortion of the body through pain, disease or disintegration works against schematised representations, whose ultimate function, as that of metaphoric representations, is to repress 'the horrifying, abject, or grotesque' nature of the human body.[62] James Elkins argues that the presence of the schematised body in representation 'is a magical gesture against the body's transgressive and continual flux'.[63] In *All That Fall*, Beckett systematically rejects this gesture in favour of explicit representations of suffering and the body's inherently deviant disposition.

Beckett's grasp of the phenomenology of sound and his astute use of it in *All That Fall* not only provide an explanation for the play's striking visual power, which creates both a more vivid spatial realm than Beckett's stage drama and an acute sense of embodied characters in the immediate absence of bodies; it also helps to explain why Beckett was so opposed to any stage adaptations of the play. As Beckett famously said about *All That Fall*, 'to "act" it is to kill it. Even the reduced visual dimension it will receive from the simplest and most static of readings... will be destructive of whatever quality it may have and which depends on the whole thing's *coming out of the dark*.'[64] As Linda Ben-Zvi has pointed out, '[c]ertain writers may create plays without anchoring them to particular forms, but Beckett is not such a writer. In each case he writes with a specific medium in mind. Those who have worked with him on these projects... have commented on Beckett's acute sense of the problems and possibilities of the form in question.'[65] A visual realisation of *All That Fall* would be harmful because it would distract from the primacy of the listening process on which the play's embodying and transporting qualities depend.[66]

Instead of being nonspatial, therefore, *All That Fall* uses sound's spatialising quality to evoke a vivid and multidimensional topography. By relying on sound, the play, paradoxically, only emphasises the situatedness and facticity of its characters. Similarly, the play's emphasis on the predicament of the body on the levels of story (arduous walk to the station and back), formal structure (use of sounds of physical suffering and exertion), plot (body of the dead child) and thematic content (physical suffering), reveals the play's insistent focus on exteriority and the embodied nature of subjectivity.

Embers, Beckett's second radio play, completed in 1959, is the story of Henry, a man who cannot stop speaking to himself, his dead father and his wife, Ada.[67] Henry's monologues are mainly about the events of his own past life. In addition, Henry narrates an apparently unrelated story about two men, Bolton and Holloway. In the course of the play, the auditor not only hears Henry's voice, but also a dialogue between Henry and Ada, together with two scenes that feature the couple's daughter, Addie, and her music and riding masters. Either in the background, whenever a pause is indicated, or foregrounded by means of an increase in volume, the auditors hear the sound of the sea that Henry is trying to escape.[68] In addition, there is a sound of hooves, a drip, Ada and Henry's laughter and Addie's wail. Most significantly, the audience hear the crunching of Henry's footsteps on the shingle. Ada's footsteps, as she joins Henry on the shore, are conspicuously absent. Absent, too, is the sound of the embers that give the play its title, although Henry makes mention of their '[s]hifting, lapsing, furtive like, dreadful sound' which he later refers to as the 'sound of dying'.[69] In a letter to Barbara Bray dated 11 March 1959, Beckett wrote that he preferred the ebb of embers to that of the sea, 'because followed by no flow'.[70]

The critical readings of *Embers* echo those of *All That Fall*. For Hugh Kenner, *Embers* locks the listener 'inside the word spinner's prison': the fictive world becomes more real than the 'present world', which 'is an occasion for delusions and testy imperatives'.[71] John Fletcher and John Spurling conclude that 'the world of [the play's] protagonist Henry is firmly interiorized, since the sounds he hears (and we hear) are mainly in his head.'[72] In Clas Zilliacus's early reading, *Embers*, likewise, centres around Henry's subjective view of the world: 'it is one man's world: The interplay between Henry and other characters takes place in Henry's mind.'[73] Martin Esslin comes to a similar conclusion: 'the voices are all internal: Henry's internal monologue as he tries unsuccessfully to conjure up his dead father's presence, and later the voices of his wife and daughter and her instructors, which materialize in his memory.'[74] David Alpaugh, for his part, has offered a psychoanalytical reading of the play, in which *Embers* becomes the story of Henry's repression of 'oceanic awareness'.[75] Finally, for Marjorie Perloff, in a more recent reading, the play's 'sounding of disembodied voices makes it the perfect vehicle for the dance of death that is its subject'.[76] These readings, however, pay little attention to Beckett's exploitation of the duplicitous nature of hearing. Beckett himself famously remarked that '*Cendres* repose sur un ambiguïté: le personnage a-t-il une hallucination ou est-il en présence de la réalité? La réalisation scenique détruirait l'ambiguïté.'[77] [*Embers* relies on ambiguity: are the characters hallucinations or are they real? A scenic realisation would destroy the ambiguity.][78]

Embers, more than Beckett's other radio plays, thematises hearing, for Henry spends his time listening to diverse sounds. Didier Anzieu, who has written about the envelope of sound that surrounds the subject, suggests that sound not only forms an environment in which the subject takes shelter, but also functions as a force or container that shapes the subject.[79] Anzieu stresses the importance of the dual nature of the sonorous space, which consists of sounds emitted by the subject and other sounds that originate in the environment surrounding the subject. The envelope of sound, like the skin, hence embodies a dialectic between interiority and exteriority, epitomised, perhaps, in the tympanum of the ear, which itself consists of a skin.

Hearing itself, furthermore, can be both endogenous and exogenous: we integrate 'the gurgling of the viscera, the cracking of the bones, the thudding and pulsing of the blood, even the firing of the neurones' effortlessly into our experience.[80] As Don Ihde puts it, 'I hear not only the voices of the world, in some sense I "hear" myself or from myself.'[81] Because we are more certain of a sound than we are of where it comes from, sound, at times, renders problematic the distinction between the endogenous and the exogenous.[82]

Although all sounds have a physical origin, sounds themselves are transitory and ephemeral. Partly because of the evanescent nature of the acoustic, hearing is more prone to miscalculations than vision.[83] Furthermore, we can also have a vivid acoustic memory or imagination: 'Auditorily Beethoven was able to imaginatively "hear" an entire symphony at will. Even after deafness his "inner hearing" did not fail him as the magnificent Ninth Symphony so well shows.'[84] In sonorous experience, 'sensation, perception, emotion, interpretation and imagination mingle in connection with stimuli made up of sounds and silences, in a density that cannot always find appropriate words to describe it.'[85]

Hearing is, in several ways, a duplicitous sense. In *Embers*, Beckett exploits to the full this characteristic of the acoustic, for the different sounds in the play function precisely as equivocal structuring devices that, more audaciously than in *All That Fall*, serve to complicate notions of spatial configuration. The appearance within one scene of sounds that identify another sound space, such as the persistence of the sound of the sea even when the sound space is not that of the shore, or the mysterious recurrence of the sound of hooves, associated with Addie's riding lesson, serves to complicate notions of the origin of the various sounds in the play. The different spaces in *Embers* permeate one another through the sonorous overlap.

While *Embers* is similar to *All That Fall* in its multiplication of spatial dimensions, it also highlights another type of sonorous transport – a temporal one. When Henry is talking with his wife, Ada, and wants to walk to the water's edge, Ada says, 'Don't stand there thinking about it...Don't stand there staring...Don't wet your good boots.'[86] Her voice triggers off a(nother) memory, and Henry, after mumbling, 'Don't, don't...' is transported back twenty years in time to a love-making scene between the two.[87] For just as sound, as we have seen, transgresses spatial boundaries, so it can similarly trigger temporal leaps: 'Because sound can put us in spaces it can also take us out of them, replacing actual and particular spaces with remembered or imagined spaces.'[88] Sound, furthermore, is itself inherently temporal by nature: not only does it lack boundaries in time, giving the subject no respite from 'sonorous perception, which is active day and night and only stops with death or total deafness', as is the agonising fate of Henry, who cannot get away from the sound of the sea; sound also surrounds us with a 360-degree range, instead of only facing us, as vision does.[89] In this way, sound not only implies the futurity of sight, with its connotations of 'looking ahead', but also, and most importantly for Beckett, the past, that which we believe we have left behind.[90] In addition to the past tense, sound, with its instantly fleeting quality, implies the here and now of the present, barely comprehensible, and even the future, that which we hear ahead of us and gradually move towards, or which we simply anticipate, as in the case of listening to music.

As a result of the transgressive quality of sound, 'the radio medium makes it possible to shift ground at a moment's notice and to [collapse] time. Past and present are often indistinguishable.'[91] In *Embers*, only the stage directions inform us that the scene triggered by the sound of Ada's words (the repetition of 'don't' when she addresses Henry) constitutes a twenty-year leap back in time, although we are aware of a change in the linearity of the narrative sequence. Hearing does not merely summon a multidimensional spatial realm; it can also evoke a similarly complex temporal landscape. Because sound is by nature wandering and centrifugal, it carries the auditor away; it makes the subject wander, dissolving semblances of stable identity.

Sound, however, can also work against principles of transport, for intense and loud noises turn the sonorous environment into a rigid space that the auditor can neither transgress nor escape. This is the role of Ada's amplified cry of pain that not only brings the love-making scene to an end, but also startles the auditor to a physical awareness of the act of listening: 'Intense noise cannot be heard, or merely heard. Such noise forces hearing to spill across into the other senses: we do not merely apprehend noise, we undergo it; shaken and scattered, we become ourselves noised, or noisy. We start to hear with our skin and skull and teeth.'[92]

Ada's scream resituates both Henry and the auditors back in the present tense.[93] We hear Henry's '*Boots laborious on the shingle*' and the sea, now '*calm and faint*'.[94] If the evocation of Ada and her mysteriously monotonous and whispering voice imply Henry's memory or imagination (for the fact that we do not hear Ada's footfalls may well indicate she is dead), and hence suggest a certain degree of interiority in *Embers*, the scream that cuts through Henry's reveries, bringing him to a physical awareness of the auditory experience, functions in the play as a marker of exteriority. Furthermore, the other sharp and differentiated sounds that abound in *Embers*, and that are set not only against the amorphous 'sucking' of the sea, but against other scenes that could be categorised as flashbacks, participate in a similar dialectic, functioning much as Ada's piercing scream: the '[v]*iolent slam of the door*' that is heard twice when Henry is reminiscing about his father; the recurrent sound of hooves, '*walking on hard road*'; the sound of Addie's music master thumping and hammering the correct note on the piano; the din of Addie's wail, '*amplified to paroxysm*' when she is being scolded by her music master, and the manner in which Henry dashes the two stones together, '[c]*lash. "Stone!" and clash amplified*', in an act of despair.[95] Frances Dyson remarks that because sound is present both externally and 'internally as a resonance or vibration, sound erodes the limits of the culturally well-established body'.[96] Sounds, like scents and flavours, literally enter our bodies; they come into contact with surfaces that generally remain out of bounds.[97] Hearing, in other words, is not merely located in the ear: just as the ear 'consists in part of a skin, so the skin itself is a kind of ear'.[98] Intense sounds that resonate in the body bring the ambiguity of hearing to an end, for as the overlap between hearing and touch suggests, sonorous perception could well be considered 'more earthly and materialistic than vision'.[99]

As Michel Serres has observed, one can 'put the ear on the other side of the window, projecting it great distances, holding it at a great distance from the body'.[100] While acoustic perception grants the expansion of spatial and temporal boundaries, hearing does not, however, allow the body to be left behind. If *All That Fall* focused on the spatialising quality of sound, *Embers* brings the auditor to an awareness of sound's temporal character. Both plays, however, foreground the material nature of acoustic perception. In the first play this is mediated through an emphasis on the physical origin of sound; in the second, through the play's focus on the embodied nature of hearing. *Embers* and *All That Fall*, in short, are simultaneously based on the transgressive and binding qualities of the acoustic: they derive their strength from Beckett's keen understanding of the phenomenology of sonorous perception.

Krapp's Last Tape, written in 1958, inaugurates a new phase in Beckett's work for the stage, for from this play onwards the act of listening becomes 'the prime visual image of Beckett's drama'.[101] The stage directions describe Krapp's initial listening posture in the following manner: '*leaning forward, elbows on table, hand cupping ear towards machine, face front*'.[102] Not only, in other words, should the audience become aware of the utter concentration with which Krapp gives himself to the act of listening; his entire posture, 'bent or twisted over the machine', and his physical immobility and terseness make the act ever more acute.[103] Pierre Chabert who, in 1975, worked with Beckett in the Théâtre d'Orsay production of the play, asserts that the author 'frequently insisted on the tension present in the act of listening'.[104] Chabert, furthermore, draws attention to the importance given in *Krapp's Last Tape* to all things sonorous, and goes on to specify 'the noises of the body [such as] Krapp's breath, panting slightly', and 'the sounds of Krapp moving on the stage'.[105] Chabert adds that the objects on stage are themselves 'chosen because of the noises that they can supply', and mentions, amongst other things, the speeded-up voice when Krapp is winding the tape forward, which Beckett himself, in his 1969 Berlin Schiller production notebook, comically referred to as 'Quatschgeräusch'.[106] In the Schiller-Theater production, Beckett also replaced the cardboard boxes holding the spools of tape with metallic ones, to ensure that the sound of the tins crashing on to the floor would be made piercingly perceptible. Beckett wrote in the same production notebook: 'As much noise as poss. with objects throughout.'[107] The author's concern with sound, furthermore, also manifests itself on the level of language. Beckett, referring to the scene of the girl in the punt, once told James Knowlson that 'if you take a single syllable out of those lines, you destroy the sound of the lapping of the water on the side of the boat'.[108] It is also significant that in his contemporaneously written 'Suggestions for T.V. Krapp', Beckett proposed the use of two cameras, A and B, the latter of which 'listens and its activity is affected by words spoken'.[109] In the same text, Beckett makes reference to the protagonist by saying, 'Krapp though hard of hearing hears acutely'; he adds, 'camera [B] is Krapp's hearing plus acute eye'.[110]

One of the most influential readings of *Krapp's Last Tape* has been James Knowlson's detailed analysis of the play. Knowlson argues that it is constructed around polar oppositions such as dark and light, fire and water and opening and closing eyes that all represent the dichotomy between sense and spirit Krapp is trying to overcome.[111] Themes such as artistic creativity and love have also attracted critics' attention.[112] Less, however, has been written on the significance of sound and technology in the play. In an essay on the poetics of orality and tape-recorded voices, Michael Davidson remarks that in *Krapp's Last Tape*, Beckett projects 'the tape recorder as an ultimate agent of mind control, a machine capable of replacing human communication with a prerecorded script'.[113] Steven Connor and Katherine Hayles have addressed the topic in innovative ways: the former has shown how the play works against a metaphysics of presence, while the latter has argued that in *Krapp's Last Tape*, the voice is gradually transferred from Krapp on to the surrogate body of the machine, a line also pursued by Daniel Albright, for whom the 'soundtrack of Krapp's life has become the life itself'.[114] For Yoshiki Tajiri, in turn, sound technology in the play serves to exteriorise 'phenomena in the skull'.[115]

Notoriously, voice in Western culture has been associated with unmediated presence, as Jacques Derrida has argued in his critique of the 'phenomenology of presence'. The spoken word has been invested with agency and immediacy and has therefore been perceived as 'authentic' and 'uncorrupted', while the written word, according to this received bias, has been taken out of its original context and further 'contaminated' by rhetoric. The telephone and the radio, early examples of auditory media, however, took advantage of sound's transgressive qualities by exploiting the principle of *spatial transport* that voice and sound offer. The sinking of the *Titanic* in 1912, for instance, was followed on the radio in a number of countries. On 16 April 1912, *The Times* (London) commented on the 'expanded range of experience made possible by the wireless': 'We recognise with a sense near to awe that we have been almost witness of a great ship in her death agonies.'[116] What most fascinated early commentators about the telephone, in turn, was not so much its message-conveying capacity as 'its faithful preservation of the individuating tones and accidents of speech and even the non-verbal sounds of the body'.[117] *The Times* characterised this revolutionary potential of the telephone by remarking that 'There is no reason why a man should not hold conversation with a son at the Antipodes, distinguishing his voice, and if the instrument be applied as a stethoscope, hear his heart throb.'[118]

The physical presence of the interlocutor was now no longer a condition of speech, although it was implied by the manner in which the telephone transmitted the embodied quality of voice. Prior to the popularisation of inscription technologies, the telephone and radio, however, functioned in the present tense. Hence, they partially 'continued to participate in the phenomenology of presence through the simultaneity that they produced and that produced them'.[119] Inscription technologies exploited sound's capacity for *temporal transport*; it now became possible to travel back in time and re-listen to a sound event: 'Our power to transport ourselves with sound [became] reinforced by the power to transport sound itself.'[120] The most crucial consequence of inscription techniques was the manner in which they distanced sound from the conceit of interiority; 'from the necessity of human agency and metaphysical presence'.[121] A humorous example of this occurs in the Hades episode of James Joyce's *Ulysses* (1922). Bloom, attending the funeral of Paddy Dignam, observes all the graves at the cemetery and, worrying about how one could possibly remember all the dead, fantasises about placing a gramophone in each grave:

Besides how could you remember everybody? Eyes, walk, voice. Well, the voice, yes: gramophone. Have a gramophone in every grave or keep it in the house. After dinner on a Sunday. Put on poor old greatgrandfather Kraahraark! Hello-hellohello amawfullyglad kraark awfullygladaseeragain hellohello amarawf kopthsth. Remind you of the voice like the photograph reminds you of the face.[122]

Although seemingly promising to reproduce the fullness and authenticity of voice, the inscription of sound, through re-production, forms the *antithesis* of 'unmediated presence'.[123] The audiotape, finally, exploiting both the spatially and temporally transgressive qualities of sound, added a further dimension to the already existing features of phonograph disks: magnetic audiotape, by being both permanent and mutable, permitted the erasure and rewriting of sound. Sophisticated studio equipment, furthermore, ceased to be a precondition of the storage of acoustic information; anyone who had the appropriate equipment could now capture sound on tape.

The importance that recording techniques held for Beckett in devising *Krapp's Last Tape* is made clear in his letter to Donald McWhinnie, written in the March of 1958. Beckett had previously informed McWhinnie that he was writing a stage monologue specifically for Patrick Magee; he now added that a tape recorder would figure in the play, and asked McWhinnie to send him the operating instructions for such a machine, so that Beckett could make certain he knew exactly how the device functioned.[124] Although Valdemar Poulsen, as early as 1898, had patented the principle of storing acoustic data on a metallic surface, it was not until the second half of the 1950s that, with the development of magnetic film tape, tape recorders reached popular consumption.[125] Beckett, therefore, was not only using cutting-edge technology; in a rare concern for the verisimilitude of the play, he situated *Krapp's Last Tape* in the future, in order to make plausible the thirty-year flashbacks that the tapes effect.[126] Beckett himself, by 1958, was already familiar with tapes, for the BBC had sent him a recording of *All That Fall* on account of the poor radio transmission Beckett had encountered on both occasions the play had been broadcast.[127]

As we have seen, magnetic audiotape turns sound into an empirical object, 'capable of being seen, read, written, and drawn directly'.[128] It is precisely this reversibility, tangibility and manipulability of sound that Beckett sets out to examine in *Krapp's Last Tape*: the status of sound as a near-physical object that has the ability to make us relive the past. One thinks of Steven Connor's words:

Our world is a world of multiple times; of variable, manufactured nows. This is largely because our world is a world of recordings, replications and action replays; and above all a world of replicable sounds. Such a world is characterised by multiple rhythms, durations and temporalities; by temporal comings, goings and crossings, of rifts and loops and pleats in the fabric of linear time.[129]

The play's temporal sedimentation is brought about by the manipulation of the tapes. The noises on stage mark the present tense, while the different dimensions of the past are conjured up by the recorded voice. Beckett wanted to ensure that the body leaves its trace on the tape recording: he made the difference in voice quality explicit by indicating

that the voice on tape should be *'clearly Krapp's at a much earlier time'*.[130]
Katherine Hayles writes: 'The play between the voices is an aural invitation
to the audience to speculate on differences and similarities, across time and
technology, even before the voices articulate words and sentences.'[131]

The verb 'to record' comes from the Latin *recordare*, meaning '[t]o get
by heart, to commit to memory, to go over in one's mind'.[132] The verb
conflates the distinction between technology and human memory, bringing
to mind Heidegger's argument that technology, rather than functioning
as the antithesis of nature, is in fact endemic to it.[133] The tapes in the play
become saturated with memories Krapp has 'got by heart'. A case in point
are the observations Krapp records on his final tape:

Lie propped up in the dark – and wander. Be again in the dingle on a Christmas
Eve, gathering holly, the red-berried. [*Pause.*] Be again on Croghan on a Sunday
morning, in the haze, with the bitch, stop and listen to the bells. [*Pause.*] And so
on. [*Pause.*] Be again, be again.[134]

That Krapp pauses after he mentions the different recollections, emphasises
the manner in which he halts again to see the holly and to hear the bells.

As early as 1880, a decade that would witness rapid advances in the field
of neurology, Jean-Marie Guyau compared the process of recording and
replaying sound to the mechanism of human memory:

Upon speaking into a phonograph, the vibrations of one's voice are transferred
to a point that engraves lines onto a metal plate that correspond to the uttered
sounds – uneven furrows, more or less deep, depending on the nature of
the sounds. It is quite probable that in analogous ways, invisible lines are inces-
santly carved into the brain cells, which provide a channel for nerve streams. If,
after some time, the stream encounters a channel it has already passed through, it
will once again proceed along the same path. The cells vibrate in the same way
they vibrated the first time; psychologically, these similar vibrations correspond
to an emotion or a thought analogous to the forgotten emotion or thought.[135]

In a not dissimilar manner, the metallic particles of audiotape here
function as Krapp's prosthetic memory. Krapp's furrowed face, in turn,
bears its own traces of inscription, for the 'marked skin means memory,
means never being able or willing to forget'.[136] The play hence stages
the process of remembering, but it simultaneously enacts a curious
re-membering, a piecing together of the sediments and fragments of
Krapp's life. When Krapp finally settles to record the events of his present
year, his audience consists merely of past versions of himself: 'All that old
misery. [*Pause.*] Once wasn't enough for you. [*Pause.*] Lie down across
her. [*Long pause*].'[137]

Many critics have argued that human beings make up for their less acute sense of hearing by inventing various amplifiers and other auditory aids. Marshall McLuhan suggested early on that, in essence, technology functions as an extension of the central nervous system.[138] Auditory technologies, as we have seen, mimic the physiology of the body: while the telephone uses the 'vibrations of a tympanum to induce a variable current which [is] then converted back to sound', Michel Serres, drawing on the affinity between technology and the body, compares the ear itself to a recording device: 'The labyrinth of the ear, with its complex invaginations of inner and outer, represents not a single diaphragm, or site of one-way transmission, but a complex, one might say fractal, landscape of transformations and recursions, which itself transmits as well as receives.'[139] Technology in *Krapp's Last Tape*, by transporting Krapp to different temporal and spatial realms, ultimately only serves to heighten the body's sensuous capacity. Serres writes: 'The I thinks only when it is beside itself...I only really live beside myself; beside myself I think, meditate, know...I exist beside myself.'[140] Or as Guyau put it, 'To understand is to remember.'[141] This is made clear in the play in the manner in which Krapp needs a drink after each intense recollection: '*gets up, goes backstage into darkness. Ten seconds. Pop of cork. Ten seconds. Second cork. Ten seconds. Third cork. Ten seconds. Brief burst of quavering song.*'[142] For McLuhan, 'all media are fragments of ourselves' and the influence of any one medium upon us 'tends to bring the other senses into play in a new relation'.[143] We have seen how auditory innovations exploit the defining characteristics of sound; in *Krapp's Last Tape*, Beckett shows us how technologies of inscription both mimic and enhance the mechanisms of the human body.

The subject's affinity with technology in *Krapp's Last Tape* has further implications: 'the thirty-nine-year-old looking back at his earlier self and the sixty-nine-year-old who is doing the same' indicate not only that technology provides a means of escape from the confines of constricting identity, but more importantly that identity, like Krapp's tapes, is perpetually written anew.[144] As the thirty-nine-year-old Krapp on tape puts it, after listening to 'an old year': 'Hard to believe I was ever that young whelp. The voice! Jesus! And the aspirations!'[145] Audiotapes, as Beckett acknowledged, function as an opportune trope for identity, because of their simultaneously permanent and mutable nature: they epitomise both the stative and active aspects of subjectivity.

That Time, another memory play, written in English between 1974 and 1975, not only follows a similar thematic to *Krapp's Last Tape*; it also further exploits recording techniques to explore the transgressive qualities of sound. In *That Time*, we again have an elderly male figure, called Listener, alone on stage. He has an '[o]*ld white face, long flaring white hair as if seen from above outspread*'.[146] Listener's breath, which is described as '*audible, slow and regular*', functions as an acoustic marker of the present tense.[147] The past is evoked by the three voices that are described in the following manner:

> Moments of one and the same voice A B C relay one another without solution of continuity . . . Yet the switch from one to another must be clearly faintly perceptible. If threefold source and context prove insufficient to produce this effect it should be assisted mechanically (e.g. threefold pitch).[148]

The first voice, A, belongs to a middle-aged narrator returning to a childhood location.[149] The second voice we hear, namely C, evokes memories of a town, most probably London, as the recurring references to the Portrait Gallery would indicate. The third voice, B, brings back memories of an adolescent love-affair. The here and now of the stage, in other words, is invaded by the there and then. The spectator, however, rapidly becomes aware that the memories evoked are not as clear-cut as would at first appear. The three voices that summon different temporal and spatial dimensions are themselves permeated with further temporal and spatial shifts, echoing the *mise en abyme* in *Krapp's Last Tape*. Voice A not only spectates his childhood landscapes with adult eyes; there are also passages within the polyphonic monologue that have a child focaliser: 'talking to yourself who else out loud imaginary conversations there was childhood for you ten or eleven on a stone among the giant nettles making it up now one voice now another till you were hoarse and they all sounded the same'.[150] Voice C, likewise, not only remembers the Portrait Gallery and the 'eyes when they opened a vast oil black with age and dirt'; there are also memories of a birth: 'always having tuning-points and never but the one the first and last that time curled up worm in slime when they lugged you out and wiped you off and straightened you up never another after that'.[151] Voice B, finally, not only remembers a first adolescent love-affair, but also appears to have recollections of a pre-natal nature: 'suddenly there in whatever scenes perhaps way back in childhood or the womb'.[152] We are, as in the case of *Krapp's Last Tape*, faced with a monologue of kinds, but monologue in Beckett is rarely if ever single or unified; it tends, in Beckett, 'paradoxically, to yield more voices than one'.[153]

That Time has received less critical attention than Beckett's major plays, or even many of the shorter plays. James Knowlson and John Pilling, who were amongst the first critics to write about the play, remarked on 'the disproportion between the visual and the aural elements' in *That Time*. Knowlson and Pilling added that Beckett himself 'was very much aware that *That Time* lay "on the very edge of what was possible in the theatre" '.[154] Bernard Beckerman, who was equally sceptical about the play, argued that *That Time* produced 'a striking visual image and an intriguing literary text, but not an effective theatricalization of the speaker-listener complex'.[155] In the 1980s, critics such as Antoni Libera and Stan Gontarski focused on the structural aspects of the play.[156] Anna McMullan, in turn, has analysed *Cette fois*, the French version of the play, in which, she observes, a 'space which is usually associated with the visual is dominated by the verbal, the mimetic by the diegetic'.[157] She examines the manner in which the play undermines categories of time and space and identity and difference. Less attention, however, has been dedicated to the importance of sound and hearing in the play.

In *That Time*, as we have seen, the voice, and by extension the subject, is divided against itself through diverse spatial and temporal positioning, epitomising the paradoxes present in vocalic expression:

My voice defines me because it draws me into coincidence with myself, accomplishes me in a way which goes beyond mere belonging, association, or instrumental use. And yet my voice is also most essentially itself and my own in the ways in which it parts or passes from me. Nothing else about me defines me so intimately as my voice, precisely because there is no other feature of my self whose nature it is thus to move from me to the world, and to move me into the world. If my voice is mine because it comes from me, it can only be known as mine because it also goes from me. My voice is, literally, my way of taking leave of my senses. What I say goes.[158]

This vocalic division is also emphasised in the play's title, which consists of a pronoun that, like all demonstrative pronouns, is inherently spatial by nature, combined with a noun that, in turn, foregrounds the temporal nature of the split. McMullan observes that 'While the stage image stresses the "here and now" of the stage present, the text recreates other spaces and other times, opening up a vast perspective of the history of an individual from birth to old age and even beyond.'[159] The 'clearly faintly' perceptible shifts from A to B to C, in other words, serve a similar purpose as the rewinding of the tapes and the changing of the spools in *Krapp's Last Tape*. The shifting voice moves both Listener and the audience back and forth between different spatio-temporal dimensions. The silences, for their part, return both Listener and the audience back to the present tense. Walter Asmus, in his rehearsal notes for the German première of the play, writes:

Beckett comments on the silence after each of the three parts: In these moments the man comes back to the present. While he was listening to his voice he was in the past. During the listening everything is closed. In the silence he is startled to find himself in the present; everything is open. It is not decided whether he opens his eyes and the voice stops for that reason or whether the voice stops and therefore he opens his eyes.[160]

Echoes of *That Time* and other Beckett plays can perhaps be found in Don DeLillo's novel *The Body Artist* (2001), which abounds in instances of Proustian, embodied memory. In the novel, a curious ghost, whom the bereaved protagonist, Lauren, names Mr Tuttle (because '[s]he thought it would make him easier to see'), begins to repeat conversations she has had with her dead husband:[161]

It was Rey's voice she was hearing... things she'd known in Rey's voice, and only Rey's... This was not some communication with the dead. It was Rey alive in the course of a talk he'd had with her, in this room, not long after they'd come here. She was sure of this, recalling how they'd gone upstairs and dropped into a night of tossing sensation, drifts of sex, confession and pale sleep.[162]

Mr Tuttle functions as a curious recording device, and the voices he reproduces, much as the recorded voices in Beckett's plays, have an uncanny quality of embodying the past.

That Time differs from *All That Fall, Embers* and *Krapp's Last Tape* precisely in being based almost solely on the embodying qualities of the human voice. It does not, like the other three plays, make abundant use of other sounds. Steven Connor writes that 'phenomenologically, the fact that an unassigned voice must always imply a body means that it will always partly supply it as well'.[163] Although the spectator is under the impression that Listener hears his own 'inner' voice,

so strong is the embodying power of the voice, that this process occurs not only in the case of voices that seem separated from their obvious or natural sources, but also in voices, or patterned vocal inflections, or postures, that have a clearly identifiable source, but seem in various ways excessive to that source. This voice then conjures for itself a different kind of body; an imaginary body which may contradict, compete with, replace, or even reshape the actual, visible body of the speaker.[164]

The visual image of Listener, which resembles that of a man on his death bed, '*flaring white hair as if seen from above outspread*', is out of sync with the voiced images of the child, the adolescent and the young man that are conjured up by the reproduced monologue on stage.[165] By positing the vocally conjured bodies side by side with the protagonist, the play highlights the crude materiality of the passage of time, revealing Listener's stark physical non-coincidence with himself. The traces left by the passage of time on the protagonist's ravaged body are made explicit in the stage directions that mention Listener's grey hair, his creased, white face and his smile, *'toothless for preference'*.[166] Beckett may well have chosen to write *That Time* and *Krapp's Last Tape* for the stage rather than for purely aural media, because the stage, by positing the protagonist next to the bodies evoked by the recorded voice, enabled him to focus attention on the theme of physical non-identity.

By transporting the listener to different spatio-temporal dimensions, sound sets the subject apart from itself, doubling, tripling and remaking the body and, in the process, reminding the subject of its perpetual non-coincidence with itself. In *Proust*, Beckett quotes the author:

'We imagine that the object of our desire is a being that can be laid down before us, enclosed within a body. Alas! it is the extension of that being to all the points of space and time that it has occupied and will occupy. If we do not possess contact with such a place and such an hour we do not possess that being.'[167]

The fact that we are temporal and spatial beings constitutes part of our identity. However, in emphasising the centrality of the body and its surroundings to the construction of identity, Beckett also comes to the realisation that the spatial, temporal and corporeal shifts we experience inevitably translate into a dissolution of identity.[168] The subject is dispersed by the spaces that it occupies. The body's own uninterrupted flux only adds to the plight of dissolution. As the narrator of *That Time* puts it, 'never the same but the same as what for God's sake did you ever say I to yourself in your life'.[169]

Although Beckett's use of sound has often been considered a marker of privileged interiority, on closer inspection, Beckett exploits the spatially and temporally transgressive qualities of the acoustic to emphasise the materially grounded nature of subjectivity. Beckett makes use of inscription technologies not only to enhance the transporting qualities of sound, but also to highlight the prosthetic nature of the devices. Beckett's insistence on the subject's non-coincidence with itself is highlighted by his use of sound technologies that, by reconfiguring categories of time and space, and thereby doubling and tripling the listening subject, serve only to augment its sensuous capacity.

CHAPTER 4

Skin deep

> We might say indeed that modern man has an epidermis rather than
> a soul.   James Joyce

During the 1960s, Beckett wrote a series of shorter prose fictions that have
acquired an enigmatic place in their author's canon. The series begins
with *All Strange Away*, which dates from 1963–4, and *Imagination Dead
Imagine*, which appeared a year later in 1965; continues with *Ping*, which
appeared in 1966, and concludes with *The Lost Ones*, a novella which has
appeared in three different English-language versions, the first of which
dates from 1971.[1] These short prose works are closely linked with one
another, if not intertwined, not only because all four share similar imagery
of bodies in austere spaces, geometrical descriptions and a fluctuating light,
but also because they share a common genetic. *Imagination Dead Imagine*
is, as Stan Gontarski has called it, an 'evolutionary descendant' of *All
Strange Away*, and *Bing* (the French version of *Ping*), as Beckett himself
said, 'may be regarded as the result or miniaturisation of "Le Dépeupleur"
abandoned because of its intractable complexities'.[2] As Leslie Hill observes,
'plott[ing] from the working drafts of *Bing*',

> it appears as though *Bing* began as a gloss on *Le Dépeupleur* as well as, to some
> extent, a part of it. In the initial versions, therefore, *Bing* seems to be devoted to
> exploring or detailing what it might be possible to say about a body's life in the
> niches described in *Le Dépeupleur*.[3]

The Lost Ones, which is the longest of the group of texts that have often
been referred to as Beckett's prose fragments, describes the life, in a
cylinder, of 'two hundred bodies in all round numbers'.[4] The bodies are
divided into four groups, according to their activity and motility: those
who are constantly searching; 'those who sometimes pause'; the sedentary searchers who rarely move; and finally the vanquished, who appear
motionless.[5] *All Strange Away*, *Imagination Dead Imagine* and *Ping* are

similar, but in them, individual bodies rather than a community become the focus of the narrator's attention.

What has most puzzled critics about these works is the peculiarity of their setting and subject matter, together with the oddity of their linguistic register. In the case of *The Lost Ones*, which to date has received the most critical attention, the abundance of measurement and precise numerical information about the space that the bodies inhabit, accompanied by the curious inaccuracy and inconsistency of the information given, has proved baffling enough to arouse discussion about the possible mistakes Beckett made when writing or translating the work.[6]

For some, *The Lost Ones* has functioned as an allegory of the human condition or as a parable of the authorial process, whilst for others, the realm of science or even science fiction has offered a frame of reference.[7] A closer look at the changing narrative strategies of *The Lost Ones* and the group of works it belongs to, however, suggests a different account. Rather than merely representing the narrator's movement behind the works, or functioning as simple tropes of the human condition, these stories engage in a probing examination of the nature of perception and the embodied state of subjectivity that is in contrast with the affirmative tone of humanist-existentialist readings of Beckett. At stake, therefore, in the re-reading I propose, are more fundamental questions about the contradictory nature of embodiment in Beckett as the very essence of a precarious identity, which is itself repeatedly undermined through a series of negations.

Even a casual glance at the short texts suffices to call attention to their difference from Beckett's earlier fictional works. Perhaps the most obvious and yet striking change is the abandonment of the first-person narrator as the texts' principal vehicle, still present in the four novellas (1946), the Trilogy (1947–50), the *Texts for Nothing* (1950–2) and *How It Is* (1964).[8] Closely connected with the shift to second- and third-person narratives is a major deconstructive move: instead of trying to penetrate an inner core or nucleus, in a manner typical of Western thought at least since the Renaissance, Beckett is fascinated in these works by the outside, the exterior, the surface of being. The so-called cylinder works, in other words, form a group of narratives that have in common a strikingly discernible quality of surface exploration, in which sense objects only are described and experienced: 'None looks within himself where none can be.'[9]

Apart from abandoning the first-person narrator, these works also have a shared thematic interest that is worked into the texts through the third-person descriptions, namely, a perceptible questioning and withering of the sense of vision within the narrative environments.[10] In *The Lost Ones*, the nature of the light in the cylinder is such that it obscures rather than aids vision: 'Light in a word that not only dims but blurs into the bargain.'[11] As Sylvie Henning says, the light has paradoxical effects: 'At the same time it enlightens, it also obscures and confuses, by making it difficult for the eye to adapt. The sense of sight is impaired and eventually ruined by the oscillating murky yellow.'[12] As the detached narrative voice of *The Lost Ones* puts it:

> It might safely be maintained that the eye grows used to these conditions and in the end adapts to them were it not that just the contrary is to be observed in the slow deterioration of vision ruined by this fiery flickering murk and by the incessant straining for ever vain with concomitant moral distress and its repercussion on the organ.[13]

It is in the nature of this light to provide 'illumination of the broad surface of things while obscuring the more troublesome irregularities'.[14] The problem of vision is replicated in *Ping*, where it is the very whiteness of the illuminated walls and planes that works to undermine the discriminatory nature of sight; to the eye, the surfaces become almost indistinguishable from one another, making the white narrated skin of Ping all but intermingle with its surroundings: 'bare white body fixed one yard white on white invisible'.[15] The body itself becomes reduced to a featureless, indistinguishable blank: 'Nose ears white holes mouth white seam like sewn invisible.'[16] In *Imagination Dead Imagine*, too, 'all shines with the same white shine, ground, wall, vault, bodies, no shadow'.[17] The distinguishing markers disappear: 'long black hair gone, long black lashes on white cheekbone gone, glare from above for features on this bonewhite undoubted face right profile still hungering for missing lashes'.[18] The undifferentiated surfaces threaten selfhood, for 'merging in the white ground were it not for the long hair of strangely imperfect whiteness, the white body of a woman finally'.[19] There is a sense in which this dissolution of individuality in the works is even oddly pleasurable and compelling.

Verbal communication, the supreme mode of interaction between interior consciousnesses, is also negated, giving way in this group of texts to gesture and posture, while voice is replaced by fluctuations of heat and light, with '[b]rief murmurs only just almost never'.[20] We are faced with a question of 'sitting, standing, walking, kneeling, crawling, lying, creeping, all any length, no paper, no pins, no candle, no matches', all else being reduced to 'silent flesh'.[21] Not only, in other words, do these works question vision; there is also a move away from sound. Because of the rubbery surface of the floor and walls, even footfalls cannot be heard: 'The only sounds worthy of the name result from the manipulation of the ladders or the thud of bodies striking against one another or of one against itself as when in sudden fury it beats its breast. Thus flesh and bone subsist.'[22] The remaining sounds, in other words, are corporeal, with even the murmur of the fluctuating light reminiscent of regular intakes of breath, 'Its restlessness at long intervals suddenly stilled like panting.'[23] A kiss, the narrator says, because of the effect of the climate on the mucous membrane, 'makes an indescribable sound'.[24]

The bodies, in the cylinder of *The Lost Ones*, situate the ladders they carry in the desired location not with the aid of sight but by means of tactile exploration; as the narrator informs us, the bodies 'are required to hug the wall at all times eddywise', instead of simply finding their way with the help of vision.[25] Eric Levy has suggested that the eye, in *The Lost Ones*, in fact functions more as a symbol of the need to search than as the organ of vision as such, which would explain the recurring references to vision even after the faltering eyesight of the bodies in the work is established.[26] For the niches themselves, once the climbers begin to ascend, are found by means of touch.[27] The fact that surfaces, the sense of touch and the skin in general are emphasised in *The Lost Ones* is made clear by the narrator's comments on the '[c]onsequences of this climate to the skin' and on the way the skin performs in the cylinder in comparison to the eye:[28]

The effect of this climate on the soul is not to be underestimated. But it suffers certainly less than the skin whose entire defensive system from sweat to goose bumps is under constant stress. It continues none the less feebly to resist and indeed honourably compared to the eye which with the best will in the world it is difficult not to consign at the close of all its efforts to nothing short of blindness.[29]

Touch, in other words, becomes a 'common sense' in the cylinder, not only because the skin, as Didier Anzieu has observed, acts as a 'surface containing pockets and cavities where the [other] sense organs...are located', but because when light fluctuations can no longer be seen, the accompanying heat fluctuations can still be felt.[30] Communication itself becomes tactile, with aural messages in *The Lost Ones* replaced by thumps and blows. When one of the climbers that chose to halt on the ladders (instead of entering one of the niches) loses track of time, thus violating the 'climbers' code':

It is in order then for him due next for the ladder to climb in the wake of the offender and by means of one or more thumps on the back bring him back to a sense of his surroundings. Upon which he unfailingly hastens to descend preceded by his successor who has then merely to take over the ladder subject to the usual conditions.[31]

In the phenomenologically reduced cylinder world of the Lost Ones, the skin functions as a medium through which the characters perceive the external world, judging time through the oscillating heat fluctuations, and assaying space by means of the skin's visualising ability, achieved through the tactile exploration of surfaces. The importance of touch in *The Lost Ones*, like many of the novella's diverse characteristics, is replicated in the other cylinder works. In *All Strange Away*, the narrator urges, 'hands, imagine hands. Imagine hands', and goes on to add, 'something in this hand, imagine later, something soft, clench tight, then lax and still any length, then tight again, so on, imagine later'.[32] There is a striking emphasis on tactile verbs: 'Imagine him kissing, caressing, licking, sucking, fucking and buggering all this stuff, no sound.'[33] The narrator makes several mentions of body parts that touch the walls and planes, and much is made of self-touching, and of squeezing, clenching and crushing in the text.[34]

The sedentary searchers in *The Lost Ones* are said to be sensitive to tactile encounters, for a 'sedentary searcher stepped on instead of over is capable of such an outburst of fury as to throw the entire cylinder into a ferment'.[35] There is, in the case of the sedentary searchers, an agonising nature to touch, for the skin functions as a common sense also because of its inability to reject stimuli. The sedentary searchers may control vision, but the skin 'can neither close like the eyes or the mouth, nor be stopped up like the ears or the nose'.[36] It remains forever vigilant, never allowing the sedentary searchers to suspend their relationship to the world they inhabit. In the last section of *The Lost Ones*, the narrator again mentions 'the horror of contact' of the 'withered ones', who are 'compelled to brush together without ceasing'.[37] The horror of this when the world is not of one's choosing is tremendous, and the Beckettian canon, as we know, is littered with glimpses of this horror.

Although the bodies in the cylinder at first seem almost indistinguishable from one another, or at least from the particular group of searchers they belong to, there are, however, certain identifying markers that receive attention in the text. One of these is hair, for the woman who is described as 'mechanically clutching to her breast a mite' is said to have white hair, while the woman vanquished, referred to as the 'north', as we shall later see, has 'red hair tarnished by the light'.[38] Another distinguishing marker is age, for, somewhat curiously, there are bodies of all age groups, 'from old age to infancy', in the cylinder.[39] Perhaps the most significant form of identification, however, occurs through the (even) closer examination of the skin, for 'the skin of a climber alone on his ladder or in the depths of a tunnel glistens all over with the same red-yellow glister and even some of its folds and recesses in so far as the air enters in'.[40] There are even times, the narrator tells us, 'when a body has to be brought to a stand and disposed in a certain position to permit the inspection at close hand of a particular part or the search for a scar or birthblot for example'.[41]

The nudity of the bodies is significant, for there is a distinct obsession with the phenomenology of the skin in the cylinder works. It is, after all, the skin that functions as a register of experience which exposes us to the world. Embryologically, the skin and the nervous system have the same developmental origins, which entails that the 'nervous system is...a buried part of the skin' or inversely, that the skin functions as the exposed part of our nervous system.[42] The expression *skin-deep*, used to denote shallowness, may therefore in fact be a misguided one, if we see the skin as extending to the innermost centre of our being, 'all known without within'.[43] The skin not only reveals the age and health of the subject, but also the traumas and worries we believe belong to the secret core of our being. The scars, wrinkles and lines caused by anxiety that bear witness to our mishaps and that are recurring identifying markers virtually throughout the Beckettian canon therefore reinforce the interpretation of the skin as an external nervous system that carries the inscription of life's crises and misgivings. The skin, in other words, is the external nervous system in this aspect, too, that it reflects that degree of past and present well-being or lack of equilibrium that we cannot hide from the world.

The skin in *The Lost Ones* therefore functions not only as an organ of perception, but also as the marker or betrayer of identity; as Anzieu says, 'The skin shields the equilibrium of our internal functioning from exogenous disruptions, but in its form, texture, colouring, and scars, it preserves the marks of those disruptions.'[44] The outer markers of identity, replicated in the case of the cylinder itself, with its shifting measurements, in other words, become more oscillating, complex and determining of identity than any inner ones. The skins of the Lost Ones, as a result of the climate conditions of the cylinder, are said to change colour and texture, for the 'desiccation of the envelope robs nudity of much of its charm as pink turns grey and transforms into a rustling of nettles the natural succulence of flesh against flesh'.[45] In *Ping*, too, inscriptions appear on the skin: 'White scars invisible same white as flesh torn of old given rose only just.'[46] Beckett's focus on scars, much like any deliberate injury inflicted on the skin, such as self-harming, may 'be an assault upon the signifying function of the skin. In that the scar signifies that something *real* – some exceeding of mere signification – has taken place, the scar can become the figure for the violent erasure of the epidermal grounding of figurality.'[47]

The title of *The Lost Ones* stems from *Le Dépeupleur*, which in turn famously originates in Lamartine's *Méditations poétiques*, specifically in the rather moving line 'Un seul être vous manque, et tout est dépeuplé!'[48] The problem in Beckett's novella, regardless of its amorous nature in Lamartine, is, in essence, that of restrictive selfhood. There is a sense, in *The Lost Ones*, in which the bodies are trapped *within* surfaces, in the very exteriority of being, whether of the cylinder, from which all but the vanquished are searching to escape, or of their own skins and bodies that 'brush together with a rustle of dry leaves'.[49] Because of the adverse conditions of the cylinder, 'The mucous membrane itself is affected which would not greatly matter were it not for its hampering effect on the work of love.'[50] Whatever the searchers are after, the narrator however tells us, it is not a question simply of physical love.[51]

The only instance when the bodies are immune from the examinations of the searchers is when queuing for a ladder:

Obliged for want of space to huddle together over long periods they appear to the observer a mere jumble of mingled flesh. Woe the rash searcher who carried away by his passion dare lay a finger on the least among them. Like a single body the whole queue falls on the offender. Of all the scenes of violence the cylinder has to offer none approaches this.[52]

Mingled through their flesh, the individual bodies become as one, for it is in the nature of the tactile that whenever one touches, one is also oneself necessarily touched, which makes it difficult to define the boundaries between the self and the world.[53] One thinks of Michel Serres's remark:

Contingency means mutual touching: world and body meet and caress in the skin. I do not like to speak of the place where my body exists as a milieu, preferring rather to say that things mingle among themselves and that I am no exception to this, that I mingle with the world which mingles itself in me. The skin intervenes in the things of the world and brings about their mingling.[54]

Touch, in other words, is inherently reflexive: through it, as Don Ihde puts it, one is 'constantly "in touch" with that' by which one is sur-rounded.[55] The skin is fundamental in situating us in the world, for while it procures the distinction between the inside and the outside, it also brings the two together in a way which is characteristic of no other part of the body. Although the skin, in other words, is a discriminatory organ, it also collapses boundaries between the self and the world, effecting the release from restrictive selfhood, intermingling us with the world or with the other in a manner that brings us to a state of coexistence which is also a dizzying proximation of nonexistence.[56] Sartre writes, 'To let [my hand] run indifferently over the length of her body, to reduce my hand to a soft brushing almost stripped of meaning, to a pure existence, to a pure matter, slightly silky, slightly satiny, slightly rough – this is to give up for oneself being the one who establishes references and unfolds distances; it is to be made pure mucous membrane.'[57]

The idea of intermingling in *The Lost Ones* is reinforced by the sedentary searchers and the vanquished bodies that become themselves topographical features of the landscape of the abode. As the narrator informs us, 'There does none the less exist a north in the guise of one of the vanquished or better one of the women vanquished or better still the woman vanquished.'[58] The yellow, white and grey monochrome shades of the different cylinder works reinstate the idea of intermingling, making it at times difficult, as we have seen, for the narrator-observer to detect the difference between the surface of the bodies and their world, and hence making vision itself participate in the epidermal intermingling which the works evoke. Even the peculiar organic quality of the cylinder functions to undermine the difference between the bodies and their world, for despite the machine connotations of its shape, the cylinder has a distinctly natural constitution. Not only are its heat and light fluctuations reminiscent of the rhythm of heartbeat or of respiration, but the rubbery nature of the surface is itself suggestive of skin, while the cylinder's tunnels and niches bring to mind the orifices and cavities of the body. 'A more or less wide mouth', the narrator tells us, gives the inhabitants access to the niches.[59] The sense of entrapment the Lost Ones experience only consolidates the corporeal nature of the cylinder, for the characters can no more escape from the confines of their 'abode' than they can from the predicament of the body. The word 'abode' with which the narrative opens, stems, as Susan Brienza has observed, from the Middle English word 'abood', 'meaning "a waiting, delay, [and most significantly] stay" '.[60]

I suggest, in short, that Beckett turns his focus on the tactile because of the way in which touch collapses the boundaries between the active and the passive, the endogenous and the exogenous and the concrete and the abstract, hence complicating the preconceived categories and binarisms through which we organise our perceptions and thought patterns. Although touch is a concrete sense that involves physical contact and therefore, on occasion, gives us a stronger sense of 'reality' than do the other senses, confirming not only the presence of the sense object but that of ourselves, there is also a sense in which the tactile is too intimate, too close to our bodily being or to the sensory objects we perceive for us to be able to experience the otherness of our surroundings or of the world through it.[61] In this way, the skin *refuses* the premise of subjectivity as interiority, denying the subject the possibility of a separation from the outside world. The very tension between individuality and its dissolution that functions as the driving force of subjectivity, that

restless, dissatisfied energy which is the stuff of life[,] is always shadowed by that desire to *become unbound*; that is, the desire for oblivion, for a dissolution of consciousness, the irresistible desire to regress back to a state of zero tension before consciousness, before life, before effort, before lack.[62]

It is perhaps this very tension that explains why the skin, which is also a vehicle of procreation, should so acutely epitomise the complex link between individuality and its loss. There is an anticipation of this loss in the intermingling with the world that touch effects, explaining, in part, the intricate interrelationship between desire and destruction. If interiority, in other words, is experienced as individuality, then exteriority seems to function as its antithesis, epitomising the very dissolution and betrayal of selfhood. The skin, more than any other organ, is in touch with both these aspects of subjectivity.

The enclosures the Beckettian characters are ceaselessly seeking can partly be explained by the ambiguous dynamics between interiority and exteriority, individuality and its dissolution, that form such a crucial aspect of subjectivity. On the one hand, the Beckettian enclosures function as a second skin of kinds, embodying the characters' need to hide from the world in which one is exposed by one's embodied being, denied autonomous subjectivity and subjected to an interaction with one's surroundings. On the other hand, however, the Beckettian quests themselves, in the very need the characters portray to leave enclosures and hence shed their armours, enact that aspect of subjectivity that is burdened and exhausted by restrictive selfhood, willing to become dissolved in an interaction with the world. Hence, perhaps, too, the oscillating movement of the Lost Ones, torn between wandering within the different zones of the cylinder and disappearing into the solitude of the niches. As the narrator remarks about the niches, '[t]hose whom these entice no longer climb simply to get clear of the ground...To the fugitive fortunate enough to find a ladder free [a niche] offers certain refuge until the clamours subside'.[63]

The linguistic counterpart to these tropes of perpetual dissolution is discernible in the shifting registers of *The Lost Ones*, and several critics have paid attention to the peculiarity of the two opposing voices that coexist in the novella.[64] The first voice is a rational, impersonal one, distanced and permeated with irony, whilst the second register has a poetic and even sensuous quality that is often achieved by the sheer heightening effect of the incongruity of this voice with the former register.[65] David Porush describes the first voice as 'a stylistic evocation of technical and mathematical precision' and labels it 'machine language', whilst he describes the second voice as 'the *language of the flesh*, since it . . . is heir to all the ills of flesh: softness, decay, inefficiency, irrational doubt, and inconsistency'.[66] Although a rapid glance at the novella would ascertain the coexistence of the two voices within the text, and although the first register, as many critics feel, would initially appear to emit codes of certainty within the discourse, at closer scrutiny, nonetheless, something more complex is at stake in the language of *The Lost Ones*.

The rational voice, which appears to mimic the discourses of law, mathematics and science in general, as Susan Brienza and others have noted, is littered with modifiers such as 'more or less', 'scarcely', 'roughly', 'approximately', 'thereabouts' and 'sometimes' that undermine the assertive tone of the register.[67] Secondly, the discourse, as Leslie Hill has pointed out, is itself permeated with expressions of doubt and reservation, such as 'it is doubtful that'; '[i]t is as though'; '[t]hat is not quite accurate'; 'in accordance with the notion requiring as long as it holds'; and the expression which appears three times in the novella: 'if this notion is maintained'.[68] Doubt, therefore, is always already built into the register that at first appears so firm in its convictions.

A further striking quality of the 'rational' register of *The Lost Ones* is the relative absence of finite verbs or of 'active voice or human agency', together with the clichéd and peculiarly distanced nature of the voice: 'It goes without saying that only the vanquished hide their faces though not all without exception. Standing or sitting with head erect some content themselves with opening their eyes no more.'[69] Not only does the impersonal voice question and undermine subjectivity, whether that of the narrator or of the Lost Ones themselves; the recurring litotes ('not all without exception' and 'to open ones eyes no more'), which form one of the most striking linguistic features of the 'rational' register of *The Lost*

Ones, function in a manner that erases and cancels literal meaning ('not all' in place of 'some'; 'not without exception' in place of 'with some exception'; 'open no more' in place of 'keep closed'), causing a slippage in which what is signified is never mentioned, and what is mentioned is never signified, hence creating a gaping gap within the linguistic expression and hollowing out the language itself. The distance between signifier and signified, in other words, undermines and negates the unity and identity of the register.

Something similar is even at stake in the 'poetic' register, which appears to negate the 'rational' register, whilst itself being in turn negated by the latter. At first glance the 'poetic' register would appear to evoke doubt and, in opposition to the 'rational' register, proximity, especially in expressions that are suggestive of onomatopoeia, such as 'rustling', 'thud' and 'succulence', all associated with the language of the body in the works.[70] But there are also times when the voice is oddly stiff and distanced from the bodily reality of life in the cylinder. Expressions such as '[w]oe the rash searcher', or 'long vigil' bring to mind and perhaps parody the stiffness and pomposity of heroic epic poetry.[71] The use of nouns such as 'coign', 'vanquished' or 'quest', as Steven Connor observes, gives the English text a chivalric and exotic foreignness.[72] In the expression 'fain to look away', Connor draws attention to the manner in which the 'hint of medievalism . . . both mocks and heightens'.[73] Other heightening expressions are 'ambient air', 'a brief amaze' and 'ever and anon', the latter a 'literary cliché that seems to sneer in its place in the English, even as it testifies to an impulse to dignify its subject'.[74] We are, in other words, at times also dealing with an elevated language that alienates itself from the contingencies of the quotidian rather than bringing us closer to them.

Although, therefore, the 'poetic' register can at times be seen to epitomise doubt, uncertainty and proximity, and although it can be argued that the cylinder's laws of oscillation, fluctuation and negation are reproduced between the two different linguistic registers of *The Lost Ones*, there is, in fact, a *mise-en-abyme* effect. Not only is the oscillation reproduced in the flux between the registers; the laws of negation are replicated *within* the registers themselves, both of which flicker between heightened certainty and its irrevocable undoing. In this way, the unstable conditions of the cylinder recur in the linguistic expression of the work, preventing and negating any attempts towards unproblematic unity.

The Lost Ones, therefore, fundamentally questions the fixity of any register or conceptual stance, be it poetic or other. The immediacy that the text evokes through its persistent emphasis on the material realm, in other words, is foregrounded by the erratic linguistic fluctuation. It is no coincidence that the corporeal sounds, which like onomatopoeia transgress conceptual categories by moving beyond the closed system of the language of the dictionary, are the ones that persevere in the cylinder world of the bodies, nor that the sound made by a kiss, in the abode, becomes 'indescribable'.[75] Onomatopoeia is also a feature of the other cylinder pieces. Beckett first named the English translation of *Bing* 'Pfft', but revised it to *Ping*, which is equally onomatopoeic.[76] The alternative title reveals Beckett's insistence on a move beyond dictionary meaning.

Although the thematic and stylistic questions discussed might at first glance seem mere minor issues, derived from works that have sometimes been dismissed as being equally minor moments in Beckett's *oeuvre*, at stake in these apparent minutiae are much larger questions about the arc and significance of Beckett's project. For there is finally a disintegration of the self in the breakdown of registers and in the insistence on the exterior which characterise *The Lost Ones*. The dynamics between interior and surface, individuality and its loss are also epitomised in the French and the English titles of the novella, which themselves portray the loss of oneness, the disappearance of self. Even the individual cylinder texts, in their fragmentary nature, function 'like parts of an absent whole which ghost one another but do not coincide except in piecemeal fashion', thus participating in the gradual dissolution of fixed identity.[77]

The different variants of *The Lost Ones* themselves operate in a similar manner, undermining the text's coincidence with itself. The differences between the original English-language versions concern numbers and what many critics have seen as Beckett's mathematical errors and inaccuracies.[78] What has been noted less often, however, is that the shifts in measurement also figure in *All Strange Away*. The narrator first describes the measurements of the space the two bodies inhabit by saying, '[f]ive foot square, six high', but later says, '[f]or nine and nine eighteen that is four feet and more across in which to kneel'.[79] This is further corrected by the comment, '[c]eiling wrong now, down two foot, perfect cube now, three foot every way, always was', and yet later,

place no longer cube but rotunda three foot diameter eighteen inches high supporting a dome semi-circular in section as in the Pantheon at Rome or certain beehive tombs and consequently three foot from ground to vertex that is at its highest point no lower than before with loss of floor space in the neighbourhood of two square feet or six square inches per lost angle.[80]

Still later, the measurements have shifted again: 'Rotunda then two foot across and at its highest two foot high'.[81] Given the genealogy of the cylinder pieces, the clearly premeditated shifts in measurement that figure in *All Strange Away* cast doubt over speculations about Beckett's possible mistakes in *The Lost Ones*. In a paradoxical manner, therefore, any aim to correct the text of *The Lost Ones* has only contributed to the dissolution of the text, for it has made it increasingly difficult to identify the 'correct' or originary novella, which may have been Beckett's intention in publishing more than one version of the text in the first place. Somewhat strangely, therefore, the dynamics between identity and its dissolution also seem to offer an explanation to the failing mathematics of the narrator, which, within the logic of the cylinder pieces, are always doomed to become undone.

The oscillation between individuality and its loss that is produced in *The Lost Ones* through the emphasis on the tactile, the different linguistic registers and their breakdown, and the textual variants of the novella, itself reproduces its own laws of vacillation. For there is, finally, fluctuation even within the categories of unity and disintegration evoked by the text. Whilst the former signifies separateness and identity, it also simultaneously entails entrapment and confinement, an exploded facticity, qualities that are epitomised in the skin, which itself contains the capacity for both pleasure and pain. Similarly, dissolution, whilst signifying negation, loss and ultimate extinction, concurrently always suggests release, a '*redemption from redemption*',[82] turning Beckett's strange novella, finally, into an intricate web that vacillates and flickers in its own erratic light.

CHAPTER 5

Come and go

I still remember the day when, flat on my face by way of rest, in defiance of the rules, I suddenly cried, striking my brow, Christ, there's crawling, I never thought of that.[1]

From early on in his writing, Beckett foregrounded motility and its problems in his work. Whether we are dealing with Murphy's wanderings through London, Watt's singular walk, Molloy's bicycle, crutches and crawling, Vladimir and Estragon's restless pacing within the confines of the stage or the eerie rhythmic choreography of *Quad I & II*, which bear a curious resemblance to chronophotographs and early films of motion studies, motility in Beckett is not only a recurring motif but one that is overtly foregrounded and problematised. Motility tends to be either forced upon the characters, as in the case of *Murphy* or the narrator of *The Expelled*; harshly stilted through the maiming of the body and its annexes, as in *Molloy* or *Endgame* (1957); or finally strikingly present in its near-absence, as in the cases of *Malone Dies*, *The Unnamable* and *Happy Days* (1961). Furthermore, 'Beckett's suppression of any emotional, sexual, psychological or metaphorical detail allows movement itself to become the subject' of the scenes which dramatise it.[2] As John Pilling has observed, 'The received idea of Beckett as a writer obsessively exploring themes of stasis and inaction misrepresents a matter – like most other matters in this connection – of considerable complexity, in which arguably the dominant factors are quite otherwise.'[3]

Whether it is a matter of cycling, walking, swinging, rolling, trembling, falling or crawling, motility in Beckett is simultaneously marked by a near impossibility and, at least after the early works, a compelling persistence to proceed at all costs. Coinciding with this impossibility is a gradual slowing down both of the physical motion of the characters and of the reader's progress through the work, with linguistic deviation accompanying and paralleling the characters' physical deterioration in the text.

In Beckett's Trilogy, for instance, 'bodily movement is as laborious and painful as . . . narrative movement is to become'.[4] Enoch Brater, writing about *Rockaby* (1980), draws attention to the fact that it is as much the language as the rocking figure of W that moves 'to and fro': 'Hard phonemes match the back-and-forth rhythm of the chair's rock: "stop her eyes/ rock her off/ rock her off." Each line of printed text thus coincides with one complete revolution made by the rocking chair's arc-shaped course.'[5] Furthermore, the movements in the play, just as the language and the light, are subject to a gradual contraction.[6] The rocking motion itself is described as 'Slight' and 'Slow' in the opening stage directions of the play.[7] As Steven Connor argues, Beckett is 'the most important inaugurator of a mode of aesthetic defection from speed', both in the textual and in the purely narrative sense.[8] Beckett, in other words, goes against the grain by looking 'for ways of turning from speed or promptness, or punctuality' and by being, instead, a writer of 'insensible elapse'.[9] A case in point is the entropic decline detectable in the shift from *Quad I* to *Quad II*, as if what preoccupied Beckett in these works were the process of deterioration itself.[10]

Accounts of motility in Beckett have often been plagued by a fate similar to that of the body: instead of focusing on movement *per se*, critics have treated motility as a trope; movement, in other words, has been approached not from the point of view of its significance but rather as signification. In his essay on Beckett's fictional topography, Robin Lee points out that 'Movement in space is commonly used in fiction to represent the movement towards fuller understanding.'[11] Using *More Pricks Than Kicks* as his example, Lee adds that for Belacqua, however, one place leads to another, 'but none offering any final resolution. No place is *the* place, the final place', which in Lee's interpretation, turns the crisis into an epistemological one.[12] For Janet Menzies, writing about bicycles in Beckett, 'plot in *Watt* becomes a device for moving characters; Beckett emphasises this in *Watt* by making the movement of characters itself his plot'.[13] In Menzies' essay, in other words, movement in *Watt* is read as a trope for narrative. Instead of being a mere trope, however, movement in the novel takes the place of dialogue in characterisation:

Watt's way of advancing due east, for example, was to turn his bust as far as possible towards the north and at the same time to fling out his right leg as far as possible towards the south, and then to turn his bust as far as possible towards the south and at the same time to fling out his left leg as far as possible towards the north, and then again to turn his bust as far as possible towards the north and to fling out his right leg as far as possible towards the south, and then again to turn his bust as far as possible towards the south and to fling out his left leg as far as possible towards the north, and so on, over and over again, many many times, until he reached his destination, and could sit down.[14]

Watt's walk, besides curiously bringing to mind nineteenth-century neurological motion studies in their fascination with the disorderly body, is what identifies him in the novel.[15] It is what we remember about Watt, and as such, it functions as yet another instance of Beckett's insistence on the material and the physical, as opposed to the conceptual and the metaphysical.[16] In a similar manner, it is not what Molloy or Moran say in the first part of the Trilogy that remains with us, rather, it is the manner in which the two move that moves us; it is their impetus to proceed painfully and brutally and at all costs that we retain from the novel.

We have, much like Molloy and Moran, come full circle, for our topic brings us back to Merleau-Ponty, who, as something of an exception amongst philosophers, deals with the question of motility. For Merleau-Ponty, motility translates into bodily intentionality: 'to move one's body is to aim at things through it; it is to allow oneself to respond to their call'.[17] The term 'intentionality' originates in the Latin verb *intendo*, meaning ' "to point (at)" or "aim (at)" or "extend (toward)". Phenomena with intentionality thus point outside of themselves to something else: whatever they are of or about.'[18] Intentionality as the essence of motility in Merleau-Ponty hence functions as a propulsive notion; it is that which orientates our actions and gestures and in a more general sense makes us tick.

Merleau-Ponty's account of intentionality, however, differs substantially from previous phenomenological accounts of the topic.[19] Whilst Husserl offers us a transcendental version of intentionality, in Heidegger's account all motivation is ultimately triggered by our need to acquire an identity or a 'way to be'. For Merleau-Ponty, instead, intentionality can exist without representation; motility, in other words, can be 'purposive without the agent entertaining a purpose'.[20] Dreyfus interprets this in the following manner:

when one's situation deviates from some optimal body–environment relationship, one's motion takes one closer to that optimum and thereby relieves the 'tension' of the deviation. One does not need a goal or intention to act. One's body is simply solicited by the situation to get into equilibrium with it.[21]

For Merleau-Ponty, the body is 'a potentiality of movement, and the perceptual field is an invitation to action'.[22] Because of the notion of 'maximal grip', according to which we 'always tend to reduce a sense of disequilibrium', motility takes the form of an endless process of physical adjustment to the world:

higher animals and human beings are always trying to get a maximum grip on their situation. Merleau-Ponty's inspiration for his notion of maximal grip comes from perception and manipulation. When we are looking at something, we tend, without thinking about it, to find the best distance for taking in both the thing as a whole and its different parts. When grasping something, we tend to grab it in such a way as to get the best grip on it.[23]

In Beckett, however, as we have already seen in passing, the concept of intentionality is problematised. Things may appeal to the characters, but seldom in their expected sense: stones are gathered in order to be sucked; a broken pipe is kept for no apparent reason at all. Indeed, stones are sucked for no discernible aim, and although Malone uses his pencil for writing, it inspires little genuine enthusiasm; writing, as crawling, is rather a means of 'going on'. Furthermore, if this going has a particular slowness to it, rather than a velocity, Beckett can also be identified as a writer of fatigue and exhaustion instead of energy.[24] In Deleuze's final essay before his death, appropriately entitled 'The Exhausted', he argues precisely this point. As his translator paraphrases, 'exhaustion is without any aim whatsoever: it becomes the logical conclusion of . . . ateleology.'[25] Although Deleuze argues for a textual genealogy of the exhaustion of possibilities in Beckett's work, the question of ateleology and the problematisation of intentionality appear early in Beckett's writing. The short story 'Ding-Dong', for instance, opens with a mention that Belacqua 'enlivened his last phase of solipsism . . . with the belief that the best thing he had to do was to move constantly from place to place. He did not know how this conclusion had been gained, but that it was not thanks to his preferring one place to another he felt sure.'[26] Leslie Hill writes:

Journeying, for Beckett, as was shown in the early story, 'Ding-Dong', is a con-tradictory process, an alternating movement of egress and regress, attraction and repulsion, desire and loathing, displacement and stasis . . . The space of jour-neying, like writing, becomes a space of indifference, according to the particular inflexion given the word by Beckett's work, of movements made and then undone, advanced but annulled, of opposites set up and then abolished, of unity assumed but then divided.[27]

In the novel *Mercier and Camier*, journeying is similarly 'portrayed as unmotivated, arbitrary, directionless, full of halts, false starts, returns, revisions and indecisions'.[28]

The problematisation of teleology is further highlighted by Angela Moorjani, who argues that *Molloy* both follows and parodies the traditional genre of quest narrative.[29] Although both parts of *Molloy* clearly tell the story of a quest, no final goal is reached. The quest, deprived of a reachable goal, becomes devoid of meaning, destructive even, ultimately producing only physical deterioration; to go somewhere in these quests is always to end up somewhere else than planned, and in the process, the categories of self and other, subject and object, pursuer and pursued are switched around until the opposites merge into one. Intentionality and teleology are interrogated, frustrated and ultimately toyed with. Robin Lee makes an even more striking point: 'The journey and the narrative are analogues one of the other, and to begin either is viewed as a necessary *faux pas*. To journey is to journey to the end, not of the journey, but of journeying.'[30]

Beckett began writing *Molloy*, the first part of the Trilogy, in Dublin in 1947, whilst on a visit to his mother, who by this time was suffering from Parkinson's disease.[31] By now, Beckett was already permanently resident in Paris, where he wrote the bulk of the French version of the Trilogy, which he completed in 1950. *Molloy* and *Malone meurt* were first published in Paris in 1951; *L'Innommable* appeared in print two years later, in 1953. In 1955, *Molloy*, translated jointly by Beckett and Patrick Bowles, was published in English; *Malone Dies*, translated by Beckett alone, appeared in 1956; and *The Unnamable*, also translated by Beckett, was published in 1958.

Molloy consists of two parallel parts of equal length, the one structurally mirror-imaging the other. The Trilogy begins with *Molloy*, the narrator, lying in his mother's bed in his mother's room, wondering how he actually got there. The beginning of the novel is, in fact, the end of the narrative, a point in story-time which occurs later than the end of the first part, and perhaps later even than the second part of the novel. The real beginning of the story, the initiation of the quest, in turn, is a false beginning, for the narrator is not about to set off on a quest at all; he is only viewing the quest in retrospect, lying, as he now is, in his mother's bed: 'Here is my beginning. Because they kept it apparently, I took a lot of trouble with it. Here it is. It gave me a lot of trouble. It was the beginning, do you understand? Whereas now it's nearly the end.'[32]

One of the first difficulties the reader is faced with when reading *Molloy* is the lack of contextual definition in the novel. Not only do the relationships and rationale between places, people and things cease to exist. The landscape remains abstract and unrefined, expressionistic even: 'the laws [that] apply to it are radically different from those of a naturalistic topography'.[33] We are in no specific town and in no specific country. The narrative, in other words, is situated in no verifiable cultural or geographical landscape, although it does, for many critics, bring to mind the author's native Ireland.[34] Not only, furthermore, do the landscapes in *Molloy* present themselves as incomprehensible, they also lack continuity. The narrator does not present us with *a* landscape, but with fragments of one: 'And perhaps it was A one day at one place, then C another at another, then a third the rock and I, and so on for the other components, the cows, the sky, the sea, the mountains.'[35] And not merely spatial, but temporal organisation breaks down: 'I am perhaps confusing several different occasions, and different times, deep down, and deep down is my dwelling, oh not deepest down, somewhere between the mud and the scum.'[36] Beckett's prose, in this sense, departs radically from the unified landscapes of Romantic and even modernist fiction; in the case of the latter, identity and cultural values may be breaking down, but landscape still holds together, as Joyce's Dublin, Woolf's London or D. H. Lawrence's Nottinghamshire testify. This process in Beckett is further accentuated in the *Texts for Nothing*, where the relationship between perception, experience and expression is made even more problematic: 'All mingles, times and tenses, at first I only had been here, now I'm here still, soon I won't be here yet.'[37] It is equally detectable in various manuscripts, where Beckett's progressive abstraction and paring down of the texts is strikingly evident.

The extraordinary lack of contextual definition in *Molloy* extends itself to the characters of the novel. The protagonists have no nationality, there is confusion about their social and parental ties; even the characters' names, not to mention their ages, are in the end unclear to us. When the policeman who arrests Molloy asks him for his papers, Molloy recounts the event in the following manner: 'Your papers, he said, I knew it a moment later. Not at all, I said, not at all. Your papers! he cried. Ah my papers. Now the only papers I carry with me are bits of newspaper, to wipe myself, you understand, when I have a stool.'[38] Beckett's tramps come curiously close, in their specific problematisation of goal-oriented intentionality, to cases of ambulatory automatism, a disorder that appears almost solely to have affected men and of which an entire epidemic broke out in France between 1887 and 1909.[39] This is how one of the contemporaries of the epidemic characterised the malady:

By the term ambulatory automatism is understood a pathological syndrome appearing in the form of intermittent attacks during which the patient, carried away by an irresistible impulse, leaves his home and makes an excursion or journey justified by no reasonable motive. The attack ended, the subject unexpectedly finds himself on an unknown road or in a strange town. Swearing by all the gods never again to quit his penates, he returns home but sooner or later a new attack provokes a new escapade.[40]

As Hacking points out, we are dealing with a form of amnesia; in particular, 'the *fugueur* tended to lose touch with exactly those facts that bureaucrats use to identify us: proper name, place of birth, domicile, married or single?, relatives, educational history, job'.[41] If this does not sound Beckettian enough, some *fugueurs* even travelled on bicycles. The 1994 descendant of the disorder, now termed 'dissociative fugue' by the American Psychiatric Association, also lists the following symptom: 'Confusion about personal identity or assumption of new identity (partial or complete).'[42] We are, in other words, not only dealing with amnesia but also a type of multiple personality disorder, whose appearance in Beckett's work may at least in part be triggered by the author's knowledge of the surrealists' simulated psychoses. In 1928, Beckett translated 'The Fiftieth Anniversary of Hysteria', written by Louis Aragon and André Breton, which advocated hysteria not as 'a pathological phenomenon' but as 'a supreme form of expression'.[43] In 1930, he translated passages of *The Immaculate Conception* by Breton and Paul Éluard. The book's essays simulate mental illnesses for literary effect, 'maladies virtual in each one of us [that] could replace most advantageously the ballad, the sonnet, the epic, the poem without head or tail, and other decrepit modes'.[44] For the surrealists, madness librated language from convention, which in turn enabled the linguistic experimentation endemic to modernist writing. Simulation as an aesthetic strategy, Hal Foster has argued, is more radical than abstraction, which, through its cancellation of representation, only preserves it in place. Simulation unfounds representation, 'pulls the real out from underneath it. Indeed, simulation confounds the entire opposition of representation and abstraction conventionally considered to control modern art.'[45]

Case studies of ambulatory automatism have intriguing parallels with Molloy, who forgets his name and place of origin, and who by some accounts is even doubled in the initially so systematic and stern figure of Moran in the second part of the novel. There are, however, also striking points of divergence between the characters of the Trilogy and Hacking's *fugueurs*: 'The prototypical *fugueur* was an honest craftsman, artisan, clerk, or regularly employed laborer – or a conscript. He was not your Paris lawyer, nor was he a tramp.'[46]

Molloy, in the novel, proceeds to narrate what he does appear to know: the outlines of his quest for his mother. Molloy has begun his journey on a bicycle and on crutches:

crippled though I was, I was no mean cyclist, at that period. This is how I went about it. I fastened my crutches to the cross-bar, one on either side, I propped the foot of my stiff leg (I forget which, now they're both stiff) on the projecting front axle, and I pedalled with the other.[47]

Gradually, however, the bicycle ceases to serve, as not only is one of Molloy's legs stiff, but the other one becomes so too, eventually allow-ing Molloy only to roll or crawl. The lack of contextual definition, in other words, functions in a manner which forces us to focus our attention on what *is* described in minute detail: the very action of moving itself. A similar course of events is repeated in the second part of the novel, in which the initially fit and organised Moran, who sets off in search of Molloy, experiences not only the loss of his bicycle, but a rapid physical deterioration almost identical to Molloy's, and which furthermore cul-minates in Moran landing in a ditch, just as Molloy himself does, at the end of his narrative.[48]

Although the novel foregrounds Molloy's and Moran's movement through space, it would be a mistake, as we have seen, to understand this in any conventional, teleological sense, even bearing in mind the fact that both Molloy's and Moran's journey have a goal of kinds, albeit one of which they regularly lose sight: 'I took my sick leg in my hands and passed it over the frame. I went. I had forgotten where I was going.'[49] The world itself resists the protagonists' efforts, for nature, as landscape, functions as a misleading, incomprehensible sign in the novel, a con-stantly shifting signifier, which prevents the characters from finding their way, both in the literal and metaphorical meaning of the phrase. Molloy mentions the 'treacherous hills' and later adds that 'often where only one escarpment is discerned, and one crest, in reality there are two, two escarp-ments, two crests, riven by a valley'.[50] The landscapes are labyrinthine: in order to progress in a straight line, Molloy goes round in circles, because, in Molloy's reading, the misleading signifiers of the landscape cause one to go round in circles when one thinks one is progressing forward in a linear fashion. Molloy says:

having heard, or more probably read somewhere, in the days when I thought I would be well advised to educate myself, or amuse myself, or stupefy myself, or kill time, that when a man in a forest thinks he is going forward in a straight line, in reality he is going in a circle, I did my best to go in a circle, hoping in this way to go in a straight line.[51]

Not only the hills, but the whole landscape presents itself as traitorous, alien and other.[52] Traditional sense-making binaries, such as linear and circular, collapse into one and cease to function. And, Molloy adds, 'I confuse east and west, the poles too, I invert them readily.'[53] As the French word *sens* indicates, direction and meaning are intertwined. What is purposive for Molloy, who by his own account moves in 'spirals', however, is not so much the direction or the end result of the movement, as the action of moving itself.[54] The narrator of *From an Abandoned Work*, written a few years after *Malone Dies*, puts it thus: 'I have never in my life been on my way anywhere, but simply on my way.'[55] As Duerfahrd suggests, 'Molloy's movements deracinate all sense of direction, freeing movement itself from the oppositions of exhaustion and exertion, rest and motion.'[56] In this respect Molloy's locomotion differs radically from Watt's, in which directionalities are emphasised to the point of being parodied.[57]

What is furthermore characteristic of Molloy's and Moran's journeying is the protagonists' harrowing insistence to keep going. The most significant feature about the compulsive mobility itself, however, is the fact that it is forever threatening to come to a halt: the tics, twitches, jerks, aches and falls that impede the forward thrust of the quest repeatedly menace the characters' advance.[58] In a similar vein the spatial scope given to the external world diminishes successively throughout the Trilogy as the characters' mobility becomes ever more restricted: Molloy ends up in his mother's room, Moran at the edge of the forest and finally back in his house, Malone in bed and the unnamable in a jar. Here is an example of the accumulating impediments to motility that Molloy faces:

I had hardly left the shore, harried by the dread of waking one fine day, far from my mother, with my two legs as stiff as my crutches, when they suddenly began to gallop, my weak points did, and their weakness became literally the weakness of death, with all the disadvantages that this entails, when they are not vital points. I fix at this period the dastardly desertion of my toes, so to speak in the thick of the fray.[59]

What is weak becomes ever more so, and as if this were not ghastly enough, Molloy loses his toes. The curious emphasis on feet and toes in Beckett brings to mind Bataille's observation that feet are base because of the scandal associated with the mud in which they reside.[60] Because of its inextricable link with matter, the very substance mankind for the past two thousand years has done its utmost to transcend, Bataille writes, 'a toe (always more or less tainted and humiliating) can be conceived as psychologically analogous to a man's brutal fall, that is, to death'.[61] In *First Love*, written shortly before the Trilogy, Beckett's narrator makes an amusing inventory of the markers of mortality and decay linked with toes and feet: 'the corn, the cramp, the kibe, the bunion, the hammer toe, the nail ingrown, the fallen arch, the common blain, the club foot, duck foot, goose foot, pigeon foot, flat foot, trench foot and other curiosities'.[62] Theodor Adorno, in his contrastingly humourless tone, takes the association of death and matter a step further, pointing out that death itself has become external and strange: 'that death does not constitute the entirety of existence...is the very reason why a man who is not yet debilitated will experience death and its envoys, the ailments, as heterogeneous and alien to the ego'.[63] With *Molloy*, Beckett reverses Adorno's paradigm, for not only does Molloy have a problem with his toes; even his limbs stiffen and weaken and wither into the bargain: 'it was shortening', Molloy curiously remarks about his ailing and unyielding leg. The ailments, in other words, become second nature to our protagonist. Despite the growing pain and discomfort, Molloy goes on:

Flat on my belly, using my crutches like grapnels, I plunged them ahead of me into the undergrowth, and when I felt they had a hold, I pulled myself forward, with an effort of the wrists. For my wrists were still quite strong, fortunately, in spite of my decrepitude, though all swollen and racked by a kind of chronic arthritis probably.[64]

Motility is not only starkly foregrounded through the lack of contextual definition and the endless impediments that threaten to bring the motion to an end; the body's potential for movement is also questioned to the point of being parodied, as if in anticipation of the second and third parts of the Trilogy: 'I cannot stoop, neither can I kneel, because of my infirmity, and if ever I stoop, forgetting who I am, or kneel, make no mistake, it will not be me, but another.'[65] It is as if the body itself were torn between the ailments that constitute its resistance to motility and its endless potential for different types of movement once a particular form of locomotion has ceased to be viable. There appears, after all, to be little in the novel's phenomenal world to invite the characters' terrifying onward thrust: 'there were no words for the want of need in which I was perishing'.[66] Finally, far from a physical adjustment to the world, what is achieved through the relentless motility is but a growing sense of disequilibrium. On the topic of his failing legs, Molloy remarks:

> I was therefore obliged to stop more and more often, I shall never weary of repeating it, and to lie down, in defiance of the rules, now prone, now supine, now on one side, now on the other, and as much as possible with the feet higher than the head, to dislodge the clots. And to lie with the feet higher than the head, when your legs are stiff, is no easy matter.[67]

The arduous motility in *Molloy*, in short, is triggered by a dynamic that differs substantially from Merleau-Ponty's affirmative notion of bodily or 'organic' intentionality. There is little comfort or hold to be found in *Molloy*'s world. The notion of an 'optimal body–environment relationship' is presented as an unattainable illusion:

> of my two eyes only one functioning more or less correctly, I misjudged the distance separating me from the other world, and often I stretched out my hand for what was far beyond my reach, and often I knocked against obstacles scarcely visible on the horizon.[68]

Motility in *Molloy*, in short, appears to be set off by a different dynamic. When Lousse is defending Molloy from the mob, after he has run over her dog and killed it, Molloy says, 'There emanated such tedium from this droning voice that I was making ready to move on when the unavoidable police constable rose up before me.'[69] Similarly, after Molloy has been repulsed by the green tea and dry bread the social worker at the police station has given him, he says, 'panic-stricken, I flung it all far from me. I did not let it fall, no, but with a compulsive thrust of both my hands I threw it to the ground, where it smashed to smithereens, or against the wall, far from me, with all my strength.'[70] Whilst a residual degree of intentionality can still be found in *Molloy*, one of Molloy's most recurrent impulses in the novel is to withdraw or flee. Far from summoning Molloy, in other words, the world with its objects and beings perturbs or even repels him. Instead of moving towards objects, Beckett's characters as often as not move away from them, which turns their action into a form of *negative intentionality*: a movement triggered by evasion. This notion has more in common with spontaneous impulse than with directionality. Its logic generates a compulsive motility that is exhausting rather than energising. In the context of Beckett's comings and goings, the tics, twitches and falls we so frequently witness in the works announce the underlying dynamics of equivocation, the logic of evasion that is forever threatening to reverse any neat trajectory the quests may appear to be taking. If we believe, as is often asserted, that there is no such thing as an accident, then the falls and twitches Beckett's characters are so prone to should be read as an abrupt and extreme form of the dynamics of negativity; a tear or rupture in that neat fabric of motion that Bergson correctly identified as continuous, but that we all one day shall cease to form a part of.[71]

The second novel of the Trilogy, *Malone Dies*, both continues and compresses the ateleological quests that Molloy and Moran initiate. In *Malone Dies*, we again have an old man, this time a dying one (all of Beckett's characters are dying), alone in a room, writing in bed. In order to pass the time, Malone decides to tell himself stories, only here the narrator does not claim to write about his own life, as he did in both parts of *Molloy*: 'I think I shall be able to tell myself four stories, each on a different theme. One about a man, another about a woman, a third about a thing and finally one about an animal, a bird probably.'[72] Malone also attempts to make an inventory of his possessions. Eventually, Malone ends up writing about Sapo(scat), a boy whose name he later changes to Macmann, and who towards the end of the novel enters an asylum, the 'House of St John of God', living much like Molloy and the narrating Malone himself do. The vagabond protagonist of the first part of the Trilogy has in short become a moribund.[73] We as readers are faced not with stasis but with a form of suspended motion that will erupt not only into the physical act of writing but into a myriad of different forms of movement that take the characteristic mode of Beckett's mature work: miniaturisation.[74]

Malone Dies opens with yet another interrogation into the enabling nature of motility and bodily intentionality: 'My body is what is called, unadvisedly perhaps, impotent. There is virtually nothing it can do. Sometimes I miss not being able to crawl around anymore...My arms, once they are in position, can exert a certain force. But I find it hard to guide them. Perhaps the red nucleus has faded.'[75] Malone's voluntary movements are so restricted that he can reach at objects only with the aid of his prosthetic stick: 'It has a hook at one end. Thanks to it I can control the furthest recesses of my abode.'[76] When Malone makes a conscious effort to move anything other than his arms, his body fails to respond:

I have demanded certain movements of my legs and even feet. I know them well and could feel the effort they made to obey. I have lived with them that little space of time, filled with drama, between the message received and the piteous response. To old dogs the hour comes when, whistled by their master setting forth with his stick at dawn, they cannot spring after him.[77]

Motility as intentionality becomes a problematic notion, for Malone is not lacking in intent but in response. Furthermore, the shaking, trembling and convulsions Malone's body is subject to constitute a motion over which Malone appears to have but scant control: 'I tremble a little, but only a little.'[78] In a gruelling passage, which perhaps has overtones of Beckett's mother's rapidly deteriorating health, Malone recounts his bodily experiences, which appear to describe the sensation caused by convulsing and the overall loss of physical control:

to me at least and for as long as I can remember the sensation is familiar of a blind and tired hand delving feebly in my particles and letting them trickle between its fingers. And sometimes, when all is quiet, I feel it plunged in me up to the elbow, but gentle, and as though sleeping. But soon it stirs, wakes, fondles, clutches, ransacks, ravages, avenging its failure to scatter me with one sweep.[79]

An exogenous force takes over Malone's debilitated body, which, instead of disrupting, absorbs the energy of the shock, blow or illness, borrowing 'its resistance from what it resists'.[80] The shaking body hence becomes a dynamic impetus rather than a passive attribute, sending the strength of the imposing force back to itself. It is for this very resistance of the decrepit body to what invades it that shaking and trembling become the site at which power and weakness meet:

trembling involves the meeting and exchange of a strength and a weakness, a form and a deforming impact. A strength meets a weakness that is not quite weak enough simply to absorb it, to collapse and vanish under the blow. Indeed, if the weakness were total, the blow would be lost, like a sword that cleft only air.[81]

If the dialectics of shaking 'reinvent the power of weakness and abasement', then the actual weakness of Malone's shaking body lies in its inability to get a grip:

The debility of the shaking hand lies in its incapacity to grasp, of the tremulous foot its inability properly to plant its weight. Shaking prohibits the concussive encounter with the world necessary to its grasping. Shaking prohibits and dissolves edges, faces, clean lines of contact.[82]

Shaking reveals the impossibility of an optimal body–world relationship, of any notion of maximal grip. Malone writes of his fictional Macmann: 'he was incapable of picking his steps and choosing where to put down his feet...And even had he been so he would have been so to no great purpose, so little was he master of his movements.'[83] Beckett's uncoordinated, shaking beings cannot grasp the world; they can, at most, shake or rattle it in return. In this way, shaking becomes an ironic comment on the phenomenology of 'gripping'; shaking, in short, does to gripping what blurring does to vision. Shaking itself hence becomes a form of negation, an acknowledgement of the fictional nature of the subject's mastery over the object. Because of the nature of shaking, which is contagious and spreads over anything that comes into its vicinity, shaking and trembling become the site in which self and world collapse: the world invades the shaking body, which in turn infects its surroundings with its trembling.

Trembling, shaking and convulsing, however, are not only caused by exogenous sources but can, even more significantly in Beckett, be endogenous by nature, triggered by 'an inner impulse or desire which moves from the inside outwards', tearing at the body.[84] One thinks of Krapp, split between past desires and present inertia, and his shaking hands and the clinking of the glass as he is pouring himself a drink. But more significantly in the case of the Trilogy, shaking and trembling, in their internal dynamics, bring to mind Freud's ideas of the conflicting desires and impulses that rule and govern our behaviour. More pertinently, Freud's thinking contains its own theory of organic intentionality, brought forth most radically in his essay 'Beyond the Pleasure Principle', in which he famously and controversially argues that '"*the aim of all life is death*"'.[85] Beckett is said to have liked the essay, and according to Gottfried Büttner, he linked his own fondness for stones with 'Freud's view that human beings have a prebirth nostalgia to return to the mineral state'.[86] Life, writes Freud in the essay, is a form of tension whose goal is to cancel itself out:

Seen in this light, the theoretical importance of the instincts of self-preservation, of self-assertion and of mastery greatly diminishes. They are component instincts whose function it is to assure that the organism shall follow its own path to death, and to ward off any possible ways of returning to inorganic existence other than those which are immanent in the organism itself.[87]

Each being creates its own death and must die in its own fashion. Hence, Freud explains, death becomes the ultimate aim even of the life instincts, whose true goal, despite appearances to the contrary, is to assure that the organism dies in its own appropriate manner. This, in turn, results in 'the paradoxical situation that the living organism struggles most energetically against events (dangers, in fact) which might help it to attain its life's aim rapidly – by a kind of short-circuit'.[88] As Malone himself points out, 'I could die today, if I wished, merely by making a little effort. But it is just as well to let myself die, quietly, without rushing things.'[89] What is important, from our point of view, is Freud's summing up of instinctual life:

It is as though the life of the organism moved with a vacillating rhythm. One group of instincts rushes forward so as to reach the final aim of life as swiftly as possible; but when a particular stage in the advance has been reached, the other group jerks back to a certain point to make a fresh start and so prolong the journey.[90]

Freud's essay would suggest that what at first sight appear to be involuntary actions, a body out of control, may after all be something rather more distinctive: a body operating under different notions of control.

Beckett's endless comings and goings embody life's vacillating rhythm through the broken syntax of the different forms of movement manifest in the works.[91] Not only do we have the surface level of egress and regress; each coming contains its own holding or turning back; each going is forever threatening to lose itself in an abrupt lapse. The deeper we look, in fact, the more layers of oscillation we encounter. Shaking, itself repeated and miniaturised in the beating of the heart or the rhythmical intake and outtake of breath, epitomises Beckettian motility precisely because of its emphatically dilatory nature.

Like all motion in Beckett, shaking contains 'a drawing back, or delay of what it portends; . . . a rippling or stuttering of time'.[92] Shaking is a coming that hesitates to arrive; a going that falters from reaching its goal, which explains its recurrence in so much of the Beckettian *oeuvre*.[93] It is the force of life and death struggling in the body, the will to go on and the desire for stasis, the oscillation between a movement and a holding back that is already manifest in the disruptions that the endless fallings, stumblings, convulsions and tics in Beckett represent, much like the tiny disturbances in the rhythmic regularity of the beating heart, indicative, themselves, both of a strength and a weakness.[94] Shaking is ultimately but a minute manifestation of the Beckettian quest: ateleological, compulsive and tardy.

In convulsing, shaking and trembling, finally, the body rehearses its ultimate decomposition:

The word 'convulsion' comes from *con-vellere*, meaning to tear apart, to pull into all directions. The prefix 'con' works to add the sense of pulling together; convulsion is a way of pulling yourself together, as well as being torn apart. It is the enactment of a dismemberment, the body torn into tiny pieces, that is nevertheless held in one place. Convulsion is a held-together-coming-apart.[95]

Motility not only figures strongly in Malone's own story, but it is also present on a metafictional level in Malone's narrative about Macmann, where it bears a similar dynamic to that of his own tale. Malone recounts:

to tell the truth [Macmann] was by temperament more reptile than bird and could suffer extensive mutilation and survive, happier sitting than standing and lying down than sitting, so that he sat and lay down at the least pretext and only rose again when the élan vital or struggle for life began to prod him in the arse again.[96]

It is as if Macmann, just as Molloy and Moran in the previous novel, felt more of an affinity with the pull of the mud than with vertical, spiritual aspirations. In Malone's narrative the whole body mingles with the mud and base matter that Bataille associated with feet. So fond is Macmann of the supine position that when he later in the narrative grows restless, he does not get up but begins to roll on the ground in a manner resembling a cylinder: 'Now it was not the first time that Macmann rolled upon the ground, but he had always done so without ulterior locomotive motive.'[97] The distinction Beckett's characters repeatedly make in favour of horizontal motion brings us back to Bataille, who writes,

Although blood flows within the body from high to low and from low to high in equal quantities, there is a prejudice that supports what elevates, and human life is erroneously considered to be an elevation. The division of the universe into subterranean hell and a perfectly pure heaven is an indelible conception, mud and darkness being the *principles* of evil as light and celestial space are the *principles* of good: with feet in the mud but heads almost in the light, people obstinately imagine a tide that will forever elevate them into pure space. In fact human life includes rage upon discovering that it is really a question of a reciprocal motion from ordure to the ideal, and from the ideal to ordure, a rage that can easily be passed on to an organ as *low* as the foot.[98]

The elevation of the vertical gradually gives way in *Molloy* and in *Malone Dies* to the more base principles of the horizontal. More accurately even, the distinction between 'elevation' and 'descent' is first interrogated in the Trilogy through the recurrent fallings and stumblings that disturb the characters' forward thrust and ultimately abandoned in the levelling out that the horizontal effects.[99] In fact, 'The pull of the ground, the compulsion of down, is always at work in Beckett's world.'[100] *How It Is* offers one of the most extreme manifestations of Beckett's mud crawlers.

During his six-week stay in London, in the summer of 1932, Beckett is said to have whiled away the time in the reading room of the British

Museum. Amongst the several things he read that summer figured the Gnostics, whose dualist doctrine may have left a trace in Beckett's early writing, most notably in the novel *Murphy*, published in 1938, which explores and ultimately parodies dualist themes.[101] Bataille shared Beckett's interest and, in his essay on Gnosticism and materialism, he offers a new reading of Gnostic practices. More specifically, Bataille writes of the crude emphasis on the body in Gnostic rites, interpreting this as the Gnostics' desire to disconcert the 'human spirit and idealism before something base, to the extent that one recognised the helplessness of superior principles'.[102] Bataille goes on to add that 'the image of this base matter . . . alone, by its incongruity and by an overwhelming lack of respect, permits the intellect to escape from the constraints of idealism'.[103] Theodor Adorno, in his *Negative Dialectics*, says something similar to Bataille, although with very different implications: 'The more our consciousness is extricated from animality and comes to strike us as solid and lasting in its forms, the more stubbornly will it resist anything that would cause it to doubt its own eternity.'[104] Although Beckett's writing has more ways than one of reversing the paradigm identified by Adorno, one of its most acute is the manner in which the characters fail to observe the otherness of the abject. The characters of the Trilogy, for instance, are not offended or repulsed by their own faeces. This failure to recognize the abject as other entails that conventional, received approaches to questions of subjectivity and embodiment will no longer serve when we are confronted with Beckett's writing. The incorporation of the abject into Beckett's work as that-which-is-not-other collapses the distinction between the spiritual and the material, for the abject is akin to shaking in that it demolishes clear lines of demarcation between the subject and its world.

Through the incessant fallings, rollings and crawlings, all of which bring the body ever closer to earth, Beckettian characters are ceaselessly reminded of their own inescapable materiality. If the exclusion of waste and (superfluous) matter is an integral part of the construction of subjectivity, then the lapsing motility and failing body in Beckett, no longer respecting these divisions, bring the characters to the border of their condition as autonomous beings, to the threshold of a place where the subject is not. Andrew Gibson, in his discussion of narrative and monstrosity, writes that Beckett 'is not merely relativising the dimensions of the human, but working into his representations of the human that surrounding context of the inhuman which an anthropocentric and humanistic ontology excludes or annihilates'.[105] As Kristeva puts it, it is 'not lack of cleanliness or health that causes abjection but what disturbs identity, system, order. What does not respect borders, positions, rules. The in-between, the ambiguous, the composite.'[106] The abject is neither subject nor object, but a 'something that I do not recognise as a thing. A weight of meaninglessness...which crushes me.'[107]

The final part of the Trilogy, *The Unnamable*, is itself not only littered with references to the abject, but has a narrator that seems to embody everything we hold abject, whether this be faeces, bodily fluids or physical deformity: 'were it not for the distant testimony of my palms, my soles, which I have not yet been able to quash, I would gladly give myself the shape, if not the consistency, of an egg, with two holes no matter where to prevent it from bursting, for the consistency is more like that of mucilage'.[108] The unnamable describes itself in a state of near stasis: 'the days of sticks are over, here I can count on my body alone, my body incapable of the smallest movement and whose very eyes can no longer close as they once could'.[109] Virtually nothing remains of the enabling power of intent; we have but a 'human scrap kept in a jar festooned with Chinese lanterns'.[110] In the unnamable's own obsessive fictions, motility takes on a nightmare appearance of compulsive, senseless rotation: 'Going nowhere, coming from nowhere, Malone passes...Malone appears and disappears with the punctuality of clockwork, always at the same remove, the same velocity, in the same direction, the same attitude.'[111]

Recent readings of *The Unnamable* have tended, often brilliantly, to focus on the question of language and signification in the novel. However, as Christopher Ricks remarks, there are

moments in Beckett's fiction when something horribly real is set before us, and when it would seem to me a perverse derogation from the art to insist that words, oh fascinatingly used of course, are all there is. These moments speak of the body's failing, as well as of the brain's failing to get its instructions heeded by the body.[112]

Although the Beckettian body is necessarily 'affected by the aporetic nature of Beckett's narrative discourse' in that it is, at times, without doubt, 'afflicted with indeterminacy',[113] to shrug off as a failure of language all the physical apprehension and suffering would be to disregard the manner in which Beckett also occasionally manages to work his way round the problem of aporia.

Linguistic readings of *The Unnamable* fail to take into account the fact that we are faced with a terrifying work: bewildering, at times repugnant and terse; offensive and deeply moving, all at one and the same time. *The Unnamable* is, in many ways, a novel about horror: the horror of that which we cannot recognize and simultaneously know only too well. For

'*The Unnamable* is by no means the opposite of a familiar conception of humanity. Rather, the degree of its divergence from that conception is undecidable.'[114]

Through its 'monstrous versions of the human', or more specifically of the human body, *The Unnamable* reveals and exposes the falsity of a thinking that 'seeks to attach all singularity to known and recognised identities'.[115] Gibson, writing about Michel Foucault, observes:

> On the far side of the world of the acceptable or manageable body . . . there is necessarily also a realm of physical monstrosity to which belongs the inadmissibility, even the horror or disaster of the aberrant body. This zone is the bodily equivalent – even the bodily representation – of epistemic illegitimacy.[116]

For Adorno, another specialist in horror (*das Grauen*), true terror is caused by 'the abstractness of modern life, its invariance, its universality, its (virtual) absence of particularity, its characteristic lifelessness'.[117] We can no longer recognize ourselves in the face of modern abstraction, which stems from the simultaneous fulfilment and betrayal of Enlightenment thought. The modern condition originates in a metaphysical or epistemological violence perpetrated by reason or concepts on the particularity of material things. The very possibility of subjectivity, of that which makes for the unique, has hence become eradicated.

Paradoxically, however, something redemptive can also grow out of the repugnance that modern identity-thinking causes in us. Extreme revulsion or horror (the Adornian sublime) generates what Adorno calls *Schauder* or 'shuddering': a form of inverted wonder that stands in opposition to expressions of pure conceptual identity.[118] The power and relevance of shuddering lies in the fact that it is an immediate, involuntary, emphatically *somatic* reaction. As such, it bypasses concepts and the conceptual categories that we impose upon the world.

In the face of identity-thinking, Beckettian characters, as Adorno has acknowledged, form an outrage.[119] They all appear to be variations one of the other, disconcerting and confusing our conventional notion of character, whilst simultaneously implying that the very notion of character has become an impossibility: 'I seem to speak, it is not I, about me, it is not about me.'[120] Furthermore, not only do the characters themselves shun different forms of identification; they also avoid becoming easy objects of identification by virtue of their otherness and revulsion, taken to its extreme precisely in the final novel of the Trilogy: 'it is a great smooth ball I carry on my shoulders, featureless, but for the eyes, of which only the sockets remain'.[121] For *Schauder* can also have another, more primitive, source. It can emerge as a primordial reaction to non-identity, to that which we experience as other.[122] *Schauder*, in this second (albeit not unrelated) meaning, is akin to a sensation of fear. It produces 'an impulsive somatic experience that momentarily registers the presence of what occasions it. It thus stands in a more intimate relation to its other (to the non-identical) than concepts and categories do.'[123]

If Beckettian characters evoke in us shuddering, a physical sensation of horror, then they do so primarily because of their emphatically abject or monstrous nature. Which is to say that it is their bodily predicament and physical repugnance, often brought forth through the painful and grotesque forms of motion, that stubbornly resist conceptual categorisation and at times transgress the limits of discourse. The characters' language may consist of a peculiar 'syntax of weakness', a clichéd and dead speech, but their bodies retain their idiosyncratic nature through their own syntax of weakness, the singular combination of disability and ingenuity of which all motion in Beckett consists.[124] If the abject body in *Malone Dies* threatens the characters' subjectivity, then the body can simultaneously be seen as the very salvation and refuge of that subjectivity, once again revealing itself as the locus of a weakness and a strength. The monstrous body unsettles us not only because it threatens to be our own, but because, often to our great embarrassment and anguish, it is always already our own. For the body finally refuses to conform to homogenising codes and categories, insisting on its irreducible, albeit agonising particularity. It is, in short, through its aberrations, its resistance to preimposed identity, that the body in Beckett, so often repulsive and strange, arouses in us a shudder that Adorno, in his appreciative writings about Beckett, failed fully to acknowledge or value.[125] For despite Adorno's insistence on materiality, his writing portrays an overemphasis on interiority that Beckett's writing, as we have seen, leaves behind.

The motif of trembling that we encountered in *Malone Dies* now presents itself in a new light. The narrator of *The Unnamable*, stuck in a bizarre glass jar outside an eating-house, imagines itself as the tympanum of an ear:

perhaps that's what I feel, an outside and an inside and me in the middle, perhaps that's what I am, the thing that divides the world in two, on the one side the outside, on the other the inside, that can be as thin as foil, I'm neither one side nor the other, I'm in the middle, I'm the partition, I've two surfaces and no thickness, perhaps that's what I feel, myself vibrating, I'm the tympanum, on the one hand the mind, on the other the world, I don't belong to either.[126]

Motility in *The Unnamable* has been reduced to mere shuddering, producing a peculiar kind of body that resonates and has become sonorous.[127]
The unnamable trembles between the categories of subject and non-
subject, being itself the border or membrane that brings together the two.
The aberrant, unruly nature of the body threatens the subject's identity
or, more specifically, its coincidence with itself. For trembling doubles
and triples the body into a succession of fading images: flickering and
trembling by nature duplicate whatever they subject. Adorno writes:

Shudder, radically opposed to the conventional idea of experience [*Erlebnis*],
provides no particular satisfaction for the I; it bears no similarity to desire.
Rather, it is a memento of the liquidation of the I, which, shaken, perceives its
own limitedness and finitude.[128]

Shuddering, like convulsing, is hence akin to shattering (*Schauder –
Erschütterung – erschüttern*): 'For a few moments the I becomes aware, in
real terms, of the possibility of letting self-preservation fall away, though it
does not actually succeed in realising this possibility . . . In its immediacy
the shudder feels the potential as if it were actual.'[129] Shuddering, through
its kinship to shattering and its somatic and disconcertingly unruly nature,
hence further threatens the constraints of an ideology of pure identity.[130]

Accordingly, the amorphous body, however, is a site that cannot be
pinned down. It thus creates an independent space over which conceptual
thought loses its hold. Whilst the body's resistance to preconceived categories threatens the subject's autonomy, it simultaneously forms the
precondition of sovereign subjectivity. The vacillation within this double
bind in which the unnamable resides spreads itself over the space of the
novel, which infects its reader with its trembling.[131]

* * *

Waiting for Godot, Beckett's most famous work, is contemporaneous
with the Trilogy, for the play was written between *Malone Dies* and *The
Unnamable*, 'as a relaxation, to get away from the awful prose I was
writing at that time'.[132] *En attendant Godot* was written rapidly, in one
single exercise book, between October 1948 and January 1949, but the play
was not staged until January 1953, after Beckett's future wife, Suzanne
Deschevaux-Dumesnil, had managed to get Roger Blin interested in the
project.[133] Beckett translated *En attendant Godot* into English in 1953, but
again the play awaited production, this time until 1955, in part as a result
of predictable censorship problems.[134] *Waiting for Godot* did not appear
in print until still later, in 1956. Because of the overnight success of the

play in Paris, Beckett had by this time consolidated his reputation as one of the major playwrights of the century.

Early readings of the play focused on the existential condition of man. True to the existentialist line of thinking, these readings aimed to accommodate the negativity of the play into an ultimately positive and redemptive investment of meaning in man's subjective freedom. A variant of the humanist readings were the religious views. Critics such as G. S. Fraser saw *Godot* as a profoundly Christian play, and argued that Vladimir and Estragon's attitude 'represents the state of tension and uncertainty in which the average Christian must live in this world, avoiding presumption, and also avoiding despair'.[135]

The humanist readings were followed by linguistic ones, mostly post-structuralist in orientation. More in sync with the complexity of Beckett's work, these readings, however, tended to disregard the important emphasis on the physical and tangible elements in the play.[136] *Godot*, Beckett said, when discussing the play with actors at the Schiller-Theater in Berlin, gives confusion 'a shape through repetition, repetition of themes. Not only themes in the script, but also themes of the body.'[137]

The story of *Godot* is well known, and often summed up in Vivian Mercier's witty 'nothing happens, twice'.[138] Vladimir and Estragon, two tramps, await the arrival of Godot. While they wait, they encounter Pozzo and Lucky, whose master–slave relationship bewilders them. Godot does not appear; instead, a young boy informs Didi and Gogo that Godot will arrive tomorrow. In the second act of the play, the action of the first act is repeated, with the difference that Pozzo is now blind and Lucky dumb, and the tree that forms part of the sparse stage props has in the second act sprouted leaves. The play, like its contemporaneous Trilogy, abounds in instances of limping, falling, crawling, '*sagging*', staggering, tottering and reeling.[139]

Vladimir and Estragon form one of the several 'pseudocouples' in Beckett's writing. We learn in the course of the play that the two have been together 'fifty years perhaps' or as Didi later on in the play puts it, 'half a century'.[140] The tramps reminisce about grape-harvesting; share expressions such as the facetious 'Que voulez-vouz?'; are of a similar age and even boast similar gestures: both tramps, for instance, have a habit of fiddling, Vladimir with his hat and Estragon with his boot – what Beckett later was to call the 'Hat Boot analogy'.[141] Both tramps also take off their hats as a sign of concentration. As all long-term pseudocouples, in other words, the two protagonists are much alike.[142]

Although Vladimir and Estragon then, against dramatic conventions, are similar 'types', the spectator, however, is also able to tell the two apart with relative ease. For despite the experiences, verbal expressions, habits and clothing that Didi and Gogo share, the two are also strikingly different. Although the stage directions do not specify what the two tramps should be like in build, 'the casting and the costuming of the characters in productions with which Beckett was closely associated tended to be extremely consistent. Estragon was short and Vladimir was tall and lean in build.'[143] Each protagonist, furthermore, has an idiosyncratic gait, one which is specified in the stage directions: Didi walks with *'short, stiff strides, legs wide apart'*, whereas Gogo, on account of the kick he receives from Lucky and the recurrent trouble he has with his feet and boots, is repeatedly forced to limp.[144]

Whilst Beckett, from the very first production of *En attendant Godot*, was regularly involved in the staging of the play, he waited until 1975 before agreeing to direct *Godot*. When he finally did, it was the German *Warten auf Godot* at the Schiller-Theater in Berlin that Beckett took on.[145] The production notebooks Beckett kept, published in 1993, together with the changes he made both to the original dialogue and, most notably, to the stage directions of the play, reveal the growing importance to the author of the characters' movements on stage.[146] In the Schiller notebook Beckett writes: 'establish at outset 2 caged dynamics, E sluggish, V restless. + perpetual separation and reunion of V/E'.[147] The two tramps, in other words, not only walk in their own distinct manner, they even move with a different pace, rhythm and intensity. In the beginning of Act II, for instance, Vladimir moves *'feverishly about the stage'* while Estragon, for his part, *'slowly crosses'* it.[148] There are, furthermore, other somatic differences between the two characters, such as the fact that Vladimir has stinking breath, whilst in Estragon's case it is his feet that let off a stench. When Pozzo, in the second act of the play, is lying on the ground unable to get up, he distinguishes between Didi and Gogo precisely because the latter 'stinks so'.[149] Even the tramps' ailments differ. When Gogo is nursing his aching foot, Didi replies, 'No one ever suffers but you. I don't count. I'd like to hear what you'd say if you had what I have.'[150] Whatever it is Didi has, we learn it prevents him from laughing. Early commentators tended to interpret the difference between Didi and Gogo in intellectual terms, but the 'themes of the body', the tramps' difference in somatic terms, appear to have been equally significant for Beckett.

The corporeal themes in *Waiting for Godot* are further accentuated through the play's costuming. In the Schiller production, as in the San Quentin one, whose direction Beckett collaborated on, the two tramps

wore ill-fitting and mismatched halves of each other's coats and trousers. In Schiller, in the first act Estragon wore his own light coat and Vladimir's dark trousers, which were too large for him, while Vladimir wore his own dark coat and Estragon's light trousers, which were too short for him. In San Quentin the same exchange applied with Estragon wearing a light striped coat and Vladimir wearing light striped trousers. In the second act of both the Schiller and San Quentin productions, they swapped items of clothing so that either the coat or the trousers again failed to fit.[151]

The matching trousers and coats serve to accentuate the characters' similarity in social demeanour and circumstance, but by being ill-fitting, the clothes also strikingly foreground Vladimir and Estragon's physical discrepancy. Vladimir's tallness is highlighted and made humorous through the short trousers that he wears. Similarly, Gogo's more modest build and stature is made prominent through the fact that, when he loosens the 'cord' that holds his trousers up, they 'fall about his ankles'.[152] When, in the second act, the tramps start rotating the three hats that are in their possession, namely their own and Lucky's, and more specifically when Estragon puts on Vladimir's hat, the added stage directions '*There is a great disparity of size. The effect is grotesque*' appear in the Schiller version.[153] Similarly, when Vladimir puts on Estragon's hat, the words '*Grotesque disparity*' are again inserted.[154] This is also the case when Estragon '*adjusts Lucky's hat on his head*'.[155] One of the purposes of the 'hat trick', in other words, is to foreground the physical difference between the three characters in humorous terms, which also attests to the influence of the grotesque tradition in the play's preparation, as Beckett's own, later stage directions indicate. Build and stature are also accentuated in the scene in which the tramps contemplate hanging themselves. If Gogo goes first and the bough does not break under his weight (given that he is the lighter of the two), it may break when Didi attempts to hang himself, which would cause a new problem: 'Gogo light – bough not break – Gogo dead. Didi heavy – bough break – Didi alone.'[156]

The difference between Pozzo and Lucky, the play's second pseudo-couple, is similarly negotiated through the characters' bodily discrepancy. Although the stage directions, as before, do not specify the physical attributes of the two characters, 'Lucky has tended to be of slight build but not notably small...Pozzo has tended to be portly but not obese.'[157]

Pozzo's gestures are theatrical and pompous, and he even asks the two tramps what his performance has been like, as Estragon's 'tray tray tray bong' testifies.[158] Lucky's gestures, in contrast, are failing and feeble: after his speech, Lucky keeps collapsing. He '*totters, reels, sags*', but finally '*succeeds in remaining on his feet*'.[159] Although Lucky's shaking is not specified in the stage directions, it has been one of his recurring traits since the play's first performance in Paris. Jean Martin, the first actor to play the role, writes:

I asked a doctor friend of mine to tell me of any illness which produced symptoms including slurred words and shaking movements but without affecting the thought process. I therefore studied 'Parkinson's Disease' and adopted a personality who trembled nervously and had difficulties with his speech...I would stand, unsteadily, on the ball of my left foot while my left knee and my arms trembled. I kept the trembling accentuated, more or less, all the time my fellow actors were on stage.[160]

At one of the rehearsals, the 'presence of the servant [Lucky], trembling, talkative, humiliated and battered, provoked a negative reaction, with cries of laughter and disgust'.[161] The rehearsal, because of the reaction of the cast, had to be interrupted, but Beckett and Blin themselves, according to Martin, were convinced by the incident 'that we were on the right track and Sam told me to change nothing'.[162] To add to the physical discrepancy between the two characters, Lucky has long white hair that '*falls about his face*', whilst Pozzo, in stark contrast, is '*completely bald*'.[163] The costumes again both highlight the connection between the two characters, whilst also accentuating the differences, for in the Schiller production, 'Lucky's shoes are the same colour as Pozzo's hat, his checked waistcoat matches Pozzo's checked trousers, as his grey trousers do Pozzo's grey jacket.'[164] The similarities in dress, in other words, make the fact that the two have been together for 'nearly sixty years' clear in tangible, material terms. Yet Lucky is thin and withered and, as Pozzo himself points out, 'Compared to him I look like a young man.'[165]

As a student of Romance languages, Beckett was closely acquainted with the grotesque tradition, and, more specifically, its master, Rabelais, in whose work the body plays a crucial role. In 1926, on his first trip to France as an undergraduate, Beckett visited Rabelais' birthplace and grave.[166] We also know that in July 1935, Beckett purchased and subsequently read Rabelais's *Pantagruel* in the Génie de France edition.[167] Beckett, furthermore, made copious notes on his reading of Rabelais, now held at Trinity College Dublin, and even wrote a summary of the

Encyclopaedia Britannica entry on the author.[168] On 23 September of that same year, Beckett wrote to Thomas MacGreevy: 'I have got stuck in the Rabelais again, on the voyage round the world to consult the oracle of the Boule.'[169]

In his major work, *Rabelais and His World*, Mikhail Bakhtin offers his most sustained analysis of the significance of the body in the grotesque tradition. Unlike the more recent 'bodily canon', which features smooth, finished, completed, individualised and 'strictly limited' bodies – not unlike the sovereign subjects that Heidegger identified with modernity – the grotesque tradition focuses on the orifices, organs, fluids and other emissions of the body, foregrounding the subject's affinity with the world.[170] The significance of the various orifices of the body, namely mouth, genitals, anus and nose, is precisely that they collapse the confines between the body and its surroundings, facilitating their mutual intermingling. Bakhtin goes on to say: 'Eating, drinking, defecation and other elimination (sweating, blowing of the nose, sneezing), as well as copulation, pregnancy and dismemberment' attest to the collapsing boundary between self, other and world.[171] The tradition's stylistic attributes, namely hyperbole, excess, exaggeration and clowning, serve only to heighten these effects, in which the thrust is always downwards, affirming the materiality of the body. Bakhtin adds that 'all that is sacred and exalted is rethought on the level of the material bodily stratum or else combined and mixed with its images'.[172]

Waiting for Godot abounds in various images of oozing. Indeed, in the play, as Estragon puts it, 'Everything oozes.'[173] Lucky weeps, Gogo bleeds and Didi makes an allusion to semen in his mention of erections and shrieking mandrakes. Gogo's feet stink because they are sweaty. Pozzo *'clears his throat, spits'*, while Didi pisses better when Gogo is not around.[174] Lucky has a 'running sore' on his neck and Estragon a wound that is '[b]eginning to fester'.[175] Both vomit and excrement are evoked in Estragon's line, 'I've puked my puke of a life away here, I tell you! Here! In the Cackon country!'[176] The grotesque emphasis on various orifices and bodily oozings in the play is striking.[177] It serves to highlight the characters' affinity with the world of matter, which is also a prominent feature of a number of other Beckett works. One of the most arresting examples is *Play* (1963), in which, as Beckett's stage directions have it, '[f]aces so lost to age and aspect as to seem almost part of urns'.[178] As Billie Whitelaw has said, discussing her experience of performing in the National Theatre production of *Play*, Beckett 'wanted the effect of the face disintegrating like the urns'. She adds that the stage makeup was 'a mixture of porridge

oats, cruder oats, oatmeal, mixed with liquefied jelly and surgical glue . . .
As this stuff dried, it stuck to your face like a crazy face pack and as you
spoke, bits of it flicked off our faces. As the play went on we saw that bits
of us were falling off.'[179]

Bakhtin, furthermore, stresses that in the grotesque tradition, the inner
organs of the body, such as 'blood, bowels, heart' acquire extraordinary
significance.[180] In *Waiting for Godot*, Pozzo makes mention of his heart
(twice), lungs and stomach. Two forms of bacteria, one the cause of a
venereal disease, are also mentioned in Estragon's abusive cry, 'Gonococcus!
Spirochaete!' which perhaps, as in *Malone Dies*, evoke the prostate.[181]
Abuse itself is a prominent characteristic of the grotesque-carnivalesque
tradition, for, Bakthin writes, 'The downward movement is also expressed
in curses and abuses. They, too, dig a grave, but this is a bodily, creative
grave.'[182] In addition, Bakhtin singles out various protrusive body parts
as characteristic of the grotesque tradition's penchant for hyperbole and
exaggeration. We learn that Estragon's foot is '[s]welling visibly'; the
tramps discuss the possibility of an erection and the nose is evoked
through references to stinking feet, breath and Pozzo's fart.[183] Lucky, for
his part, has a 'goiter' and eyes '[g]oggling out of his head'.[184] The new
bodily canon, in contrast, 'is completely alien to hyperbolization'.[185] Bakhtin
also emphasizes the importance of eating, drinking and swallowing in
grotesque realism, which, likewise, figure prominently in *Waiting for
Godot*. The tramps chew and suck on carrots, turnips and radishes. The
stage directions, '[c]hews, swallows' are inserted when Estragon chomps at
his carrot, and Pozzo, in turn, *'eats his chicken voraciously'*.[186] The references to religion in *Waiting for Godot* intermingle with profane, embodied
ones. Both Didi and Christ, we learn, go barefoot, with the distinction
that, where Christ lived, 'it was warm, it was dry!' and 'they crucified
quick'.[187] The collapsing distinction between imagery of life and death, a
feature Bakhtin defines as crucial to the grotesque tradition, is of course
evident in Pozzo's famous lines in Act II: 'They give birth astride of a
grave, the light gleams an instant, then it's night once more.'[188] *Breath*
(1969), which features no dialogue, only a birth and death cry, is one of
many other instances of the blurred boundary between life and death in
the Beckettian canon.

While Beckett, in *Waiting for Godot* and other works, is clearly
influenced by the grotesque tradition, and, like Rabelais, makes use of its
emphasis on the visceral body to subvert hierarchical values and to
emphasise the subject's affinity with its surroundings, he however makes
one crucial departure from the tradition. For Bakhtin stresses the 'joyful,

triumphant' nature of '[m]an's encounter with the world' in grotesque literature.[189] In grotesque realism, Bakhtin stresses, the 'limits between man and the world are erased, to man's advantage'.[190] While play, humour, hyperbole and exaggeration are clearly aspects of Beckett's play, and while they undoubtedly produce laughter in the spectator, this ultimately does not offer the redemption Bakhtin identifies with the grotesque tradition. Beckett, in other words, whilst adopting the grotesque body of the carnivalesque tradition, abandons its affirmative, triumphant overtones. This is played out in the formal qualities of the play, for Beckett famously called *Waiting for Godot* a 'tragi-comedy'. If the humorous elements of the play lack the redemptive quality they might have had in the grotesque tradition, missing, too, is the elevation of classical, Aristotelian tragedy. Beckett abandons closure, catharsis and the grand heroes of classical drama. His plays, instead, are 'populated by those who fall below the tragic, those who fluff their big moment, and fail to rise to their dramatic occasions'.[191] Furthermore, '[i]f tragic figures meet with a fall, Beckett's figures fail to rise to a height from which a fall would be possible' in the first place.[192] In fact, Beckett's drama questions not only the heroic notion of character that classical tragedy advanced, but, in its problematisation of identity, any coherent notion of character at all. Beckett's writings call into question the whole notion of meaning which classical dramatic form offered the spectator. 'Tragedy is too high-brow [and] portentous... for the deflation and debunkery of Beckett's work', and the material, bodily suffering the drama presents belongs more to the realm of comedy than lofty tragedy.[193] Terry Eagleton argues that Beckett's 'farce and bathos may spell the ruin of hope, but they also undercut the terrorism of noble ideas, maintaining a pact with ordinariness, which is a negative version of solidarity'.[194] In its focus on the body and brute materiality, *Waiting for Godot* belongs to the genre of comedy, for comedy is precisely 'the eruption of materiality into the spiritual purity of tragic action and desire'.[195] However, as Simon Critchley has argued, in the modern world, the only truly tragic genre may after all be comedy, precisely for its relentless emphasis on materiality, for lacking the elevation and redemption of classical tragedy: 'Tragedy is insufficiently tragic because it is too heroic. Only comedy is truly tragic. And it is tragic by not being a tragedy.'[196]

* * *

Elin Diamond has argued that *Waiting for Godot* explores notions of power by assimilating politics to questions of identity. More specifically, she refers to fascism and its 'identificatory fantasies'.[197] In *Godot*, Pozzo informs the two tramps that 'I cannot go for long without the society of my likes [*He puts on his glasses and looks at the two likes*] even when the likeness is an imperfect one.'[198] Pozzo's comment triggers off an identificatory process in the two tramps, who thereafter either court Pozzo's approval or protest against him, as can be evidenced in the varying ways in which Didi and Gogo approach Lucky. The two tramps, for instance, both start abusing Lucky as a result of Pozzo's manipulation; on the other hand Vladimir is also appalled at the way in which Pozzo treats his 'carrier'. Diamond, in short, argues that 'Beckett sets forth a "political imaginary" – Pozzo's "society of my likes" – which the tramps reproduce and resist.'[199]

The argument about identificatory processes could be taken a step further, for Pozzo himself fails to live up to his own ideals and expectations, 'the society of [his] likes'.[200] This becomes evident in the second act of the play, where Pozzo re-enters the stage, now blind and helpless, in stark contrast with the pompous and inflated figure encountered in the first act. Lucky for his part has already undergone a process of physical decline when Didi and Gogo meet him in the first act of the play, for they learn that Lucky used to think and dance beautifully, but now resembles a physical wreck. This process is taken a step further in the second act, for not only is Lucky feeble, he is now also dumb. It is the body that once again refuses to conform to the codes of identity-thinking. In this respect, the body, yet again, is simultaneously the focal point of a weakness and a strength. For whatever the identificatory ideology, the body can be guaranteed not to live up to it. As Beckett shows us, any achievement of likeness, even of the body to itself, must by definition always remain imperfect and incomplete, which is also the key to the body's non-conformist force.

What, in short, appear to be constitutive of identity in *Waiting for Godot* are the characters' physical experiences, such as their stature, ailments, mobility, poise and Estragon getting beaten in the ditch. The fact that none of these conditions is stable only further serves to accentuate the dynamics of non-identity: because the characters are embodied beings, they are in constant flux; yet for the very same reason, they remain stubbornly individuated.

In his treatment of motility and the grotesque body, which serve to foreground the importance of embodiment in Beckett's work, the author subverts a number of cultural givens. Firstly, instead of being a propulsive notion, as in phenomenological accounts of the topic, motility in Beckett portrays a dialectic which incorporates the negative. Secondly, what appears to be a loss of control, namely the body's inertia or convulsing, turns out to be a body functioning under a different logic of control. Finally, the body has conventionally been considered the enemy of subjectivity, in that its temptations and decay threaten to infect the subject's autonomy. In the Trilogy and in *Waiting for Godot*, the body's amorphous and unpredictable nature at first glance constitute precisely its harrowing weakness. Yet on closer inspection the unruliness of the body also forms its dissident and individuating power, yet again revealing Beckett's resistance to simple dichotomies. What is constitutive of the demise of subjectivity is also its precondition. The body's weakness in Beckett turns out to be a form of strength.

CHAPTER 6

Seeing ghosts

Technology figures prominently in Beckett's work. His fascination with radio, film and television are obvious examples, but the textual strategies of modernist writing can themselves be seen as analogous to technology; in Beckett's work, this is further perpetuated by the endless repetitions and permutations in the texts which, as Hugh Kenner has argued, anticipate information code and function as a 'proto-computer-language'.[1] Technology also has a prominent actual presence in Beckett's writing. The stage and media works famously incorporate a tape recorder (*Krapp's Last Tape*), megaphone (*What Where*) and loudspeakers (*That Time*), as well as other prosthetic devices such as a telescope (*Endgame*), spectacles (*Happy Days*) and lenses (*Film*). Examples of prostheses can also be found in the prose works, most obviously in Molloy's bicycle and crutches, Malone's stick or the 'phial' in *The Calmative*, which functions as one of the several markers of medical technologies in Beckett's writing.[2] Here, I shall focus on the ambiguous role of technology in Beckett's television plays, with particular emphasis on perceptual technologies.

The five senses, as Merleau-Ponty has emphasised, function as the interface between the self and the world, and therefore mediate and bring into being the relationship between the subject and its surroundings. Beckett's work, though containing some points of divergence with Merleau-Ponty's writing, does share its interest in perception, as the minute attention Beckett devotes in his writing to the experience of seeing, hearing and touching testifies. One can even characterise certain of Beckett's works as phenomenological reductions into the nature and functioning of the various senses.

As Karl Marx observed in *Das Kapital*, originally published in 1867, the human senses have a history, and one of the most radical paradigm shifts in that history occurs during the so-called Second Industrial Revolution, in which major perceptual technologies, such as the telephone, gramophone, photography and cinematography, enter popular consumption.

Furthermore, medical practices were revolutionised by such ground-breaking visualising techniques as the X-ray, invented in 1895 by Wilhelm Röntgen, which also had a radical impact on the popular imagination. As Ezra Pound argued: 'You can no more take machines out of the modern mind, than you can take the shield of Achilles out of the *Iliad*.'[3]

One of the recurrent ways of making sense of new technologies has been to conceptualise them precisely in relation to the human body, as forms of prosthetic devices that function either as instances of organ- or sensory extension, in a positive sense, or as a form of organ replacement, to make up for an individual deficiency or lack.[4] An example of the former would be the telephone, which enhances the perceptual powers of the human ear and, as we have seen, was modelled on the anatomy of the ear, with its vibrating tympanum. As an example of a technological device that was originally designed to supplement a lack, one could offer the typewriter, first devised in order to enable the blind to write. Freud, one of the most famous early commentators on technology, indeed argued that 'With every tool man is perfecting his own organs, whether motor or sensory, or is removing the limits to their functioning.'[5] In 1930, Freud wrote in his now seminal essay *Civilization and Its Discontents* that:

Man has, as it were, become a kind of prosthetic God. When he puts on all his auxiliary organs he is truly magnificent; but those organs have not grown on to him and they still give him much trouble at times.[6]

Machines, Freud argues, either augment or constrict the body. Technology, therefore, can be seen not merely as an enhancement, but also as a subtraction from the living body.[7]

Beckett, whose works pay minute attention to both different forms of perception and technology, examines, particularly in his mature work, the manner in which these auxiliary organs change the way in which we see, hear and more generally perceive the world, producing in us a double-perception that differs from earlier modes of perceiving. If perception establishes our relationship to the world, then perceptual technologies, by default, have an impact on that relationship, and Beckett, ever attuned to these questions, sets out to examine this impact.

Beckett's television plays, as well as his late drama, are famous for the dissociation of protagonist from voice. As examples one could give *Eh Joe*, *Ghost Trio* and *. . . but the clouds . . .*, as well as the stage plays *That Time*, *Footfalls* and *Rockaby*, to mention but a few. Critics have proposed a number of ways of approaching this dissociation or doubling in Beckett's drama, suggesting, for instance, that the dissociated voices stage the inner monologue of the self-reflexive mind. However, especially in cases in which the monologue is overtly and explicitly technologically mediated, as in the case of *Ghost Trio*, these kinds of interpretations pose a number of problems. What I shall argue instead, then, is that these plays stage an analysis of the manner in which perceptual technologies produce in us a bifurcation or double-take of different modes of perception.

The association of vision with knowledge, as we have seen, has a long tradition in Western thought, dating at least as far back as Plato. However, this association, while not exactly changed in the last hundred years or so, does become modified with the advent of new technologies, and in particular, of course, technologies of perception, those prosthetic devices that Freud and other thinkers, such as the media critic Marshall McLuhan, have characterised as enhancing the human senses.

In the second half of the nineteenth century, or more accurately towards its end, new technologies emerged that were designed to 'chart, explore, and record sensory phenomena that [it] had never before been possible to perceive'.[8] Étienne-Jules Marey's stop-motion photographs of flying birds and running horses turned physiological action invisible to the human eye into visual records and data.[9] Early photographic procedures had not been 'sensitive enough to record moving subjects', and 'anything that moved produced a blur on the silver plate'.[10] To study the flight of birds, Marey invented a camera, the *fusil photographique*, which resembled a 'small portable rifle that took twelve pictures...at intervals of 1/720 of a second'.[11] The images could then be combined to represent movement. This invention of 1882 was followed by Marey's chrono-photographs, which consisted of multiple exposures on single glass plates using a rotating, slotted-disk shutter. With the arrival in France in 1888 of George Eastman's photographic paper, Marey was able further to improve his invention. Chronophotography had an important impact on both science, for instance studies of muscle function, and on the arts – as an example, one could, for instance, give twentieth-century photography; many even consider Marey the real inventor of motion film. In 1894 Marey adapted the motion-picture camera to the microscope, and subsequently inaugurated microscopic film, which further enhanced the discrepancy between the now fallible human eye and technologically mediated vision.

In 1895, Wilhelm Röntgen developed the X-ray, which exposed the human skeleton and other organs within the now *living* body. This device, which for the first time turned the body inside out without surgical intervention, made human beings more aware of their state of

embodied being by revealing physiological processes and detailed ana-
tomical information previously unavailable in living subjects. X-rays,
furthermore, not only collapsed the distinction between the inside and
the outside of the body, but also between 'the public and the private;
specialized knowledge and popular fantasy; and scientific discourse, high
art, and popular culture'.[12] However, the X-ray and other imaging techniques that followed in its wake also somewhat problematically reproduced images of the body that reduced it to graphs and information code,
suggesting that the body could be rewritten. Imaging techniques therefore
had a drastic and duplicitous impact on the way in which twentieth-
century artists, intellectuals and the popular imagination conceived of the
question of embodiment.

The awe that X-ray technology produced in the early years of the twentieth century is recorded in Thomas Mann's novel *The Magic Mountain*
(1924), which opens in the year 1907. The novel is set in a sanatorium in
the Swiss alps, and when its protagonist, Hans Castorp, first witnesses
his cousin Joachim have an X-ray, he is particularly taken, baffled even,
at the sight of 'something like a bag, a strange, animal shape, darkly
visible behind the middle column, or more on the right side of it – the
spectator's right. It expanded and contracted regularly, a little after the
fashion of a swimming jelly-fish.'[13] What Hans Castorp sees, of course, is
his cousin Joachim's heart, and the experience is so strange and intimate
that he feels apologetic and mildly embarrassed about peering into the
inside of his companion's body. The narrator goes on to say that 'Hans
Castorp gazed without wearying at Joachim's graveyard shape and bony
tenement, this lean *memento mori*, this scaffolding for mortal flesh to hang
on.'[14] Fascinated, Castorp then requests that an X-ray be taken of his own
hand. The impact of the image is striking:

Hans Castorp saw exactly what he should have expected to see, but which no
man was ever intended to see and which he himself had never presumed he
would be able to see: he saw his own grave. Under that light, he saw the process
of corruption anticipated, saw the flesh in which he moved decomposed,
expunged, dissolved into airy nothingness – and inside was the delicately turned
skeleton of his right hand and around the last joint of the ring finger, dangling
black and loose, the signet ring his grandfather had bequeathed him... With
the eyes of his Tienappel forebear – penetrating, clairvoyant eyes – he beheld
a familiar part of his body, and for the first time in his life he understood that
he would die.[15]

This passage reveals the acute awareness of embodiment that imaging
techniques can produce, as well as the manner in which modernist

literature resists the body's reduction to mere text or code, insisting, instead, on the body's fleshly, visceral nature. There is also a distinct sense of wonder in the way Mann renders this experience, giving us an intimation of the fact that, in the modern world, wonder may reside less in a search for transcendental, otherworldly phenomena, than in material, commonplace experiences such as seeing or hearing, augmented now or liberated through various technological advances.

Both Marey's and Röntgen's methods enhanced the human eye and appropriated scopic ideas of knowledge, whilst simultaneously underscoring the limitations and lack in human, embodied vision. The radical new visual technologies, in other words, opened up a gap between subjective, human, ultimately fallible vision, and the so-called objective vision of technology and visual inscription methods. This awareness of the limitations of human vision had already begun in the first half of the nineteenth century, and even the end of the eighteenth, with studies on such issues as retinal afterimages, as Jonathan Crary has argued. However, figures like Goethe, in the early nineteenth century, treated the topic much more thoroughly than previous researchers had done. The importance of afterimages was that they revealed 'the presence of sensation in the absence of stimulus' – in other words, that the eye, on occasion, perceived things that were not there.[16] Several studies were conducted, for instance, to measure afterimages, and although their length varied according to circumstance, the discovery was made that the images lasted, on average, one third of a second. These kinds of revelations, in turn, triggered the development of a number of devices, initially for the 'purposes of scientific observation but... quickly converted into forms of popular entertainment', such as the 'thaumatrope (literally, "wonder-turner") first popularised in London by Dr. John Paris in 1825'.[17] Another gadget was the stereoscope that produced three-dimensional images by emulating the functioning of human vision.

As early as the 1930s, Beckett had an interest in and an awareness of the impact of technology on perception, as can be evinced in his 'Psychology Notes', now held at Trinity College Dublin. Beckett's notes, for instance, contain observations on Gestalt theorists' studies of the 'psychology of motion pictures'.[18] In these notes, which in themselves are strikingly technical, Beckett writes:

Wertheimer studied conditions under which motion does or does not appear. Two simple lines, presented at an interval of 1 sec or 1/5 sec, were seen according to fact, one line & then the other. Reducing this interval the appearance of motion began. At 1/15 sec a clear motion ensued, one line seeming to move across to second. At 1/30 sec no apparent motion, but simultaneous juxtaposition.[19]

Beckett goes on to comment how, in Wertheimer's study, the subject did not comprehend a succession of impressions, but rather a process of perpetual change. This leads Beckett to conclude that motion is 'not inferred but actually sensed . . . The visual images (inexplicable in terms of physiology of the retina) are not inferred associatively by higher centres, but result from a complex of sensory factors of which the retinal stimulation is only one', a comment which foregrounds the primacy of perception over cognition.[20]

In *The Calmative* and *The End*, as we have seen, Beckett similarly questions our received notions of vision, foregrounding the vulnerable eye of flesh over the disembodied eye of Western metaphysics. Molloy, in the Trilogy, wanders in a landscape he finds treacherous and alien, one that he can no longer master by casting his gaze over it. Molloy has to conclude, for instance, that even though certain objects on the horizon may appear to be close, in reality they are probably much farther than the eye suspects. A reversal of this experience occurs in *Texts for Nothing*, where the narrator reports: 'Out of the corner of my eye I observe the writing hand, all dimmed and blurred by the – by the reverse of farness.'[21] The knowledge rendered by the human eye is inaccurate and misleading; in fact, not really *knowledge* at all. Instead, the human eye and the information it renders is perspectival, and perception, memory and imagination have a tendency to exchange functions and merge into one.

Beckett's 1975 television play, *Ghost Trio*, features a male protagonist, F, alone in a room, in an attitude of intense expectation. Twice in the course of the play F, thinking he hears someone, gets up, looks behind window and door and subsequently resumes his opening posture, '*bowed over cassette*'.[22] The music F is listening to on his cassette player is Beethoven's Piano Trio No. 5 in D Minor, whose 'unofficial title' was the 'Ghost' Trio.[23] In addition, we hear V, a woman's colourless and mechanical voice, describing the set and F's actions.

Ghost Trio, which is considered by many Beckett's finest work for television, and characterised by Michael Billington as 'a mesmeric piece of painting for the TV', offers one of the most probing analyses of the new bifurcated experience of seeing.[24] As critics such as Jonathan Crary and Laura Danius have observed, technology, whilst underscoring the limitations of the human eye, also liberates it from its association with knowledge, enabling a more sensuous, aestheticized experience of vision. This is reflected

in the multiple movements in the visual arts modernity has experienced –
impressionism, post-impressionism, expressionism and so on – that privilege
colour over line, beauty over fact, and Beckett's numerous writings on the
visual arts reflect his awareness of and interest in these new modes of seeing. Beckett, furthermore, is not alone in his discovery. A number of
modernist writers comment, in their idiosyncratic ways, on the new-found
liberation of the eye. In her essay 'Street Haunting: A London Adventure'
(1930), Virgina Woolf, for instance, distances vision from its received
association with the rational and the empirical by observing that:

the eye has this strange property: it rests only on beauty; like a butterfly it seeks
colour and basks in warmth. On a winter's night like this, when nature has been
at pains to polish and preen herself, it brings back the prettiest trophies, breaks
off little lumps of emerald and coral as if the whole earth were made of precious
stone.[25]

In her essay, Woolf even describes the modern self in aesthetic, painterly
terms: 'we are streaked, variegated, all of a mixture; the colours have run'.[26]

Modernist art works, in other words, begin to explore the subjective
nature of perceptual experience. Modernism, that is to say, 'increasingly
thinks of the sensory world as unique and individual'.[27] Indeed, the
opening shots of *Ghost Trio*, which Daniel Albright describes as 'a game
with superimposed rectangles', bear a closer resemblance to a Mondrian
than to modern drama.[28] Furthermore, if *Film* and Beckett's first television play, *Eh Joe* (1966), already featured a pared-down setting of a man
alone in an austere room, in *Ghost Trio* this has been even further reduced:
'Whereas *Film* and *Eh Joe* offer lit spaces that include discernable naturalist
details, furniture, windows, and doors that however strangely shaped
may represent an individualised setting', *Ghost Trio* 'shows a rectangular
box, dominated by unnaturally even and smooth grey rectangles, in floor,
wall, door, window, mirror, pallet, pillow'.[29] Indeed, in the Süddeutscher
Rundfunk production, *Geistertrio*, which Beckett himself directed in
1977, even the Male Figure is at first indistinguishable from the objects
in the room, and appears himself to form but yet another rectangle.[30]
The fact that the Male Figure is unrecognisable as such until the camera
zooms in at the end of the first act once again draws attention to the
miscalculations of the human eye. Other objects, too, such as the cassette
player, Beckett's directions make clear, are at first *'not identifiable at this
range'*.[31] In fact, the props are so schematic that 'a voice-over is needed to
confirm their identity'.[32] There is in *Ghost Trio* 'a deliberate play on the
disparity between "looking" and "knowing" that leaves the spectator aware

of the strangeness and the ambiguity of what he is observing'.[33] The female voice of the play not only urges the spectator to 'Look', but to 'look closer' and to 'Look again'.[34] As Jonathan Kalb has observed, 'The imperative "look again" in part one applies not only to the rectangles but also to the rest of the play and, by extension, to the other television plays . . . "look again", Beckett seems to say, not only at the picture at hand but at the way you looked the first time, at how that may have been inadequate'.[35] *Ghost Trio*, then, is yet another example of the manner in which Beckett incorporates the 'viewer's process of viewing into his drama'.[36]

Several critics have drawn attention to *Ghost Trio*'s melodramatic subtext, and Sydney Homan, James Knowlson and others have pointed out that the play's working title was 'Tryst', which only heightens our sense of the play's sentimental subject-matter, namely, that of the Male Figure waiting for a woman who never appears. When Beckett, in 1977, directed the play at Süddeutscher Rundfunk in Stuttgart, Reinhart Müller-Freienfels, who was the director of SDR at the time, recalls looking, together with Beckett and in accordance with his wishes, for a boy with 'a moving face' for the German production of the play.[37]

The play is divided into three acts that Beckett names 'Pre-action', 'Action' and 'Re-action'. In the first two acts, 'The disembodied female voice . . . uses extradiegetic direct access: it directs the representation and equates the camera eye and the viewer's eye by giving orders to the viewer that the camera vicariously obeys.'[38] The title of the third act, namely 'Re-action', is in part explained by the fact that what the audience sees in Act II is repeated in Act III. However, the act is also a 'reaction', because what the audience now sees also changes radically, for 'the camera begins to alternate between a long view of the entire room and views that are taken from the first-person perspective of F, as if we were looking through his eyes'.[39]

There is, in other words, a discrepancy between *Ghost Trio*'s austere, geometric set with its embedded rectangles, and the play's sentimental subject-matter, that of a man waiting for a woman who never appears. This discrepancy is reflected in the two different types of focalisation we encounter in the play: that of the camera and that of F; external and internal or extradiegetic and intradiegetic, to use terms familiar from film theory.

Something similar is at stake in the sound-track of *Ghost Trio*. The voice in the play foregrounds its own technologically mediated quality,

not only by having a 'flat and unearthly' tone, as James Knowlson has
observed, but also by explicitly stating, in the opening lines of the play:

Good evening. Mine is a faint voice. Kindly tune accordingly. [*Pause.*] Good
evening. Mine is a faint voice. Kindly tune accordingly. [*Pause.*] It will not be
raised, or lowered, whatever happens.[40]

Beckett, in other words, made clear from the start of the play that the
voice is technologically mediated, and that as in the case of the camera, in
the first two acts of the play, it will not render what F, the Male Figure,
hears, but only the objectively mediated voice in all its flatness and lack
of depth. Nor will it, unlike the human voice, show affect, 'whatever
happens'.[41] As Daniel Albright has suggested, '[m]any of the voices in
Beckett's late plays seem determined to unvoice themselves', and the
'unvoicing' here has its roots in Beckett's interest in technology.[42] Never
once do we hear what F thinks he hears, namely the sound of the absent
woman that triggers his movements and prompts him to look behind
door and window. However, in Act 3, as Eric Prieto has argued:

not only are we able to hear the music from A, and for longer periods of time,
but we also hear the creaks of the door and window as they open or close, and
rain falling outside the window. It is also at this point that the camera begins to
[render] the first-person perspective of F, showing us the view out of the window
and the appearance of the boy at the door.[43]

Each of these views may also be available to F in Act 2, but because the
focalisation is that of the camera, we do not see what F sees. Beckett, in
other words, is foregrounding the difference and discrepancy between the
human eye and ear, which are tinged with emotion, memory and imagination, and the objective camera eye and recorded voice, which give us
the clinical, objective 'truth'. Beckett makes the discovery of the relentless
precision of technologically mediated perception early in his career, for
in *Proust* he comments on Marcel speaking on the telephone with his
grandmother, which makes the protagonist hear her voice anew:

he hears his grandmother's voice, or what he assumes to be her voice, because he
hears it now for the first time, in all its purity and reality, so different from the
voice that he had been accustomed to follow in the open score of her face that he
does not recognise it as hers. It is a grievous voice, its fragility unmitigated and
undisguised by the carefully arranged mask of her features, and this strange real
voice is the measure of its owner's suffering.[44]

A similar kind of exposure occurs in Beckett's first television play, *Eh Joe* (1966). The nine progressive camera close-ups of Jack MacGowran's face, in which even the pores of the skin are in the end disconcertingly visible, objectify and intensify, often in disquieting ways, the viewer's experience of seeing.

The precision of the camera and the importance of its angles in *Ghost Trio* are made explicit in the various manuscript versions of the play, held at the Beckett International Foundation Archives. Especially striking is the first holograph manuscript, which reveals the importance of the camera's perspective from the very early stages of the play's conception. Beckett plans each camera move, whether 'close up', 'near shot' or 'fade out' with meticulous detail, particularly in the so-called 'III SYNOPSIS'. The length, in seconds, of each shot, is also included in the manuscript. This attention to camera moves, though revised, finds its way through the various manuscript drafts into the final version of the play.

In a carbon typescript of *Ghost Trio* entitled 'Notes on Tryst', Beckett states, in the instructions for the camera, that 'Once set for shot it should not explore, simply stare. It stops and stares, mainly in vain.'[45] Human vision, in contrast, may have more in common with touch than static staring. Merleau-Ponty writes:

From the point of view of my body I never see as equal the six sides of the cube, even if it is made of glass, and yet the word 'cube' has a meaning; the cube itself, the cube in reality, beyond its sensible appearances, has *its* six equal sides. As I move round it, I see the front face, hitherto a square, change its shape, then disappear, while the other sides come into view and one by one become squares.[46]

The eye, in Merleau-Ponty's treatment of vision, explores the various sides of the cube in a temporal manner, moving around its surface successively, as in a caress. Beckett's treatment of human vision, in his various works, seems to attest to a similar kind of temporal, exploratory mode of seeing, which F, too, engages in in parts II ('Action') and III ('Re-action') of *Ghost Trio*.

In this way, Beckett stages the manner in which perceptual technologies, by being more objective, stark and 'reliable' than the human eye and ear, not only differ from but perhaps also liberate human perception from its association with rationality and objectivity, freeing it for sensuous, subjective and aestheticized perceptual experience. If technology does the quantifiable seeing and hearing for us, human perception is freed for qualitative sensory experience.

. . . *but the clouds* . . ., *Ghost Trio*'s companion piece, shares the former play's emphasis on human, vulnerable vision, for like F in *Ghost Trio*, M in the 1977 BBC version of... *but the clouds*... is virtually indistinguishable as a human figure in the opening shot of the play, in which he is 'sitting on invisible stool bowed over invisible table'.[47] In the SDR version of the play,... *nur noch Gewölk*..., which Beckett directed in Stuttgart in 1977, 'the basic shot of M bent over the table, which was already hard to recognize as a human figure in the BBC version, is enlarged even further so that it appears only as an obscure shape; one sees it initailly as an abstract composition and only gradually comes to read it as a partial view of a man after the camera returns to it fifteen times'.[48] The subjective, fragile nature of M's own visions of W, the woman V begs to appear, is highlighted in V's line, 'For had she never once appeared, in all that time, would I have, could I have, gone on begging, all that time?'[49]

In 'The Tower' (1928), which famously inspired Beckett to write... *but the clouds*..., William Butler Yeats writes:

> Never had I more
> Excited, passionate, fantastical
> Imagination, nor an ear and eye
> That more expected the impossible —[50]

An eye and ear that expect the impossible are what *Ghost Trio* and... *but the clouds*... stage, for both plays are about the subjective, yearning human eye and ear. James Knowlson, writing about the largo of Beethoven's Piano Trio No. 5 that Beckett chose for the music in *Ghost Trio*, observes that the bars

capture a sense of tense expectation which may be regarded as one of the main links between Beethoven's dark motifs and the play which, until very late in its preparation, Beckett had entitled *Tryst*. Before the end of the movement there is even a slight lightening of mood and a hint of hopefulness...which may well encourage the waiting figure to persist with his vigil and perhaps partially explain the strange, haunted, half-smile that flickered on the face of the actor, Klaus Herm, at the end of Beckett's production.[51]

The cassette player and the Beethoven largo that F so intently listens to, are not only a further example of the now qualitative nature of human perception — they also point, as so many of Beckett's plays, to the autonomisation of the senses, triggered precisely by such devices as the telephone, gramophone and audiotape, that no longer require the direct involvement of the full sensorium.

Ghost Trio and... *but the clouds*... can be read as examinations into the manner in which perceptual technologies such as cameras, recording devices and various imaging techniques that do the seeing and hearing for us, produce in us a double-perception that differs from earlier modes of perceiving. For Beckett's late television plays, in their historicisation of perception, suggest that while technologically mediated ways of seeing and hearing differ from the human eye and ear, they also liberate the senses from their association with rationality, and in the process, alter our perception of the world.

* * *

Various medical conditions and terminology figure prominently in Beckett's writing, as words such as 'lamina', 'larynx', 'lassata', 'laudanum', 'laxative', 'leukotrichia', 'limen', 'lochia', 'locomotor ataxy' and 'lumbago' all attest, to mention but a few of the hundreds of examples of medical terms that can be found in Beckett's writing.[52] In fact, it would be hard to find instances of non-ailing characters in Beckett's work, and as we know from James Knowlson's biography and Beckett's own correspondence, especially with Thomas MacGreevy, Beckett had plenty of firsthand experience of illness and various medical procedures, having, for instance, suffered recurring cysts on his neck; problems with his feet; anxiety attacks; and, in 1968, a series of X-rays and gruelling bronchoscopies for an abscess on the lung. Beckett's short story 'Yellow', published in *More Pricks Than Kicks* (1934), is said to be based on an operation Beckett had at the Merrion Nursing Home in December 1932, to lance a septic cyst on his neck. On the same occasion, he also had 'the joint of a painful hammer toe removed'.[53] According to James Knowlson, Beckett 'observed carefully what was happening to him in the hospital, paying meticulous attention to all the preparations for his operation. And, a couple of days after the operation, he jotted down notes on what he remembered of his experiences and feelings about the occasion.'[54]

Beckett also makes a number of humorous references to various ailments in his work, most of them real, but a few of them fictional, as the list we have seen of pathologies of the foot in *First Love* attests.[55] The best-known imaginary disease in Beckett is probably Miss Dew's 'duck's disease', which figures in *Murphy*. In *Watt*, Beckett makes a reference to haemophilia, which 'is, like enlargement of the prostate, an exclusively male disorder. But not in this work.'[56] This interest in medicine, furthermore, can already be detected in Beckett's formative years. In his 'Whoroscope Notebook', from the 1930s, Beckett makes note of the fact that the human body is 'equivalent in length to 200 000 tissue cells, or 2 million ordinary microbes', and that blood consists of '30 000 milliards of red globules & 50 milliards of white'.[57] The notebook also contains a one-line annotation that simply reads 'the Roentgen hand', by which Beckett must have meant the photograph of Wilhelm Röntgen's wife's, Bertha's, hand, which is the first known X-ray photograph of the human body, dating from 1896, and which was circulated in at least 1,100 publications, to prove that X-rays did, indeed, exist.[58] Beckett himself had early experience of X-rays; he makes mention, in a letter to Thomas MacGreevy, of an X-ray he had taken of his lungs in January 1935.[59] In *Proust*, written in 1930, Beckett refers to 'the Röntgen rays of jealousy', metaphorically highlighting the hypertrophied precision of technologically enhanced vision.[60]

Beckett also demonstrates a fascination with medical history and ideas in his work, as his earliest independently published text, *Whoroscope*, from 1930, attests, with its reference to the brothers Boot, Dutch doctors working in London, and more importantly to William Harvey – 'dear bloodswirling Harvey' – who in 1628 announced his theory of the circulation of blood, based on experimentation, comparative anatomy and calculation, and which caused great controversy in its time, as Beckett's own notes on Descartes's reactions make clear. As Hugh Culik has argued, Beckett's art incorporates various 'methods of knowing about the world', and the medical represents one of the many.[61] Culik, who has focused on Beckett's novel *Murphy*, has suggested that 'Murphy, Wylie, Kelly, Cooper, and Dew', all characters in the novel, 'are names of relatively well-known physicians. All have become eponyms for different operations, instruments, procedures, signs, methods, or tests.'[62] The references to medicine in the late work, though often more implicit than explicit, persist. In *Company*, the character lying on his back in the dark feels the 'thrust of the ground against his bones. All the way from calcaneum to bump of philogenitiveness', which four pages later is referred to as the 'occipital bump'.[63] The fragmentation of the body, so prominent in Beckett's work, further attests to a medical imagination. It is also a prominent feature of surrealist art, whose many leading proponents, such as André Breton, were either students of medicine or had acquired clinical experience during the Great War: Breton, Theodore Fraénkel, Louis Aragon and Max Beckmann all worked as doctors or orderlies in the medical services. As we know, Beckett had an intimate knowledge of surrealism through his work as a translator. Adam Piette has in addition drawn attention to the influence of Clarapède and Janet's neuropsychological case studies on Beckett's writing. He argues that Korsakoff-like syndromes, which Clarapède studied, resonate throughout Beckett's work,

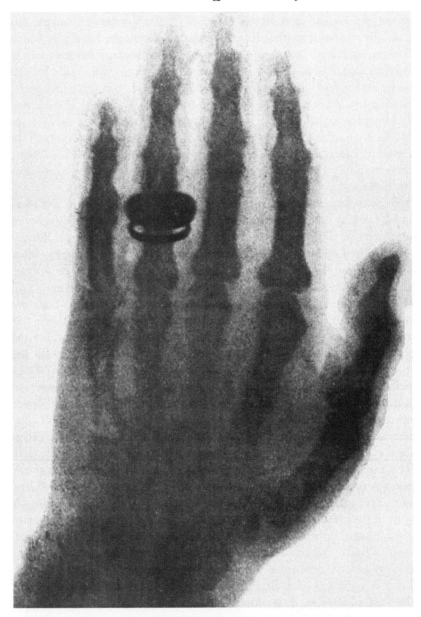

Figure 2. Bertha Röntgen's hand (1896)

in particular in *Murphy, Watt* and *Krapp's Last Tape*. Janet's famous case study of Irène, a hysteric, in turn, informs *Footfalls*.[64]

Beckett's late works are often suggestive of various medical technologies, in particular different imaging devices that form an important subcategory of perceptual technologies. Various visualising techniques, such as X-rays, scanners and probes of different kinds, not only collapse the distinction between the inside and the outside of the body; they also somewhat problematically reproduce often two-dimensional images of the body that transform or reduce the living organism into pixels, graphs and information code, hence suggesting that the body can be re-coded. The technologies used to map the body are increasingly '*digital* rather than *analog* . . ., such as the MRI image, and this means in turn that cultural concepts of the body have begun to reflect concepts of the digital'.[65] The body, in other words, by being made perceptible through various medical imaging methods, is not only made more acute; it is also rewritten, made virtual and – what amounts to the same thing – curiously disembodied.

In a number of Beckett's works, the relationship between voice, character and place is difficult to determine, casting a problematic light on questions of agency. This theme is introduced early, at least as early as *The Unnamable*, which famously opens with the questions, 'Where now? Who now? When now?'[66] A number of the later prose works also have an oddly 'framed' quality, as if they were taking place on a television or computer screen: 'Say a body. Where none. No mind. Where none. That at least. A place. Where none. For the body. To be in. Move in.'[67] The title of Beckett's final play, *What Where* (1983), also seems pertinent, and one could argue that at least since Beckett wrote his first radio play, *All That Fall*, in 1956 – another work with numerous medical references – he had an interest in technology's potential to create virtual bodies. This kind of idea of the virtual body, whose late twentieth-century manifestation is the body transferred onto screens and various monitors, can be said to have its origins in medicine, for the attempt to visualize the body has been a central aspiration in Western medicine for its entire duration, as the importance of the anatomy theatre, dissection and physiognomy attest.[68] As Bojana Kunst notes, 'with the discovery of X-rays, there has been a radical change in the depiction and decoding of the human body . . . the body is no longer approached by the intimacy (or morbidity) of direct physical contact'.[69] Numerical, graphical and pictorial evidence, which is now considered more dependable, objective and easy to transmit than data gathered at the bedside by physicians, has gained ground over palpation and other forms of physical examination.[70] Developments in medical imagining originate in 'the digitalisation and computerisation of traditional X-ray techniques'.[71] CAT scans, for instance, developed in 1967 by Godfrey Hounsfield, transmit 'fine X-rays through the patient to produce detailed cross-sections, which are computer processed to create a three-dimensional picture whose shading depends on tissue density'.[72] MRI scans, in turn, were developed in the early 1980s. Using a magnetic field '30 000 times stronger than the earth's', they afford extraordinary accuracy and fine detail of soft tissue, and are also renowned for the aesthetic appeal of the images that they produce.[73] The close relationship between medicine and aesthetics that we are familiar with from at least the Renaissance onwards, in other words, persists into postmodernity. The tactility of the conventional anatomy class has given way to 'clean technological filters where the image of the body is created by means of computers and technology; and therefore transmuted into a dematerialised graph, matrix, shadow, combination of colours and stripes, hypertexts'.[74] Furthermore, as Stanley Reiser observes, computers, with their 'power through programs to array, compare and portray the significance of data, now [also provide] the interpretive function'.[75] They analyse the virtual body of the patient and often diagnose, so that the entire process of diagnosis can occur in a virtual realm.

The manner in which these newer digital technologies differ from analogue ones is their promise of projecting full, three-dimensional computer images, rather than the flat, two-dimensional fragments of early X-rays and other visualising devices such as electrocardiographs that seemed to reduce the body to a diagram. The development of digital imaging, in turn, fuelled fantasies of virtual bodies in virtual environments, at their peak in the 1980s, and Beckett's work, always anticipatory, as several critics have observed, begins to investigate the potential and significance of these environments: 'The body again. Where none. The place again. Where none.'[76]

Nacht und Träume, written for Süddeutscher Rundfunk in 1982, at the request of Reinhart Müller-Freienfels, who was the director of SDR at the time, presents us with a dreamer, A, and his dreamt self, B, in the upper-right-hand corner of the television screen.[77] The play, in other words, reproduces or doubles the dreamer's body, or, what amounts to the same thing, turns it virtual. The play has no dialogue, but instead uses Schubert's lied, 'Nacht und Träume'. However, the sentimental effect of the lied and the play's subject-matter is curiously lessened and even made

Figure 3. *Nacht und Träume* (1983)

ironic by the peculiar *mise en abyme* of virtuality, created by the enframed image on the TV screen, which itself sports a further embedded image in the upper-right-hand corner of the monitor. In response to a query from Müller-Freienfels about whether the dreamer and his dreamt self could be played by different actors, Beckett responded, in a letter dated Paris, 5 August 1982, that 'The dreamer's face is virtually invisible. Head resemblance alone is enough. So by all means 2 separate performers for the dreamer and his dreamt self. The more so as he may be supposed to dream himself somewhat other than he is.'[78]

The virtual, dreamt self is comforted and aided by a pair of disembodied hands, whose gender Beckett wanted to keep deliberately ambiguous.[79] The left hand rests briefly on B's head; the right hand offers a cup to his lips and later wipes his brow, then rests on B's palm. After fadeout the dream is repeated, but this time 'in close-up and slower motion', as if to emphasise the dreamt, virtual self, and also foreground the medium Beckett is using, by employing television's stock signifying devices, close-ups and slow motion, both methods of underscoring a particular scene.[80] The prominent use of close-ups deprives the viewer of setting and context, and the soft focus in which the scene is shot smooths out details and distances the image, as if to further stress the virtual nature of the scene at hand.[81] The foregrounded virtuality in this play seems to entail a release from physical discomfort and suffering, a thought entertained by a number of Beckett's works, though not without a sense of irony. As Enoch Brater has observed, it seems as if the 'visualization' of the images in *Nacht und Träume*, rather than 'their meaning, were the dramatist's true subject'.[82]

The play that seems most pertinent, however, for a study of virtuality is *What Where*, and especially the two TV versions, *Was Wo*, which Beckett directed at Süddeutscher Rundfunk in 1985, and the Global Village production, which dates from 1987, and for which Beckett acted as an adviser to the directors, Stan Gontarski and John Reilly.[83] Although it was originally written for the stage, Beckett came to the conclusion, in his own words, that '*What Where* was written for the theatre, but it's much more a television play than a theatre play.'[84] Beckett was famously unhappy with the stage version, which presented problems of costume, makeup, lighting and the like, all well documented by Knowlson, Cohn and others. Before setting off to Stuttgart, Beckett drastically edited the play. He 'cut about a quarter of the German text of *Was Wo* . . . Visually, he substituted masklike faces for the full-length grey figures. For exits and entrances of Bam, Bem, Bim and Bom, he substituted fadeouts and fadeups.'[85] As Beckett himself put it in his Production Notebook for *Was Wo*, 'Bodies & movement eliminated.'[86] In preparation of his trip to Süddeutscher Rundfunk, Beckett wrote to Reinhart Müller-Frienfels, in a letter dated Paris, 13 March 1984, that:

Perhaps the clue to the whole affair is its ghostliness. The 4 are indistinguishable. Ghostly garments, ghostly speech. This should be supplied by a single & invisible speaker, either live in conjunction with the 'action', or for part-synchronisation. Bam's voice from beyond to be distinguished from the others by some form of microphonic distortion. The players would speak their words, but inaudibly.[87]

In another letter, written in German to Müller-Freienfels, and dated Paris, 5 March 1984, Beckett mentions that Bam's voice belongs to a 'noch nicht gewordenen Jenseits' (a not yet evolved world beyond).[88]

The TV play consists of four heads that are supposed to be 'indistinguishable' from one another.[89] Beckett wrote to Müller-Freienfels: 'All four to be made as alike as possible by means of costume and make-up however excessive.'[90] In his Production Notebook for *Was Wo*, Beckett added: 'Dim light. Faces blurred' and 'Only oval of face to be seen.'[91] In the TV versions, especially the Global Village production, the effect of likeness between the four figures was intensified by making the images

Figure 4. *What Where* (1988)

of Bam, Bem, Bim and Bom appear as if they had been morphed, for morphing 'makes it difficult to distinguish between one person and another, thus collapsing the boundaries between bodies that were once considered inviolable'.[92] One of the characteristics of the augmented use of digital imaging is to make 'bodies appear mutable and plastic, easily combined and reassembled'.[93] Morphing, in addition, deprives the subject of a personal and social history, which is precisely what virtual beings lack.

Bam, Bem, Bim and Bom appear to operate through a set of permutations that resemble a computer language. As Enoch Brater has argued, 'a variety of elements, some lexical, some seasonal, and some more strictly choreographic, contribute to the formulation of a sustained pattern of repetition and recognition. On this set all directions end in mathematical symmetry.'[94] To add to the machine-like quality of the play, V, represented by Bam's death mask, keeps switching off and back on again when a glitch in the system appears, 'aborting the re-enactment if . . . the words or actions are not correct'.[95] The permutations, in turn, bring to mind computer loops: Bam, Bem, Bim and Bom seem condemned to perform the same set of moves, as if caught in a set of looping instructions. In a letter to Müller-Freienfels, Beckett specified: 'Attitudes and movements strictly identical. Speech mechanical and colourless.'[96] 'Are you free?' Bam asks Bim and later Bem.[97] The design, however, 'serves no purpose, gratifies no desire; it is simply obedience to a compulsion', as if the players were losing species.[98]

Certain programming languages, such as Pascal and FORTRAN, which figure loop structures for repetition, only have one mood, the imperative.[99] This is also the mood of *What Where*, in which each character in turn is compelled, by V, to act as interrogator and victim. In directing *Was Wo*, Beckett wanted to make certain Bam was clearly set apart from Bim, Bem and Bom, and that his voice should be, and I repeat, 'distinguished from the others by some form of microphonic distortion'.[100] Beckett wanted Bam's voice to be 'distant' and to have a 'flat tone'.[101] 'S [*Stimme* (voice)] recorded separately. then playback.'[102] As Stan Gontarski observes, 'In the final version of *Was Wo* worked out with cameraman Jim Lewis, "V" [represented by Bam's death mask . . . takes] up almost one-third of the video screen.'[103]

As is now widely acknowledged, modern surveillance culture has close institutional links with medical culture:

The development of imaging technology in the detection and prevention of crime is historically and institutionally related to the development of imaging technology in the detection and prevention of disease. The technology in both institutions developed along the panoptic principle of surveillance and control, and now incorporates both photo-mechanical and computer imaging.[104]

The most obvious and often-cited example is precisely Jeremy Bentham's Panopticon, which, as Sarah Kember has argued, was but the 'epitome of a disciplinary practice already carried out across a range of institutions including schools, prisons and hospitals'.[105] In *Discipline and Punish*, Foucault describes the functioning of the Panopticon in the following manner: 'All that is needed . . . is to place a supervisor in a central tower and to shut up in each cell a madman, a patient, a condemned man, a worker or a schoolboy. By the effect of backlighting, one can observe from the tower, standing out precisely against the light, the small captive shadows in the cells of the periphery.'[106]

Not only *What Where* but a number of Beckett's prose pieces, too, seem to draw on the surveillance culture of modern medicine, staging bodies in various chambers being measured and observed in various postures: *All Strange Away*, *Imagination Dead Imagine*, *Ping* and even *Company*, which seems to offer us two different points of view, a positivist one of measurement and empirical observation, and a personalised reading of character tinged with memory and imagination. A number of Beckett's works also stage a peculiar light and various rays. In *Play*, the three protagonists 'must respond to the stimulus of a light-beam that turns their narrative on and off'.[107] As if to emphasise their lack of agency, 'The response to light is immediate.'[108] The unpublished 'Long Observation of the Ray', in its various manuscript versions, which were written between October 1975 and November 1976, also seems to suggest a clinical scenario, in which 'the only sound this faint sound as the shutter closes or opens again to reemit the ray', which again brings to mind an imaging device, scanner, or some such gadget.[109]

The bodies in the late prose pieces and TV versions of *What Where* lack agency and seem to perform their permutations as on a computer loop. As Charles Lyons has argued, the '"itness", "whatness" and "whereness" of these figures, who are almost interchangeable, does not exist'.[110] They appear like case studies of virtuality, 'poor binarised ghost[s]', the philosopher's dream.[111] *What Where* could even be considered the culmination of a theme Beckett investigated from at least Murphy's rocking-chair onwards. Sarah Kember has argued that 'When medicine represents the body it represents its "other"; the material object is sought by the rational subject.'[112] For all their promise of fullness and three-dimensionality, new medical devices, as any fantasies of virtuality, are curiously premised on erasing the body. Virtual 'bodies are thin and never attain the thickness of flesh. The fantasy that says we can simultaneously have the powers and capacities of the technologizing medium without its ambiguous limitations, so thoroughly incorporated into ourselves that it becomes a living body, is a fantasy of desire.'[113]

The fantasy of the body as virtual is premised on the idea of the body as code or information, which in turn has a long history, dating at least as far back as the Renaissance. A contemporary example is the Human Genome Project, which renders the 'body as a kind of accessible digital map, something easily decipherable, understandable, and containable – a body that is seemingly less mysterious than the body that is popularly conceived and individually experienced'.[114] The Human Genome Project consists of an idea of the body 'transcribed into thousands of pages of code – line upon line of letters of various orderings'.[115] But as *What Where* attests, this kind of body, and the thinking or actions it might generate, are no longer human. Jean-François Lyotard writes: 'As a material ensemble, the human body hinders the separability of [its] intelligence, hinders its exile and therefore survival. But at the same time the body, our phenomenological, mortal, perceiving body is the only available *analogon* for thinking a certain complexity of thought.'[116]

The body with its various ailments and disorders is the locus of contingency in Beckett's *oeuvre*, which renders its status problematic, yet also non-negotiable. Beckett's work both investigates and resists fantasies of disembodiment, by offering us unattached hands, mouths and floating heads, fragmentation rather than wholeness. Beckett's last two TV projects can be read as case studies of virtuality – *Nacht und Träume*, perhaps, focusing on the promise of comfort and release from suffering that disembodiment might entail, while *Was Wo* and its Global Village version offer us a glimpse of its horrors.

Conclusion

I have argued for the centrality of the body in Beckett's writing, and suggested that the prereflective, sensuous body is pivotal to Beckett's mature work. Beckett shares Merleau-Ponty's notion of embodied subjectivity, manifest in his emphasis on the body's role in cognition and the wider construction of identity. The body's relation to time, in particular, is pertinent in both writers, for whom the body has a stative, time-arresting aspect, and an active, dynamic one that can be understood as time itself.

The significance of embodiment in Beckett's work can be evidenced in the extraordinary attention he devotes to sensory perception. Beckett's writing questions Western disembodied notions of vision, in which sight has been associated with rationality and autonomous subjectivity. Instead, his work focuses on the fleshly and fallible nature of the eye, which is prone to errors and miscalculations. Beckett reimagines the experience of seeing anew, casting doubt over the autonomy of the subject, which is further intensified in his examination of self-perception. Through an emphasis on the embodied eye, Beckett divulges the modern myth of individuality that rests on an untenable division between subject and world.

Beckett's emphasis on the material origin of sound and hearing, as well as his understanding of their transgressive nature, further attests to his interest in embodied experience, for hearing in Beckett's work not only grounds the subject in the body; it also allows the body to exceed itself. These effects are only augmented by auditory technologies, which serve to heighten the sensuous capacity of the ear.

Beckett's writing also devotes attention to the sense of touch. Beckett turns his focus on touch, I suggest, because the tactile collapses boundaries between interiority and exteriority, the active and the passive and the concrete and the abstract, bringing about the subject's intermingling with the world. The skin, which is both endogenous and exogenous and functions as a visible carrier of identity in Beckett's writing, hence also operates as the vehicle of its dissolution. This intermingling is further reinforced through Beckett's linguistic registers that serve to complicate notions of self-identity.

The extraordinary emphasis on different forms of motility in Beckett's writing dramatises the body's weakness and its strength, for the body in its lapsing and deviant nature not only threatens identity in Beckett's work, but also functions as its peculiar refuge. While Beckett's writing repeatedly foregrounds the body's refusal to conform to homogenising codes and categories, it simultaneously stresses its irreducible particularity. For the amorphous body in Beckett cannot be pinned down. It creates an independent space over which conceptual thought loses its hold. The characters, because they are embodied beings, find themselves in perpetual flux. Yet, for the very same reason, they remain stubbornly individuated.

The prominence of the abject, to which the failing body in Beckett pertains, further demolishes clear demarcations between the subject and its surroundings. Beckett inherits his emphasis on the material body, its oozings and protrusions, from the grotesque tradition he was intimately acquainted with. However, although adopting the tradition's penchant for the base body, Beckett leaves behind its triumphant, affirmative overtones.

Beckett's prolific foregrounding of various perceptual technologies in his work attests to his historicisation of embodied experience. By being more accurate, relentless and precise than human vision, various imaging devices serve to liberate the human eye from its association with rationality, allowing for a more sensuous, subjective and imaginative mode of seeing, which Beckett explores in his television plays. Various medical imaging techniques that unfetter the human eye, however, also problematically reduce the living body to pixels, graphs and binary code, suggesting the body's reconfiguration. Beckett explores this possibility in a number of his works, dedicating special attention to virtuality in his late television plays. If *Nacht und Träume* explores the comforting fantasy of disembodiment, *What Where*, Beckett's last play, concludes with a realization of its horrors. While technology in Beckett's writing serves to augment and enhance the perceptual powers of the subject, the binarised, post-human ghosts of *What Where* stage the effects of the body's eradication.

Over and again in his work Beckett emphasises the incarnate nature of subjectivity, while simultaneously demonstrating how vision, hearing, touch and technologically enhanced forms of perception expand the limits of the body, facilitating the subject's transgression beyond itself. The 'disembodiment' critics have so frequently found in Beckett's work may therefore more accurately be considered part of the expansion endemic to embodied being: when we sense, as Beckett's work shows us, we are always beside ourselves.

Beckett makes a weighty contribution to modernism's dialectic with materialism in his emphasis on the body's irreducibility. His writing offers one of the most sustained efforts in literature to cast light on embodied experience. Although Beckett's work denies all forms of transcendence, and hence, unlike Merleau-Ponty's writing, refuses to posit the body as a new locus of meaning, his focus on sensory perception suggests that, in a disenchanted world, sensuality emerges as a new, albeit subtle source of value. Beckett's aesthetic strategies, in their unruly rejection of notions of system, ultimately bear witness to literature's often-contested ability to represent somatic experience.

Notes

INTRODUCTION

1 See Hugh Kenner, *Samuel Beckett: Critical Study* (Glasgow: John Calder, 1962), pp. 117–32.

2 Rachel Russell, 'Ethical Bodies', in Phil Hancock, Bill Hughes, Elizabeth Jagger *et al.* (eds.), *The Body, Culture and Society* (Buckingham and Philadelphia: Open University Press, 2000), pp. 101–16 (p. 105).

3 The body, in fact, forms a locus of ambiguity in Foucault's theory. As Bryan Turner writes: 'At times [Foucault] treats the body as a real entity – as, for example, in the effects of population growth on scientific thought or in his analysis of the effect of penology on the body. Foucault appears to treat the body as a unified, concrete aspect of human history which is continuous across epochs. Such a position is, however, clearly at odds with his views on the discontinuities of history and with his argument that the body is constructed by discourse.' Ultimately, however, Turner argues, the body in Foucault 'is that which is signified by biological, physiological, medical and demographic discourses'. Bryan S. Turner, *The Body and Society: Explorations in Social Theory*, 2nd edn (London: Sage, 1996), pp. 74, 231.

4 Cixous's thinking, too, contains contradictory features. Cixous rejects biologism in her emphasis on a discourse that frees itself from the binds of the symbolic; however, her celebration of the female body would appear to embrace it. Irigaray's thinking portrays similar characteristics, most notably in its emphasis on male 'scopophilia' and the feminine orientation towards touch.

5 Anthony Giddens, *The Transformation of Intimacy: Love, Sexuality and Eroticism in Modern Societies* (Cambridge: Polity, 1992), p. 31.

6 Russell, 'Ethical Bodies', p. 108.

7 Elizabeth Jagger, 'Consumer Bodies', in Hancock, Hughes, Jagger *et al.*, *The Body, Culture and Society*, pp. 45–63 (p. 53).

8 Pierre Bourdieu, *Distinction: A Social Critique of Taste*, tr. Richard Nice (London: Routledge and Kegan Paul, 1984).

9 Turner, *Body and Society*, pp. 229–30.

10 The difficulty of addressing issues of embodiment manifests itself in the lack of an appropriate idiom. It is endemic to the body to resist conceptual categorisation.

11 I am referring here to the publication dates of the French *Molloy* and *Malone meurt*, namely 1951. The English translations appeared in print in 1955 and 1956, respectively.

12 For a discussion of gender in Beckett, see Linda Ben-Zvi's *Women in Beckett: Performance and Critical Perspectives* (Urbana and Chicago: University of Illinois Press, 1990), which is a collection of critical essays and interviews. See also Mary Bryden's *Women in Samuel Beckett's Prose and Drama: Her Own Other* (London: Macmillan, 1993), a pioneering work which offers the first sustained analysis of the topic. For a discussion of gender in Beckett's late drama, see Anna McMullan's book, *Theatre on Trial: Samuel Beckett's Later Drama* (New York and London: Routledge, 1993). See also Elin Diamond's 'Feminist Readings of Beckett', in Lois Oppenheim (ed.), *Palgrave Advances to Beckett Studies* (Basingstoke: Palgrave Macmillan, 2004), pp. 45–67. Shane Weller's *Beckett, Literature, and the Ethics of Alterity* (Basingstoke: Palgrave Macmillan, 2006) contains a consideration of Beckett's misogyny.

13 Peter Boxall, in his essay 'Beckett and Homoeroticism', has addressed the treatment of masculinity in Beckett's work in insightful ways. The essay appears in Oppenheim (ed.), *Palgrave Advances to Beckett Studies*, pp. 110–32.

14 Maurice Merleau-Ponty, *Phenomenology of Perception*, tr. Colin Smith (London: Routledge, 1992).

15 Merleau-Ponty received his *agrégation* in philosophy from the École Normale Supérieure in 1930.

16 Lois Oppenheim, *The Painted Word: Samuel Beckett's Dialogue with Art* (Ann Abor: University of Michigan Press, 2000), pp. 96, 208n8.

17 Ibid., pp. 96–7.

18 Heidegger's 'Letter on Humanism' (1946) was addressed to Beaufret. Beaufret also published his conversations with Heidegger. For more information on Beckett and Beaufret, see Shane Weller's 'Phenomenologies of the Nothing: Democritus, Heidegger, Beckett', forthcoming in Ulrika Maude and Matthew Feldman (eds.), *Beckett and Phenomenology* (New York and London: Continuum, in press).

19 We do know, for instance, that much later, in 1946, Beaufret attended Merleau-Ponty's address to the Société française de philosophie, published later as 'The Primacy of Perception and Its Philosophical Consequences'. The lecture summarised Merleau-Ponty's argument in *Phenomenology of Perception*, and the published essay includes the transcribed discussion that followed the address. See Maurice Merleau-Ponty, 'The Primacy of Perception and Its Philosophical Consequences', tr. James M. Edie, in James M. Edie (ed.), *The Primacy of Perception and Other Essays* (Evanston, IL: Northwestern University Press, 1964), pp. 12–42. In the debate, Beaufret argued in favour of Merleau-Ponty's thesis and criticised the philosopher only for not having been 'sufficiently radical': 'If phenomenology rejects "intellectualist" explanations of perception, it is not to open the door to the irrational but to close it on verbalism . . . The only reproach I would make to the author is not that he has gone "too far", but rather that he has not been sufficiently radical. The

phenomenological descriptions which he uses in fact maintain the vocabulary of idealism.' Beaufret's stance, in other words, appears to have been more radical than Merleau-Ponty's. Cited in Merleau-Ponty, 'The Primacy of Perception', pp. 41–2.

20 In a letter to MacGreevy from 1930, Beckett wrote: 'the Bowsprit comes and talks abstractions every second day and déniche books for me in the library'. Cited in James Knowlson, *Damned to Fame: The Life of Samuel Beckett* (London: Bloomsbury, 1996), p. 97.

21 According to Knowlson, Beckett became acquainted with Alberto Giacometti (1901–66) in the post-war years. The two met in late bars in the early hours of the morning. Knowlson, *Damned to Fame*, p. 371. Giacometti famously sculpted the tree for the 1961 production of *Waiting for Godot*, staged at the Odéon Théâtre in Paris. Sadly, the sculpture has been lost.

22 Anthony Uhlmann has recently argued that Beckett drew more heavily on Arnold Geulincx's (1624–69) theory of the cogito 'than on the image of Descartes's cogito'. See Anthony Uhlmann, *Samuel Beckett and the Philosophical Image* (Cambridge: Cambridge University Press, 2006), p. 77. For a fine analysis of Geulincx's influence on Beckett, see especially pp. 69–85 and 90–113. For a history and critique of Cartesian readings of Beckett's works, see Matthew Feldman, *Beckett's Books: A Cultural History of Samuel Beckett's 'Interwar Notes'*, Continuum Literary Studies Series (New York and London: Continuum, 2006).

23 The script for *Film* is reproduced in Samuel Beckett, *The Complete Dramatic Works* (London: Faber, 1990), pp. 321–34.

24 Samuel Beckett, *The Complete Short Prose, 1929–1989*, ed. S. E. Gontarski (New York: Grove Press, 1995), p. 123.

25 Hal Foster, *Prosthetic Gods* (Cambridge, MA: MIT Press, 2004), p. 109.

1 THE BODY OF MEMORY

1 Bryan S. Turner, *The Body and Society: Explorations in Social Theory*, 2nd edn (London: Sage, 1996), p. 229.

2 Samuel Beckett, *Nohow On: Company, Ill Seen Ill Said, Worstward Ho* (London: Calder, 1992), p. 5.

3 Beckett, *Complete Dramatic Works*, p. 400.

4 Pierre Chabert, 'The Body in Beckett's Theater', *Journal of Beckett Studies* 8 (1982), 23–8, 25.

5 Samuel Beckett, *The Beckett Trilogy: Molloy, Malone Dies and The Unnamable* (London: Picador, 1979), p. 170.

6 Chabert, 'The Body', 24.

7 Virginia Woolf, 'On Being Ill', in *Selected Essays*, ed. David Bradshaw, Oxford World's Classics (Oxford: Oxford University Press, 2008), pp. 101–10 (p. 101).

8 Ibid., p. 101.

9 Deirdre Bair, *Samuel Beckett: A Biography* (London: Vintage, 1990), pp. 124–5. Bair quotes the following passage from Renard's diary, an entry of 7 April 1910,

which particularly impressed Beckett: 'Last time I wanted to get up. Dead weight. A leg hangs outside. Then a trickle runs down my leg. I allow it to reach my heel before I make up my mind. It will dry in the sheets.' Bair, *Samuel Beckett*, p. 124. See also Jules Renard, *The Journals of Jules Renard*, tr. and ed. Louise Bogan and Elizabeth Roget (New York: Georges Braziller, 1964), p. 248. Anthony Cronin, in his biography of Beckett, confirms Beckett's interest in Renard and gives an account of Beckett's having read the above passage to his friend, Georges Pelorson, twice in a row. *Samuel Beckett: The Last Modernist* (London: Flamingo, 1997), p. 148. James Knowlson, in his biography, mentions the great interest with which Beckett read 'the meticulous self-analysis of Jules Renard's *Journal intime*'. Knowlson, *Damned to Fame*, p. 126. For a brief discussion of Renard's influence on various works by Beckett, see Chris Ackerley and S. E. Gontarski (eds.), *The Faber Companion to Samuel Beckett: A Reader's Guide to His Works, Life, and Thought* (London: Faber, 2006), pp. 481–2. For a detailed mapping of the entries Beckett made from Renard's *Journal intime* in his 'Dream Notebook', now held at the Beckett International Foundation Archive, University of Reading, see John Pilling (ed.), *Beckett's Dream Notebook* (Reading: Beckett International Foundation, 1999), pp. 30–4.
10 Samuel Beckett, *How It Is* (London: Calder, 1996), p. 15.
11 For an excellent analysis of Sartre's treatment of embodiment, however, see Steven Connor, 'Beckett and Sartre: The Nauseous Character of All Flesh', forthcoming in Ulrika Maude and Matthew Feldman (eds.), *Beckett and Phenomenology* (New York and London: Continuum, 2009).
12 Merleau-Ponty's ideas apply equally to both sexes, but for convenience, I will use the masculine pronoun, in line with Merleau-Ponty's own practice.
13 Merleau-Ponty, *Phenomenology of Perception*, p. 76.
14 Ibid., p. 77.
15 Ibid., p. 81.
16 Ibid., pp. 81–2.
17 Ibid., p. 82.
18 Beckett's relationship to intentionality will be revisited in chapter 5.
19 Beckett, *Trilogy*, p. 229.
20 Merleau-Ponty, *Phenomenology of Perception*, p. 85.
21 Ibid., p. 83.
22 Monika M. Langer, *Merleau-Ponty's Phenomenology of Perception: A Guide and Commentary* (London: Macmillan, 1989), p. 32.
23 Ibid., p. 46.
24 Ibid.
25 Merleau-Ponty, *Phenomenology of Perception*, p. 143.
26 Langer, *Merleau-Ponty's Phenomenology*, p. 47.
27 Merleau-Ponty, *Phenomenology of Perception*, p. 146.
28 Ibid., pp. 146–7.
29 Ibid., p. 146.

30 Shaun Gallagher writes of the almost universal rejection of Cartesian dualism in the cognitive sciences. Whilst in many cases this has meant reducing the body to the brain, 'to its representation in the somatosensory cortex', figures such as Jean Piaget and Ulric Neisser, who have emphasised the body's role in cognition, are important exceptions. Shaun Gallagher, 'Body Schema and Intentionality', in José Luis Bermúdez, Anthony Marcel and Naomi Elian (eds.), *The Body and the Self*, (Cambridge, MA: MIT Press, 1995), pp. 225–44 (p. 225).

31 Ibid., p. 226.

32 Samuel Beckett, *Proust and Three Dialogues* (London: John Calder, 1999). Beckett himself felt uneasy about his book once it was in print. In a letter to Thomas MacGreevy, dated 3 February 1931, Beckett writes of how 'juvenile' the book now appears to him, and how troubled he is, in particular, by the enthusiastic reviews it has received. Samuel Beckett, 1931, 'To Thomas Mac-Greevy, 3/2/31, 3 G Trinity College', TCD MS 10402, Manuscripts Department, Trinity College Library Dublin.

33 Beckett, *Proust*, pp. 32–3.

34 Ibid., p. 31.

35 Ibid.

36 Ibid., p. 36.

37 Steven Connor, *Samuel Beckett: Repetition, Theory and Text* (Oxford: Blackwell, 1988), pp. 47–8.

38 Beckett, *Proust*, p. 19.

39 Merleau-Ponty, *Phenomenology of Perception*, pp. 85–6.

40 Beckett, *Proust*, p. 34.

41 Ibid., pp. 36–7.

42 Yoshiki Tajiri, *Samuel Beckett and the Prosthetic Body: The Organs and Senses in Modernism* (Basingstoke: Palgrave Macmillan, 2007), p. 94.

43 Beckett, *Complete Dramatic Works*, p. 222.

44 Maurice Harmon (ed.), *No Author Better Served: The Correspondence of Samuel Beckett and Alan Schneider* (Cambridge, MA and London: Harvard University Press, 1998), p. 59.

45 Beckett, *Proust*, p. 15.

46 Pierre Chabert, 'Beckett as Director', *Gambit* 7 (1976), 41–63, 57.

47 As Beckett famously wrote to Alan Schneider, on 29 December 1957, 'My work is a matter of fundamental sounds (no joke intended), made as fully as possible, and I accept responsibility for nothing else.' Harmon, *No Author Better Served*, p. 24.

48 Beckett, *Complete Dramatic Works*, pp. 215, 218, 221.

49 'Suggestions for T. V. Krapp' is reproduced in Clas Zilliacus, *Beckett and Broadcasting: A Study of the Works of Samuel Beckett for and in Radio and Television*, Acta Academiae Aboensis, Ser. A., Humanoira 51: 2 (Åbo, Finland: Åbo Akademi, 1976), pp. 204–5.

50 For the human voice is experienced as distressingly incomplete before its source can be visually located. See Steven Connor, *Dumbstruck: A Cultural*

History of Ventriloquism (Oxford: Oxford University Press, 2000), p. 20. The unity of time, space and action collapses in the doubling, tripling, if not quadrupling of all three through the voice(s) on tape.

51 Beckett, *Complete Dramatic Works*, p. 218.

52 Ibid., p. 217.

53 Ibid., p. 220.

54 Ibid.

55 Chabert, 'Beckett as Director', 52. In the *Beckett on Film* production of the play, directed by Atom Egoyan, John Hurt, who plays Krapp, lays his head between the two spools of the tape recorder. *Krapp's Last Tape*, dir. Atom Egoyan, perf. John Hurt (RTÉ and Channel 4, 2000).

56 Chabert, 'The Body', 28.

57 Chabert, 'Beckett as Director', 52.

58 Beckett, *Complete Dramatic Works*, p. 223.

59 Ibid.

60 Merleau-Ponty, *Phenomenology of Perception*, p. 163.

61 Ibid., p. 165.

62 The working title Beckett gave the play was the 'Magee Monologue'. Knowlson, *Damned to Fame*, p. 444.

63 Connor, *Dumbstruck*, p. 5.

64 Beckett, *Complete Dramatic Works*, p. 217.

65 The quotation is from *Worstward Ho*, first published in 1983, and included in Beckett, *Nohow On*, p. 126. The passage from *Dream* I am referring to is the following: 'the thought or dream, sleeping and walking, in the morning dozing and the evening ditto, with the penny rapture, of the shining shore where underneath them the keel of their skiff would ground and grind and rasp and stay stuck for them, just the pair of them, to skip out on to the sand and gather reeds and bathe hands, faces and breasts and broach the foot-hills without any discussion, in the bright light with the keen music behind them – then that face and site preyed to such purpose on the poor fellow that he took steps to reintegrate the facts of the former and the skin of the zephyr, and so expelled her, for better or for worse, from his eye and mind.' Samuel Beckett, *Dream of Fair to Middling Women* (Dublin: Black Cat Press, 1992), p. 114. The scene is also repeated in the prose fragment 'Heard in the Dark 2', which is an early extract of the novel *Company*. The prose fragment was first published in *Journal of Beckett Studies* 5 (1979), and has been reprinted in Samuel Beckett, *Complete Short Prose*, pp. 250–2 (p. 251).

66 Beckett, *Nohow On*, p. 11. In 'Heard in the Dark 1', another early extract of the novel *Company*, first published in 1979, the second-person narrator says, 'Your father's shade is not with you anymore. It fell out long ago.' In *Samuel Beckett: The Complete Short Prose: 1929–1989*, ed. S. E. Gontarski (New York: Grove Press, 1995), pp. 247–9 (p. 248).

67 Beckett, *Complete Dramatic Works*, pp. 379–80.

68 Elaine Scarry, in her book on pain and its representation, draws attention to the rarity with which physical suffering is depicted in literature, especially

when compared to the persistence with which psychological suffering is represented in literary works. Elaine Scarry, *The Body in Pain: The Making and Unmaking of the World* (New York and Oxford: Oxford University Press, 1985), p. 11.

69 Beckett, *Trilogy*, pp. 61–2.

70 Beckett, *Complete Dramatic Works*, p. 161. Out-of-body experiences that on occasion seem to ghost Beckett's work, recent neurological research suggests, are themselves disturbances of the body schema, occasions on which the body fails to coincide with itself. A recent article in the journal *Brain* suggests that out-of-body experiences 'relate to a paroxysmal pathology of body perception and cognition (body schema). Yet, it is not known which of the many senses involved in body perception and cognition are primarily involved in the generation of OBE/AS. Thus, some authors postulated a dysfunction of proprioception and kinaesthesia, others a dysfunction of visual or vestibular processing, as well as combinatory dysfunctions between these different sensory systems.' See Olaf Blanke, Theodor Landis, Laurent Spinelli and Margitta Seeck, 'Out-of-body Experience and Autoscopy of Neurological Origin', *Brain* 127 (2004), 243–58 (244).

71 'Shifting Ground' is the English-language version of Steven Connor's 'Auf schwankendem Boden', in Sabine Folie and Michael Glasmeier (eds.), *Samuel Beckett, Bruce Nauman: Kunsthalle Wien, 4. Februar–30. April 2000*, tr. Wolfgang Astelbauer (Vienna: Die Kunsthalle, 2000), pp. 80–7. The English text can be found at www.stevenconnor.com/beckettnauman/. Last accessed on 22 February 2008.

72 Ibid.

73 Gabriel Josipovici, *Touch* (New Haven and London: Yale University Press, 1996), p. 112.

2 THE PLACE OF VISION

1 Jonathan Crary, *Techniques of the Observer: On Vision and Modernity in the Nineteenth Century* (Cambridge, MA: MIT Press, 1996); Martin Jay, *Downcast Eyes: The Denigration of Vision in Twentieth-Century French Thought* (Berkeley: University of California Press, 1993).

2 David Michael Levin, *The Opening of Vision: Nihilism and the Postmodern Situation* (New York and London: Routledge, 1988); Crary, *Techniques of the Observer*; Laura Danius, *The Senses of Modernism: Technology, Perception, and Aesthetics* (Ithaca and London: Cornell University Press, 2002).

3 See, for instance, Enoch Brater's essay, 'Dada, Surrealism, and the Genesis of *Not I*', *Modern Drama* 18 (1975), 49–59.

4 Jessica Prinz, 'Resonant Images: Beckett and German Expressionism', in Lois Oppenheim (ed.), *Samuel Beckett and the Arts: Music, Visual Art, and Non-Print Media*, Border Crossings II (New York and London: Garland, 1999), pp. 153–71.

5 Connor, *Repetition, Theory and Text*, pp. 183–4; Anna McMullan, *Theatre on Trial*.

6 Jane Alison Hale, *The Broken Window: Beckett's Dramatic Perspective* (West Lafayette: Purdue University Press, 1987).

7 Oppenheim, *The Painted Word*.

8 Steven Connor, 'Between Theatre and Theory: Long Observation of the Ray', in John Pilling and Mary Bryden (eds.), *The Ideal Core of the Onion: Reading Beckett Archives* (Reading: Beckett International Foundation, 1992), pp. 79–98.

9 Hans Jonas, *The Phenomenon of Life: Toward a Philosophical Biology* (New York: Delta, 1966), p. 148.

10 Ibid. The opposite is true of the proximity senses, as the denomination itself indicates. Touch benefits from, even requires, the closeness of the sense-object. The same applies to taste and, to a degree, smell.

11 Connor, 'Between Theatre and Theory', p. 91.

12 Thomas R. Flynn, 'Foucault and the Eclipse of Vision', in David Michael Levin (ed.), *Modernity and the Hegemony of Vision* (Berkeley: University of California Press, 1993), pp. 273–86 (p. 274).

13 Paul Ricoeur, *The Conflict of Interpretations*, tr. Don Ihde (Evanston, IL: Northwestern University Press, 1974), p. 236. As Foucault's discussion of natural history in *The Order of Things* exemplifies, in the Classical episteme (which, despite Foucault's terminology, inaugurates the modern period), the relationship of a subject to its object becomes one of direct observation. Natural history 'takes on a meaning closer to the original Greek sense of a "seeing"'. Gary Gutting, *Michel Foucault's Archaeology of Scientific Reason*, Modern European Philosophy (Cambridge: Cambridge University Press, 1989), p.163. Sight becomes the virtually exclusive sense employed in the process of observation, with the almost complete exclusion of olfactory, acoustic and tactile perceptions. Not only, however, are other sensory perceptions excluded; sight itself is used in a restricted way: colours, for instance, which belong to the so-called secondary qualities of objects, do not form an integral part of the observation of nature. What becomes important, in accordance with Cartesian thought, is the structure of the observed object: the visual is limited and filtered to render into language the forms, numbers, magnitudes and relative spatial arrangement of the objects observed. Natural history, according to Foucault, 'traverses an area of visible, simultaneous, concomitant variables, without any internal relationship of subordination or organization'. Michel Foucault, *The Order of Things: An Archaeology of the Human Sciences* (London: Routledge, 1986), p. 137. Spatiality, as is implied by Foucault's words, is the norm at the almost exclusive expense of temporality. We are faced with present visible surfaces only.

14 Martin Heidegger, 'The Age of the World Picture', in *The Question Concerning Technology and Other Essays*, tr. William Lovitt (New York: Harper and Row, 1977), pp. 115–54 (p. 129).

15 Ibid., p. 130.

16 Ibid., pp. 127, 128.

17 Ibid., p. 132.

18 Timothy Mitchell, 'The World as Exhibition', *Comparative Studies in Society and History* 31 (1989), 217–36 (223). For Descartes, the material world in its entirety was a question of *res extensa*, extended substance, a matter of nothing apart from 'divisions, shapes, and movements', as he says in section 64 of the second part of *Principles of Philosophy*, tr. Blair Reynolds, Studies in the History of Philosophy 6 (Lewiston, Queenston and Lampeter: Edwin Mellen Press, 1988), p. 20. In his search for certainty, Descartes sought to mathematize all but the *res cogitans*, the thinking substance. However, Descartes's own thinking already shows signs of doubt about the neat division he proposes: the so-called secondary qualities of objects, such as colour, texture, scent or smell, in other words everything that cannot be mathematized, belong in Descartes's thinking to the sphere of the subjective mind and become, in this way, detached from the physical world.

19 Samuel Beckett, 1932, 'To Thomas MacGreevy 18/10/32, Cooldrinagh', TCD MS 10402, Manuscripts Department, Trinity College Library Dublin.

20 Samuel Beckett, 1935, 'To Thomas MacGreevy, 8/2/35, 34 Gertrude Street S. W. 10', TCD MS 10402, Manuscripts Department, Trinity College Library Dublin.

21 Samuel Beckett, 1934, 'To Thomas MacGreevy, 8/9/34, 34 Gertrude Street, S. W. 10', TCD MS 10402, Manuscripts Department, Trinity College Library Dublin.

22 Samuel Beckett, 1934, 'To Thomas MacGreevy, Monday [undated], 34 Gertrude Street, London S.W. 10', TCD MS 10402, Manuscripts Department, Trinity College Library Dublin.

23 Cited in Dan Gunn, 'Until the gag is chewed. Samuel Beckett's Letters: eloquence and "near speechlessness"', *Times Literary Supplement* (21 April 2007), p. 15.

24 With the exception of Beckett's work on Proust, these critical writings are all reproduced in Samuel Beckett, *Disjecta: Miscellaneous Writings and a Dramatic Fragment*, ed. Ruby Cohn (London: John Calder, 1983). For a survey of Beckett's critical writings, see Rupert Wood, 'An Endgame of Aesthetics: Beckett as Essayist', in John Pilling (ed.), *Cambridge Companion to Samuel Beckett* (Cambridge: Cambridge University Press, 1994), pp. 1–16. Apart from his critical writings, Beckett's early and enduring interest in the methodology of the visual arts can be detected in his correspondence and in the 'German Diaries', which consist of six notebooks Beckett kept during his travels in Germany from 1936 to 1937, now held at the Beckett International Foundation, University of Reading. As Lawrence Harvey notes, Beckett's travels in Germany proceeded 'from town to town and from museum to museum for some six months'. Lawrence Harvey, *Samuel Beckett: Poet and Critic* (Princeton: Princeton University Press, 1970), p. 170. Furthermore, Beckett told Ann Cremin that during his visits to Germany in his youth to see his relatives, he spent ' "hours and hours in museums" '. Ann Cremin,

'Friend Game', *ARTnews* (1985), 82–9 (87). Beckett's friend, the painter Avigdor Arikha, remarked that Beckett 'could spend as much as an hour in front of a single painting, looking at it with intense concentration, savouring its forms and its colours, reading it, absorbing its minutest detail'. Knowlson, *Damned to Fame*, p. 195. Beckett also took notes on paintings, and kept lists of the titles of works he had been especially impressed by. Dougald McMillan writes that '[t]he breadth of [Beckett's] knowledge extends from ancient Chaldean to modern art. His essays and allusions indicate far more than a passing familiarity with schools of art ranging from the Norwich school of English landscape painting to the German postexpressionist movement.' McMillan also does the following detective work: 'Some measure of the kind of artistic education Beckett provided for himself in his wanderings can be gained through his allusions in the fiction. Through them his path can be traced to the National Gallery of England, the British Museum, the Louvre, the Prado, the Schatzkammer, Albertina, and the *Kunsthistorisches* museum in Vienna, the Pinacoteca in Milan, the Uffizi and Santa Croce in Florence, the Sistine Chapel in Rome, the Bishop's Palace in Würzburg, the *Stadtsgalerie* in Dresden, and the Campanella in Pisa – to name the most prominent.' Dougald McMillan, 'Samuel Beckett and the Visual Arts: The Embarrassment of Allegory', in S. E. Gontarski (ed.), *On Beckett: Essays and Criticism* (New York: Grove Press, 1986), pp. 29–45 (pp. 29–30). For interesting essays on Beckett and the visual arts, see Fionnuala Croke (ed.), *Samuel Beckett: A Passion for Paintings* (Dublin: National Gallery of Ireland, 2006).

25 Oppenheim, *Painted Word*, p. 107.

26 Beckett, *Disjecta*, p. 70.

27 Frances Morris (ed.), *Paris Post-War: Art and Existentialism 1945–55* (London: Tate Gallery, 1993), p. 171.

28 Beckett translated 'Peintres de l'empêchement' into English as 'The New Object'. The translation appeared in the unpaginated exhibition catalogue, *Geer and Bram van Velde* (New York: Samuel M. Kootz Gallery, 1948).

29 Morris, *Paris Post-War*, p. 171.

30 *Three Dialogues with Georges Duthuit* was first published in *transition* 49:5 (1949), 97–103, signed by both Beckett and Duthuit. It has since been published as *Proust and Three Dialogues* (London: Calder, 1965) and, more recently, by the same press in 1999. It is also reprinted in *Disjecta*, pp. 138–45.

31 Duthuit was the editor of *transition* from 1948 to 1950.

32 Beckett, *Disjecta*, p. 138.

33 Ibid., pp. 140, 141.

34 Merleau-Ponty, *Phenomenology of Perception*, p. 333. In 1966, in a short text entitled 'Pour Avigdor Arikha', Beckett characterised the painter's art in the following manner: 'Back and forth the gaze beating against unseeable and unmakable.' A facsimile of the first English version of the text is reproduced in Anne Atik, *How It Was: A Memoir of Samuel Beckett* (London: Faber and Faber, 2001), p. 15. The text can also be found in English and French in Beckett, *Disjecta*, p. 152.

35 Samuel Beckett, 'Lettre à Georges Duthuit 9 mars 1949–10 mars 1949', in S. E. Gontarski and Anthony Uhlmann (eds.), *Beckett after Beckett, Crosscurrents: Comparative Studies in European Literature and Philosophy* (Gainesville: University Press of Florida, 2006), pp. 15–18 (p. 16).

36 Tr. Oppenheim in *Painted Word*, pp. 107–8.

37 Beckett, 'Lettre à Georges Duthuit', p. 16.

38 Tr. Oppenheim, *Painted Word*, p. 108.

39 It is this relationship that Beckett saw Tal Coat simply accepting, hence his criticism of the painter for remaining 'on the plane of the feasible'. Beckett, *Disjecta*, p. 139.

40 Heidegger, 'Age of the World Picture', p. 133.

41 Ibid., p. 134.

42 Ibid., pp. 116–17.

43 Ibid., p. 135.

44 Samuel Beckett, 1934, 'To Thomas MacGreevy, 8/9/34, 34 Gertrude Street, S.W. 10', TCD MS 10402, Manuscripts Department, Trinity College Library Dublin.

45 Ibid.

46 Lois Oppenheim has suggested that Beckett's art criticism should be read as 'a phenomenology of vision'. Oppenheim, *Painted Word*, p. 102. Most certainly, Beckett's critical writings address issues of subjectivity and vision that later become major themes in his creative works, but as I shall argue, Beckett's *oeuvre* also centres around the renegotiation of other modes of perception, including senses other than vision. This is also true of Beckett's critical writings. A case in point is Beckett's famous letter to Axel Kaun, of 1937, in which he writes not only of language as a medium, but also of 'the sound surface, torn by enormous pauses, of Beethoven's seventh Symphony'. Samuel Beckett, 'Letter to Axel Kaun', *Disjecta*, p. 172. Furthermore, in writing about Rainer Maria Rilke's poetry, Beckett observes, '[t]here is no position here, no possibility of a position, no faculty for one. He changes his ground without ceasing, like Gide, though for different reasons.' Beckett, *Disjecta*, p. 67.

47 Maurice Merleau-Ponty, 'Cézanne's Doubt', tr. Michael B. Smith, in Galen A. Johnson (ed.), *The Merleau-Ponty Aesthetics Reader: Philosophy and Painting*, Northwestern University Studies in Phenomenology and Existential Psychology (Evanston: Northwestern University Press, 1993), pp. 59–75.

48 Ibid., p. 63.

49 Beckett, *Proust*, p. 17.

50 Merleau-Ponty, 'Cézanne's Doubt', p. 63.

51 Ibid., pp. 63, 64.

52 Émile Bernard, 'From *A Conversation with Cézanne*', in Richard Kendall (ed.), *Cézanne by Himself: Drawings, Paintings, Writings* (London: Macdonald, 1990), p. 289.

53 Merleau-Ponty, 'Cézanne's Doubt', p. 69. Cézanne exclaimed to Jules Borély: 'If only we could see with the eyes of a newborn child!' Jules Borély, 'From

Cézanne en Aix', in Kendall (ed.), *Cézanne by Himself: Drawings, Paintings, Writings*, pp. 294–6 (p. 296).

54 Galen A. Johnson, 'Phenomenology and Painting: "Cézanne's Doubt"', in *The Merleau-Ponty Aesthetics Reader: Philosophy and Painting*, pp. 3–13 (p. 13).

55 Merleau-Ponty, 'Cézanne's Doubt', p. 66.

56 Samuel Beckett, 1934, 'To Thomas MacGreevy, 8/9/34, 34 Gertrude Street, S.W. 10', TCD MS 10402, Manuscripts Department, Trinity College Library Dublin; Merleau-Ponty, 'Cézanne's Doubt', pp. 61, 67. In Cézanne's own words, 'man has spent too long seeking himself in all that he has done'. Bernard, 'From *A Conversation with Cézanne*', p. 290.

57 Merleau-Ponty, 'Cézanne's Doubt', pp. 61, 69.

58 Samuel Beckett, 'German Diaries, 28/1/37', quoted in Mark Nixon, 'Samuel Beckett's "Film Vidéo-Cassette projet"', in Ulrika Maude and David Pattie (eds.), *Beckett on TV*, special issue of *Journal of Beckett Studies* (in press).

59 Merleau-Ponty, 'Cézanne's Doubt', p. 69.

60 Beckett, *Disjecta*, p. 172.

61 Merleau-Ponty, 'Cézanne's Doubt', p. 59.

62 Samuel Beckett, 1934, 'To Thomas MacGreevy, 8/9/34, 34 Gertrude Street, S.W. 10', TCD MS 10402, Manuscripts Department, Trinity College Library Dublin.

63 Meyer Schapiro, *Paul Cézanne* (London: Thames and Hudson, 1988), p. 124.

64 Merleau-Ponty, 'Cézanne's Doubt', p. 63.

65 Samuel Beckett, 1930, 'To Thomas MacGreevy, 5/1/30, Cooldrinagh', TCD MS 10402, Manuscripts Department, Trinity College Library Dublin.

66 Samuel Beckett, 1932, 'To Thomas MacGreevy, 18/10/32, Cooldrinagh', TCD MS 10402, Manuscripts Department, Trinity College Library Dublin.

67 Samuel Beckett, 1934, 'To Thomas MacGreevy, 8/9/34, 34 Gertrude Street, S.W. 10', TCD MS 10402, Manuscripts Department, Trinity College Library Dublin.

68 Quoted in Gunn, 'Until the gag is chewed', p. 15.

69 Although I do not mean to argue here that Beckett's art historical writings contain the aesthetic programme or formula of Beckett's literary works, I am suggesting, in a view I share with a number of critics, that the problematics and methodology of the visual arts influenced Beckett's own creative enterprise.

70 *The Expelled* and *The End* were translated in collaboration with Richard Seaver. The novellas have received relatively little critical attention, most likely because they are often considered mere precursors of the canonised Trilogy of novels. In Paul Davies's view, for instance, the four novellas and the Trilogy deal with one and the same character, who 'has many different incarnations and names, as he goes from story to story'. Paul Davies, 'Three Novels and Four *Nouvelles*: Giving Up the Ghost to Be Born at Last', in Pilling (ed.), *The Cambridge Companion to Samuel Beckett*, pp. 43–66 (p. 46). Steven Connor, however, has questioned this attitude towards the novellas,

suggesting that the relationship of the four texts to the Trilogy is more
complex than has been assumed. Connor acknowledges that the events of the
novellas, like those of the three novels, 'seem to mark the stages of a life, or,
rather, a death'. However, 'What is haunting about these stories is the way
that they refuse to be definitely assigned to any fixed relationship with the
Trilogy.' Connor, *Repetition, Theory and Text*, pp. 82–5.

71 Beckett, *Complete Short Prose*, pp. 62, 73.
72 Ibid., p. 75.
73 Ibid., p. 64.
74 Ibid., p. 66.
75 Ibid., p. 70.
76 Ibid., pp. 64, 68.
77 Ibid., pp. 70, 75.
78 Ibid., pp. 66, 76.
79 Ibid., pp. 62–3.
80 Ibid., p. 69.
81 Ibid., p. 63.
82 The translation is Daniel Albright's in *Beckett and Aesthetics* (Cambridge:
Cambridge University Press, 2003), p. 50. The original French can be found
in Beckett, *Disjecta*, p. 136.
83 Beckett, *Disjecta*, p. 136.
84 Beckett, *Complete Short Prose* p. 69.
85 Ibid., pp. 66, 67.
86 Levin, *The Opening of Vision*, p. 69.
87 Beckett, *Complete Short Prose*, p. 71.
88 Ibid., p. 75.
89 Paul Rodaway, *Sensuous Geographies: Body, Sense and Place* (London and New
York: Routledge, 1994), p. 124.
90 Merleau-Ponty, *Phenomenology of Perception*, p. 239.
91 'Yield', v., III, *Oxford English Dictionary*, 2nd edn. (1989); Beckett, *Disjecta*,
p. 136.
92 Beckett, *Complete Short Prose*, p. 75.
93 Rodaway, *Sensuous Geographies*, p. 121.
94 The modern association of vision and theory stems from two main biases.
Firstly, vision has been considered free of causality and temporality. Secondly, because the object of vision is detached from the subject, and hence
has been seen as 'the thing in itself as distinct from the thing as it affects me',
sight has been associated with theoretical truth. Jonas, *The Phenomenon of
Life*, pp. 146–7. As Martin Jay observes: 'The word *theater*... shares the same
root as the word *theory*, *theoria*, which meant to look at attentively, to behold.
So too does theorem, which has allowed some commentators to emphasize
the privileging of vision in Greek mathematics, with its geometric emphasis.'
Jay, *Downcast Eyes*, p. 23. For a discussion of *theoria*, see the first chapter of
Downcast Eyes, pp. 21–82. However, as Jay remarks, 'the Greeks believed that
the eye transmitted as well as received light rays (the theory of extramission)',

and hence 'there was a certain participatory dimension in the visual process, a potential intertwining of viewer and viewed.' In the Middle Ages, however, the theory of extramission was forgotten. Jay, *Downcast Eyes*, pp. 30–1.

95 Beckett, *Complete Short Prose*, p. 65.

96 It has been claimed that vision, unlike the other senses, provides a sense of being instead of becoming. Hans Jonas writes: 'Only sight... provides the sensual basis on which the mind may conceive the idea of the eternal, that which never changes and is always present. The very contrast between eternity and temporality rests upon an idealization of "present" experienced visually as the holder of stable contents as against the fleeting succession of nonvisual sensation. In the visual presence of objects the beholder may come to rest and possess an extended *now*.' Jonas, *The Phenomenon of Life*, p. 145. In music, for instance, it is a succession of sounds rather than a single sound that we hear, all of which we need in order to be able to call our perceptions music. The same, in essence, goes for speech, the sound of a train passing by, a child's cry or an alarm informing us that something is amiss. The case is similar for tactile experiences, for one sensation is not enough to determine the shape of an object, the coarseness or softness of its surface or even its temperature. Here, too, we need a succession of stimuli in order for the information to become accessible.

97 Beckett, *Complete Short Prose*, p. 70.

98 Samuel Beckett, *Watt* (London: John Calder, 1981), p. 62.

99 Beckett, *Complete Short Prose*, p. 62.

100 Ibid., p. 63.

101 See Merleau-Ponty, *Primacy of Perception*, p. 74.

102 Beckett, *Complete Short Prose*, pp. 76–7.

103 Ibid., pp. 98, 99.

104 Ibid., p. 81.

105 Ibid., pp. 86, 91, 93.

106 Ibid., p. 93.

107 Ibid., p. 95.

108 Ibid., p. 82.

109 Ibid., p. 83.

110 Ibid., p. 98.

111 Ibid., p. 81.

112 Ibid., p. 85.

113 Jean-Paul Sartre, *Being and Nothingness: An Essay on Phenomenological Ontology*, tr. Hazel E. Barnes (London and New York: Routledge, 2007), p. 279.

114 For Sartre's account of the gaze, see the section entitled 'The Look' in *Being and Nothingness*, pp. 276–326.

115 Beckett, *Complete Short Prose*, p. 94.

116 See Connor, 'Beckett and Sartre'.

117 Beckett, *Complete Short Prose*, p. 82. The enclosures anticipate the void-like surroundings of Beckett's later prose, in which he often appears to be

undertaking philosophical experiments into sensory deprivation. Beckett himself was attracted to a similar asceticism. As late as 1985, he reportedly told Ann Cremin: 'My ideal is to live in a totally bare room, with no books, no pictures, just four empty walls.' Cremin, 'Friend Game', p. 82. So crucially do Beckettian characters interact with their surroundings, however, that when deprived of real spaces, they begin, instead, to create phantom landscapes: 'The light there was then. On your back in the dark the light there was then. Sunless cloudless brightness. You slip away at break of day and climb to your hiding place on the hillside. A nook in the gorse. East beyond the sea the faint shape of high mountain.' Beckett, *Nohow On*, pp. 19–20.

118 Beckett, *Complete Short Prose*, p. 96.
119 Ibid., p. 98.
120 Ibid., p. 96.
121 Ibid., p. 97.
122 Galen A. Johnson, 'Structures and Painting: "Indirect Language and the Voices of Silence"', in *The Merleau-Ponty Aesthetics Reader: Philosophy and Painting*, pp. 14–34 (p. 30). 'Indirect Language and the Voices of Silence' was first published in *Les Temps modernes* in two instalments, in June and July 1952. It is reproduced in *The Merleau-Ponty Aesthetics Reader*, pp. 76–120.
123 'Eye and Mind', one of Merleau-Ponty's best-known essays, was first published in *Art de France* in 1961, and is reproduced in *The Merleau-Ponty Aesthetics Reader*, pp. 121–49 (p. 130).
124 Foucault, *The Order of Things*, p. xviii.
125 Ibid., p. xvii.
126 Samuel Beckett, 1934, 'To Thomas MacGreevy, 8/9/34, 34 Gertrude Street, S.W. 10', TCD MS 10402, Manuscripts Department, Trinity College Library Dublin.
127 Samuel Beckett, 1934, 'To Thomas MacGreevy, Monday [undated], 34 Gertrude Street, London S.W. 10', TCD MS 10402, Manuscripts Department, Trinity College Library Dublin.
128 It should here be pointed out that *Film* has been produced twice. The second version was completed in 1979, with David Clark as director and Max Wall as the protagonist. I shall here limit my discussion to Schneider's version, in whose production Beckett was closely involved. Beckett made his first and only trip to America for the shooting of *Film*.
129 Beckett originally wanted Charlie Chaplin for the film, but he declined.
130 S. E. Gontarski, '*Film* and Formal Integrity', in Morris Beja, S. E. Gontarski and Pierre Astier (eds.), *Samuel Beckett: Humanistic Perspectives* (Cleveland: Ohio State University Press, 1983), pp. 129–36 (p. 132).
131 The notebook, entitled both 'Notes for Film' and 'Percipi Notes', is held at the Beckett International Foundation Archive, University of Reading, RUL MS 1227/7/6/1.
132 Beckett, *Complete Dramatic Works*, p. 325.
133 Ruby Cohn, *Back to Beckett* (Princeton: Princeton University Press, 1973), p. 208.

134 6 February 1936, quoted in Knowlson, *Damned to Fame*, p. 226.

135 Beckett, *Complete Dramatic Works*, p. 323.

136 The opening and closing scenes with the eyeball also anticipate later stage plays, such as *Not I* and *That Time*, that 'feature body parts as the primary stage image'. Gontarski, 'Film', p. 135.

137 Rosemary Pountney, 'Beckett and the Camera', *Samuel Beckett Today/ Aujourd'hui: The Savage Eye/L'oeil fauve* 4 (1995), 41–52 (43). *Film* recalls Luis Buñuel and Salvador Dalí's surrealist film, *Un chien andalou* (1929), which opens with a scene of an eye being severed with a shaving knife. The still is reproduced in Enoch Brater's *Why Beckett* (London: Thames and Hudson, 1989), p. 116. Furthermore, *Film*, as the script indicates, is set in 1929, the year of the making of *Un chien andalou*. See Sidney Feshbach, 'Unswamping a Backwater: On Samuel Beckett's *Film*', in Oppenheim (ed.), *Samuel Beckett and the Arts*, pp. 333–63 (p. 346). For an account of surrealist influences on *Film*, see Enoch Brater, 'The Thinking Eye in Beckett's *Film*', *Modern Language Quarterly* 36 (1975), 166–76, in which Brater, amongst other things, draws attention to an affinity between *Film* and René Magritte's painting, *False Mirror*, from 1928. Another possible influence can be found in Georges Bataille, who, in 1928, published his *Histoire de l'oeil*, translated into English in 1953 as *The Story of the Eye*, and published by Olympia Press, who also published Beckett's *Watt* in the same year. Feshbach, 'Unswamping a Backwater', p. 346. To add to the list of coinciding dates, Roland Barthes published his essay 'The Metaphor of the Eye' in 1963. In it, he discusses Bataille's novel. In 1963 Beckett also wrote the script for *Film*. Feshbach, 'Unswamping a Backwater', p. 346. For Barthes's essay, see his *Critical Essays*, tr. Richard Howard (Evanston, IL: Northwestern University Press, 1972), pp. 239–47.

138 'Beckett on Film', '*an edited version of a series of preproduction discussions held in New York in the summer of 1964*', is reproduced in S. E. Gontarski, *The Intent of Undoing in Samuel Beckett's Dramatic Texts* (Bloomington: Indiana University Press, 1985), pp. 187–92 (p. 192).

139 Raymond Federman, 'Film', in Lawrence Graver and Raymond Federman (eds.), *Samuel Beckett: The Critical Heritage* (London and New York: Routledge, 1979), pp. 275–83 (pp. 275–6).

140 Hugh Kenner, *A Reader's Guide to Samuel Beckett* (London: Thames & Hudson, 1988), p. 169.

141 Connor, *Repetition, Theory and Text*, p. 182.

142 Sylvie Henning, ' "Film": A Dialogue between Beckett and Berkeley', *Journal of Beckett Studies* 7 (1982), 89–99 (89); Wilma Siccama, 'Samuel Beckett's *Film* and the Dynamics of Spectation: Our Look is Turned on Us', *European Journal for Semiotic Studies* 9 (1997), 201–22 (201).

143 Tajiri, *Beckett and the Prosthetic Body*, p. 121.

144 Beckett, *Complete Dramatic Works*, p. 324. In the final, filmed version the crowd scene had to be omitted for, as a result of technical fiascos, it turned out disastrously. The director, Alan Schneider, writes of the abandoned

scene: 'The lighting was gloomy throughout. The performances, except for Buster's, were terrible. The group scenes suffered so badly from that strobe effect that they were impossible to watch. In everyone's opinion, none of the scenes involving the other actors (except the tardy couple who were bad but bearable) was even remotely usable. And the budget would not permit our going down there again to do everything over. It was another disaster, a real one.' Alan Schneider, 'On Directing Film', *Samuel Beckett Today/Aujourd'hui: The Savage Eye/L'oeil fauve* 4 (1995), 29–40 (35). The final scene is reminiscent of the opening shots of *The Cabinet of Doctor Caligari* (1919), the famous expressionist film, in which Caligari is seen walking along the walls of the city. Feshbach, 'Unswamping a Backwater', p. 345.

145 Beckett, *Complete Dramatic Works*, p. 325.
146 Ibid., p. 331.
147 Ibid., p. 327. In the recorded preproduction discussion, Beckett said that the room 'is a trap prepared for [O], with nothing in it that wasn't trapped. There is nothing in this place, this room, that isn't prepared to trap him.' Reproduced in Gontarski, *The Intent of Undoing*, p. 190.
148 Beckett, *Complete Dramatic Works*, p. 333.
149 Ibid., p. 333.
150 Ibid.
151 Ibid., p. 334.
152 Kenner, *Reader's Guide*, p. 169.
153 Beckett, *Complete Dramatic Works*, p. 331.
154 Cited in Gontarski, *The Intent of Undoing*, p. 191.
155 Gontarski, *'Film'*, p. 134.
156 Cited in Gontarski, *The Intent of Undoing*, p. 189.
157 Ibid., p. 191.
158 Ibid., p. 188.
159 Feshbach, 'Unswamping a Backwater', p. 351.
160 Beckett, *Complete Dramatic Works*, p. 323.
161 For Berkeley's ideas on perception, see *A Treatise Concerning the Principles of Human Knowledge*, which dates from 1710 and is reproduced in *Principles of Human Knowledge and Three Dialogues*, ed. Howard Robinson, Oxford World's Classics (Oxford: Oxford University Press, 1996). See also Berkeley's influential 'Essay towards a New Theory of Vision' written in 1709 and reproduced in *A New Theory of Vision and Other Select Philosophical Writings* (London: Dent, 1963), pp. 1–86.
162 For Berkeley, the external world does not exist; sense perceptions are ultimately ideas that God produces in our minds.
163 Berkeley, *Principles of Human Knowledge*, p. 196.
164 Ackerley and Gontarski suggest the influence of Jules Renard here: 'As Renard noted, many want to kill themselves but remain content with tearing up their photographs.' Ackerley and Gontarski, *The Faber Companion to Samuel Beckett*, p. 482.
165 Hale, *Broken Window*, p. 89.

166 Beckett, *Complete Dramatic* Works, p. 323. The second manuscript draft identified this as the '[s]ubject of film'. Pountney, 'Beckett and the Camera', 43.

167 The script states: 'It will not be clear until end of film that pursuing perceiver is not extraneous, but self.' Beckett, *Complete Dramatic Works*, p. 323.

168 Beckett, *Complete Dramatic Works*, p. 329.

169 Henning, ' "Film": A Dialogue', 91–2.

170 Samuel Beckett, 1932, 'To Thomas MacGreevy 18/10/32, Cooldrinagh', TCD MS 10402, Manuscripts Department, Trinity College Library Dublin.

3 HEARING BECKETT

1 Douglas Kahn and Gregory Whitehead (eds.), *Wireless Imagination: Sound, Radio, and the Avant-Garde* (Cambridge, MA: MIT Press, 1992), p. ix.

2 The play was first broadcast on the BBC Third Programme on 13 January 1957, produced by Donald McWhinnie. Mary O'Farrell played Maddy Rooney; Dan was played by James Gerard Devlin; Allan McClelland was cast as Christy; Harry Hutchinson acted the role of Mr Barrel; Patrick Magee played Mr Slocum; and Jack MacGowran, finally, the role of Tommy. For Magee and MacGowran, later to become the two great male English-language interpreters of Beckett, *All That Fall* provided a first contact with Beckett's work. Zilliacus, *Beckett and Broadcasting*, p. 65. The play is often said to mark Beckett's return to English, although Beckett had, in fact, already written *From an Abandoned Work* (1954–5) in English by the time he wrote *All That Fall*. The French translation of the play, *Tous ceux qui tombent*, was made by Roger Pinget, and is one of the very few works not translated by Beckett himself.

3 Beckett to Nancy Cunard, 5 July 1956, quoted in Bair, *Samuel Beckett*, p. 502.

4 In *The Drama in the Text*, Enoch Brater, though concentrating on the role of voice in Beckett's work, does discuss the sound qualities of voice. He writes, 'Sound, the physical nature of language, makes the energy of Beckett's thought, mood, and word coincide.' Brater adds: 'Rhythm, melody, and texture are the strategies of a highly compressed vocal style that takes the place of embodiment, *gestus*, and blocking, as will other speech acts like paraphrase, modeling, parataxis, repetition, and borrowing.' Enoch Brater, *The Drama in the Text: Beckett's Late Fiction* (New York and Oxford: Oxford University Press, 1994), pp. 16, 19. Martin Esslin, Donald McWhinnie, James Knowlson, Everett Frost and Pierre Chabert are amongst the few commentators to have written about sound in Beckett's work.

5 Martin Esslin, 'The Mind as Stage', *Theatre Quarterly* 1 (1971), 5–11 (5).

6 Martin Esslin, 'Samuel Beckett and the Art of Broadcasting', in *Meditations: Essays on Brecht, Beckett and the Media* (New York: Grove Press, 1982), pp. 125–54 (pp. 130–1). The essay has been published three times. It first appeared as an article in *Encounter* (1975). A shorter version of the essay, entitled 'Samuel Beckett and the Art of Radio', appeared in 1986, in S. E.

Gontarski (ed.), *On Beckett: Essays and Criticism* (New York: Grove Press, 1986), pp. 360–83.

7 Zilliacus, *Beckett and Broadcasting*, p. 37.

8 In their treatment of sound these critics echo philosophers such as Berkeley, Diderot and Hegel, for whom sound essentially belongs to the realm of the ideal, interior and subjective. See Jonathan Rée, *I See a Voice: A Philosophical History of Language, Deafness and the Senses* (London: HarperCollins, 1999), p. 41.

9 Kenner, *Samuel Beckett*, p.171.

10 Ibid., p. 173.

11 Esslin, 'Samuel Beckett and the Art of Radio', in S.E. Gontarski (ed.), *On Beckett: Essays and Criticism* (New York: Grove Press, 1986), p. 365.

12 Katharine Worth, 'Beckett and the Radio Medium', in John Drakakis (ed.), *British Radio Drama* (Cambridge: Cambridge University Press, 1981), pp. 191–217 (p. 193).

13 Linda Ben-Zvi, 'Samuel Beckett's Media Plays', *Modern Drama* 28 (1985), 22–37, (28, 29).

14 Robert Wilcher, ' "Out of the Dark": Beckett's Texts for Radio', in James Acheson and Kateryna Arthur (eds.), *Beckett's Later Fiction and Drama* (Basingstoke: Macmillan, 1987), pp. 1–17 (p. 7).

15 Everett C. Frost, 'Fundamental Sounds: Recording Samuel Beckett's Radio Plays', *Theatre Journal* 43 (1991), 361–76 (367).

16 Cohn, *Back to Beckett*, pp. 163, 164.

17 Thomas F. van Laan, '*All That Fall* as "a Play for Radio" ', *Modern Drama* 28 (1985), 38–47.

18 Clas Zilliacus, '*All That Fall* and Radio Language', in Oppenheim (ed.), *Samuel Beckett and the Arts*, pp. 295–310 (pp. 302, 308).

19 Alan Beck has remarked that radio drama is especially speech-oriented, 'by showcasing dialogue and making it comprehensible, above and mostly to the exclusion of other sounds'. Alan Beck, 'Point-of-Listening in Radio Plays', *Sound Journal* (1998), www.kent.ac.uk/sdfva/sound-journal. Last accessed 22 February 2008. In *Words and Music*, which Beckett completed in 1961, and in *Cascando*, which he originally wrote in French in 1962, Beckett further breaks with the conventions of radio drama by giving music the status of a character. For readings of the role of music in Beckett's work, see Mary Bryden (ed.), *Samuel Beckett and Music* (Oxford: Clarendon, 1998), a collection of essays and interviews. For an account of the use of music in Beckett's television plays, *Ghost Trio*, from 1977, and *Nacht und Träume*, from 1983, see Michael Maier, 'Nacht und Träume: Schubert, Beckett und das Fernsehen', *Acta Musicologica* 68 (1996), 167–86 and Michael Maier, 'Geistertrio: Beethovens Musik in Samuel Becketts zweitem Fernsehspiel', *Archiv für Musikwissenshaft* 57 (2000), 172–94.

20 Esslin, 'Samuel Beckett and the Art of Radio', pp. 365–6.

21 Elissa S. Guralnick, *Sight Unseen: Beckett, Pinter, Stoppard, and Other Contemporary Dramatists on Radio* (Athens, OH: Ohio University Press, 1996), p. x. This is not, however, Hugh Kenner's opinion, who writes, 'in a radio

play there is nothing to see, an elementary fact which not all radio dramatists are willing to accept. Much radio drama fights this limitation, looking for ways to offer us mental pictures. Beckett instead made a play about a blind man, and toyed with the odd fact that in a drama exclusively auditory the unheard, unspoken, is the non-existent.' Kenner, *Reader's Guide*, p. 159.

22 Jonathan Kalb, 'The Mediated Quixote: The Radio and Television Plays', in Pilling (ed.), *The Cambridge Companion to Beckett*, pp. 124–44 (p. 126); Beckett, *Complete Dramatic Works*, p. 178.

23 Kalb, 'The Mediated Quixote', pp. 128–9. In her fear, Maddy Rooney resembles other Beckett characters, such as the tramps of the four novellas, who all seek enclosures and respite from perception. Maddy's fear also anticipates *Film*, in which O, like Maddy, feels threatened by the gaze.

24 Guralnick, *Sight Unseen*, p. xvi.

25 Ventriloquism relies precisely on this psychological principle: the sound does not come from the dummy's mouth, but because we can locate no other source for the voice, our minds will synchronise the dummy's moving jaws with the words we hear.

26 Connor, *Dumbstruck*, p. 20.

27 Rudolf Arnheim, *Radio: An Art of Sound*, tr. Margaret Ludvig and Herbert Read (New York: Da Capo Press, 1972), pp. 25–6. Beckett was familiar with at least some of Arnheim's work. See Knowlson, *Damned to Fame*, p. 226. In 'La Radia' (1933), which reads much as a manifesto for sound art, Marinetti and Pino Masnata proclaim 'The utilization of the various resonances of a voice or sound in order to give a sense of the size of the place in which the voice is uttered.' F. T. Marinetti and Pino Masnata, 'La Radia', in Kahn and Whitehead (eds.), *Wireless Imagination*, pp. 265–8 (p. 268). This has, in effect, become standard practice in radio art, for in order to create a per-spective and an acoustic for each scene, 'the technicians build a "set", as it is called, in the studio, with microphones, screens (having absorbent or reflective sides), and as required, laying down carpet or wooden planks or flagstones, and with other spot equipment such as a door, steps or a window, or glasses, cups and the gravel box'. Beck, 'Point-of-Listening'.

28 Rodaway, *Sensuous Geographies*, p. 92.

29 Worth, 'Beckett and the Radio Medium', pp. 193, 197.

30 Zilliacus, *Beckett and Broadcasting*, p. 30.

31 Under McWhinnie's direction, some of the animal sounds were made by the actors themselves. In January 1957, Beckett, however, wrote to McWhinnie: 'Things I liked particularly: the double walk sound in the second half, Dan's YES and their wild laugh (marvellous)...I didn't think the animals were right.' Quoted in Knowlson, *Damned to Fame*, p. 433. Beckett, in other words, did not care for this degree of manipulation of the sound effects. McWhinnie himself writes: 'to use real animal sounds, since the actual sound of a cow mooing, a cock crowing, a sheep bleating, a dog barking, are complex struc-tures, varying in duration and melodic shape; to put these four sounds in succession would be to create a whole which is only too obviously composed

of disparate elements'. For McWhinnie's view on the man-made animal sounds, to do with an unwillingness to create a 'visual picture', 'together with the importance of creating the correct rhythm for the work, impossible to achieve by the use of "real" animal sounds', see McWhinnie's *The Art of Radio* (London: Faber, 1959), pp. 133–4.

32 Beckett, *Complete Dramatic Works*, p. 172.

33 Ibid.

34 Ibid.

35 Ibid.

36 As Alan Beck explains, 'In BBC production, directors and studio managers... talk of the "sound picture" and what is "in" and what is "out".' In this way, the cinematic distinction of onscreen and offscreen is made in radio art, for which an appropriate sonic terminology does not yet exist. Beck, 'Point-of-Listening'.

37 Touch, taste and, to some extent, smell are proximity senses.

38 Rée, *I See a Voice*, p. 38.

39 Rodaway, *Sensuous Geographies*, p. 101. Reversely, 'an absolute silence... would be without geography, location or spatial arrangement'. Rodaway, *Sensuous Geographies*, p. 96.

40 Beckett, *Complete Dramatic Works*, p. 179.

41 Ibid., p. 182.

42 Ibid., p. 183.

43 Ibid., pp. 182, 183, 190.

44 Frost, 'Fundamental Sounds', p. 367.

45 Beckett, *Complete Dramatic Works*, pp. 176, 178, 181.

46 Zilliacus, *Beckett and Broadcasting*, p. 40.

47 Ben-Zvi, 'Samuel Beckett's Media Plays', 26.

48 Beckett, *Complete Dramatic Works*, p. 198.

49 Ibid., p. 198.

50 Ibid., pp. 174, 187.

51 Ibid., pp. 180, 193.

52 Scarry, *The Body in Pain*, pp. 161–2.

53 Ibid., p. 4.

54 We know from Beckett's comments in the 'Whoroscope Notebook' that he had read the novel. He made sixteen entries on the novel in his notebook, which is held at the Beckett International Foundation, University of Reading (RUL MS 3000). Beckett appears to have had a copy of the original Spanish, but relied mostly on the French translation of the novel.

55 Miguel de Cervantes Saavedra, *The Adventures of Don Quixote*, tr. J. M. Cohen (Harmondsworth: Penguin, 1963), p. 68.

56 George Lakoff and Mark Turner, *More Than Cool Reason: A Field Guide to Poetic Metaphor* (Chicago: University of Chicago Press, 1989), p. 103.

57 Gerald Doherty, *Theorizing Lawrence: Nine Meditations on Tropological Themes*, Studies in Twentieth-Century British Literature 1 (New York: Peter Lang, 1999), p. 55. In metonymy, a corpse, for instance, does not become a trope for afterlife (as it would in the case of metaphor), but retains, instead,

its materiality. Doherty writes: 'the metaphorization of death disincarnates. It shifts the gaze away from the corpse, as the detritus of life's meanings, towards transfigurations that amplify its significance in an alternative world.' *Theorizing Lawrence*, p. 53.

58 More accurately, *quijote* means 'pieza del arnés destinada a cubrir el muslo', which is to say, the part of an armour designed to protect a muscle. J. Corominas and J. A. Pascual, *Diccionario Crítico Etimológico Castellano e Hispánico* (Madrid: Editorial Gredos, 1981), p. 727.

59 The novel is littered with examples. An early one can again be found in the windmill chapter of the first part. The servants of the two monks that Don Quijote attacks, we learn, 'fell upon Sancho and knocked him down. And, pulling every hair from his beard, they kicked him mercilessly, and left him stretched on the ground, breathless and stunned.' Cervantes, *Don Quixote*, p. 72.

60 Beckett, *Complete Dramatic Works*, p. 190.

61 Ibid., p. 174.

62 James Elkins, *Pictures of the Body: Pain and Metamorphosis* (Stanford: Stanford University Press, 1999), p. 226.

63 Ibid., p. 276.

64 Beckett to Barney Rosset of Grove Press on 27 August 1957, used as the epigraph to Zilliacus, *Beckett and Broadcasting*. Later Beckett did allow simple stage readings of the plays. Zilliacus reproduces 'the standard wording' that Grove Press used when replying to requests concerning the right to stage the radio plays: 'Mr. Beckett has specifically stated that these are meant to be radio plays, and should therefore be read, not acted. They are plays for voices and he has given permission for stage readings, but he definitely does not want the "readers" to be costumed, to use any props, to move around the stage any more than is necessary to get to the microphone, or to use any movements even when standing still. They should be read just as if it were being done over the radio and there were no audience to see the performers.' On 6 November 1964, however, Beckett wrote to Grove Press asking them to '"decline all eventual stage offers for *Cascando*"'. Zilliacus, *Beckett and Broadcasting*, pp. 175, 175n.18.

65 Ben-Zvi, 'Samuel Beckett's Media Plays', 23.

66 *Tous ceux qui tombent*, the French translation of the play, was, however, broadcast on French television on 25 January 1963. Knowlson, *Damned to Fame*, p. 799n.133. In June of the same year, Beckett wrote to John Barber: '"In a weak moment I let French T.V. do *All That Fall*, with disastrous results".' Ibid.

67 *Embers* was first broadcast on 24 June 1959, on the BBC Third Programme. It was directed by Donald McWhinnie, and had Jack MacGowran as Henry; Kathleen Michael as Ada; Kathleen Helme as Addie and Patrick Magee as the music and riding master. The production won the RAI (Radiotelevisione Italiana) prize the same year, which for its part triggered international interest in the play, resulting, amongst other foreign-language productions, in two German-language ones, with the title *Aschenglut*, and an Italian one entitled

Ceneri. For further details, see Zilliacus, *Beckett and Broadcasting*, pp. 97–8. Beckett translated the play into French in collaboration with Roger Pinget. The French version, *Cendres*, was first published in *Les Lettres nouvelles* 36 (1959).

68 As Beckett puts it in the stage directions, '[s]ea . . . *audible throughout what follows whenever a pause is indicated*'. Beckett, *Complete Dramatic Works*, p. 253. All in all, *Embers* has 228 pauses that are filled by the sound of the sea. Zilliacus, *Beckett and Broadcasting*, p. 91. The preponderance of the pauses in the BBC version of *Embers* is made clear by the fact that when Henry first addresses his dead father, the beginning of his monologue consists of forty-two seconds of text and fifty-five seconds of pauses. Zilliacus, *Beckett and Broadcasting*, p. 94.

69 Beckett, *Complete Dramatic Works*, p. 255.

70 Samuel Beckett, 1959, 'To Barbara Bray, 11/3/59, Ussy', TCD MS 10948/1/1, Manuscripts Department, Trinity College Library Dublin.

71 Kenner, *Samuel Beckett*, pp. 174, 176. Kenner has called *Embers* 'Beckett's most difficult work'. *Samuel Beckett*, p. 174.

72 John Fletcher and John Spurling, *Beckett the Playwright* (New York: Hill and Wang, 1972), p. 95.

73 Zilliacus, *Beckett and Broadcasting*, p. 82.

74 Esslin, 'Samuel Beckett and the Art of Radio', p. 368.

75 David Alpaugh, '*Embers* and the Sea: Beckettian Intimations of Mortality', *Modern Drama* 16 (1973), 317–28 (322). In a similarly psychoanalytic vein, Thomas J. Cousineau reads repetition in the play as a marker of Henry's attempt to 'establish symbolic mastery'. 'The Significance of Repetition in Beckett's *Embers*', *Southern Humanities Review* 19 (1985), 313–21 (317).

76 Marjorie Perloff, 'The Silence That Is Not Silence: Acoustic Art in Samuel Beckett's Embers', in Oppenheim (ed.), *Samuel Beckett and the Arts*, pp. 247–68 (p. 264).

77 Quoted in Rosemary Pountney, '*EMBERS*: An Interpretation', *Samuel Beckett Today/Aujourd'hui* 2 (1993), 269–73 (270).

78 My translation.

79 See Anzieu's chapter, 'The Sound Envelope', in Didier Anzieu, *Skin Ego*, tr. Chris Turner (New Haven and London: Yale University Press, 1989), pp. 157–73.

80 Steven Connor, 'Michel Serres's *Les Cinq Sens*', in Niran Abbas (ed.), *Mapping Michel Serres* (Ann Abror: University of Michigan Press, 2005), pp. 153–69 (p. 160).

81 Don Ihde, *Listening and Voice* (Athens, OH: Ohio University Press, 1976), p. 119.

82 Rée, *I See a Voice*, p. 46.

83 Ibid., p. 47.

84 Ihde, *Listening and Voice*, p. 121.

85 Édith Lecourt, 'The Musical Envelope', in Didier Anzieu (ed.), *Psychic Envelopes*, tr. Daphne Briggs (London: Karnac Books, 1990), pp. 211–35 (p. 212).

86 Beckett, *Complete Dramatic Works*, p. 259.

87 Ibid., p. 258.
88 *Noise*, by Steven Connor, prod. Tim Dee, five episodes, BBC Radio Three (24–28 February 1997).
89 Lecourt, 'The Musical Envelope', p. 211.
90 Frances Dyson, 'When Is the Ear Pierced? The Clashes of Sound, Technology, and Cyberculture', in Mary Anne Moser and Douglas MacLeod (eds.), *Immersed in Technology: Art and Virtual Environments* (Cambridge, MA: MIT Press, 1996), pp. 73–101 (pp. 74–5).
91 Perloff, 'The Silence', p. 258.
92 *Noise*, by Steven Connor.
93 Paul Rodaway points out that 'auditory perception is like all other forms of sensuous experience in that it involves the whole body whilst at the same time giving the immediate impression of sensing from a particular point or dedicated organ – touch and the finger, seeing and the eye, smell and the nose, hearing and the ear. Sensuous experience, even of a particular sense character, is always inclusive of wider body involvement.' Rodaway, *Sensuous Geographies*, p. 91. Temporal shifts are similarly effected through Henry's recollections of his father. In one of the early manuscript versions of *Embers*, now held at Trinity College Dublin, and originally entitled *Ebb*, Beckett even specified separate voices for '"Henry then"' and '"Henry now"'. See Pountney, '*EMBERS*', 269.
94 Beckett, *Complete Dramatic Works*, p. 260.
95 Ibid., pp. 256, 253, 259, 260. Paul Lawley has drawn attention to the distinction between the 'undifferentiated' sound of the sea and the other 'hard, regular sounds'. Lawley, '"Embers"; an interpretation', *Journal of Beckett Studies* 6(1980), 29.
96 Dyson, 'When Is the Ear Pierced?', p. 75.
97 Rée, *I See a Voice*, p. 35.
98 Connor, 'Michel Serres's', p. 159.
99 Rée, *I See a Voice*, p. 37. For this very reason, Jonathan Rée questions the classification of sound as a distance sense rather than a proximity sense. Deaf people often assert that there is no such thing as total deafness, because the rhythms of music, for instance, can at times be 'heard' through the feet.
100 Tr. Steven Connor in 'Michel Serres's', p. 160. The Futurists seem to have discovered sound's inherent lack of boundaries early. In the fanciful 'La Radia', Marinetti and Pino Masnata write: 'The immensification of space/ No longer visible and framable the stage becomes universal and cosmic.' They add, 'An art without time or space without yesterday or tomorrow/ The possibility of receiving broadcast stations situated in various time zones and the lack of light will destroy the hours of the day and night/ The reception and amplification of the light and the voices of the past with thermoionic valves will destroy time.' Marinetti and Masnata, 'La Radia', p. 267.
101 Bernard Beckerman, 'Beckett and the Act of Listening', in Enoch Brater (ed.), *Beckett at 80/Beckett in Context* (New York and Oxford: Oxford University Press, 1986), pp. 149–67 (p. 150).

102 Beckett, *Complete Dramatic Works*, p. 217.

103 Chabert, 'Beckett as Director', 51.

104 Ibid., p. 50.

105 Ibid., p. 57.

106 Ibid. Samuel Beckett, *The Theatrical Notebooks of Samuel Beckett*, vol. III, *Krapp's Last Tape*, ed. James Knowlson (London: Faber and Faber, 1992), p. 229. This was the first time Beckett directed *Krapp's Last Tape*. Knowlson translates 'Quatschgeräusch' as 'unintelligible gabble'. *Theatrical Notebooks* III, p. 229.

107 Beckett, *Theatrical Notebooks* III, p. 217.

108 John Haynes and James Knowlson, *Images of Beckett* (Cambridge: Cambridge University Press, 2003), p. 8.

109 'Suggestions for T.V. Krapp' is reproduced in Zilliacus, *Beckett and Broadcasting*, pp. 204–5. The notes were written towards the end of the Schiller-Theater rehearsals, after Westdeutscher Rundfunk had approached Beckett about a television version of the production.

110 Ibid., p. 205.

111 See, for instance, James Knowlson's introduction to *The Theatrical Notebooks* III, pp. xxii–xxiii.

112 See, for instance, James Acheson, 'Beckett and the Heresy of Love', in Ben-Zvi (ed.), *Women in Beckett: Performance and Critical Perspectives*, pp. 68–80 and Mary Catanzaro, 'The Voice of Absent Love in *Krapp's Last Tape* and *Company*', *Modern Drama* 32 (1989), 401–12.

113 Michael Davidson, 'Technologies of Presence: Orality and the Tapevoice of Contemporary Poetics', in Adalaide Morris (ed.), *Sound States: Innovative Poetics and Acoustical Technologies* (Chapel Hill and London: University of North Carolina Press, 1997), pp. 97–125 (p. 99).

114 Connor, *Repetition, Theory and Text*, pp. 126–31; Katharine Hayles, 'Voices out of Bodies; Bodies out of Voices: Audiotape and the Production of Subjectivity', in Morris (ed.), *Sound States: Innovative Poetics and Acoustical Technologies*, pp. 74–96; Daniel Albright, *Beckett and Aesthetics* (Cambridge: Cambridge University Press, 2003), p. 95. Connor has drawn attention to the manner in which the difference between speech and writing, listening and reading collapses in *Krapp's Last Tape* because of the possibility the tape recordings provide of re-listening, stopping and fast forwarding, just as the eye can stop and wander at will on the page. Connor, *Repetition, Theory and Text*, pp. 127–9.

115 Tajiri, *Beckett and the Prosthetic Body*, p. 161.

116 Cited in Stephen Kern, *The Culture of Time and Space 1880–1918* (Cambridge, MA and London: Harvard University Press, 2003), p. 67.

117 Steven Connor, 'The Modern Auditory I', in Roy Porter (ed.), *Rewriting the Self: Histories from the Renaissance to the Present* (London and New York: Routledge, 1997), pp. 203–23 (p. 205).

118 Quoted in Connor, 'The Modern Auditory I', p. 205.

119 Hayles, 'Voices out of Bodies', p. 76.
120 *Noise*, by Steven Connor.
121 Douglas Kahn, 'Introduction: Histories of Sound Once Removed', in Kahn and Whitehead (eds.), *Wireless Imagination: Sound, Radio, and the Avant-Garde*, pp. 1–29 (p. 18).
122 James Joyce, *Ulysses* (Harmondsworth: Penguin, 1992), p. 144.
123 Davidson, 'Technologies of Presence', p. 98.
124 Esslin, 'Art of Broadcasting', pp. 133–4.
125 For a brief survey of the history of magnetic audiotape, see Hayles, 'Voices out of Bodies', pp. 76–7.
126 In an early typescript the play is set in a 'late evening in the nineteen eighties'. RUL MS 1659, Beckett International Foundation, University of Reading.
127 Esslin, 'Art of Broadcasting', p. 134.
128 Kahn, 'Histories of Sound', p. 18.
129 *Noise*, by Steven Connor.
130 Beckett, *Complete Dramatic Works*, p. 127. The importance this held for Beckett is made clear in his letter to Alan Schneider of 4 January 1960, in which he stressed the significance of the quality of the voices in the play: 'The text recorded should be spoken obviously in a much younger and stronger voice than Krapp's for his last tape...but unmistakably his.' Harmon, *No Author Better Served*, p. 59.
131 Hayles, 'Voices out of Bodies', p. 81.
132 'Record', 1a, *OED*, 2nd edn. (1989).
133 Martin Heidegger, 'The Question Concerning Technology', in *The Question Concerning Technology and Other Essays*, tr. William Lovitt (New York: Harper and Row, 1977), pp. 3–35.
134 Beckett, *Complete Dramatic Works*, p. 223.
135 Quoted in Friedrich A. Kittler, *Gramophone, Film, Typewriter*, tr. Geoffrey Winthorp-Young and Michael Wutz (Stanford: Stanford University Press, 1999), pp. 30–1.
136 Steven Connor, *The Book of Skin* (London: Reaktion Books, 2004), p. 86.
137 Beckett, *Complete Dramatic Works*, p. 223.
138 Marshall McLuhan, *Understanding Media: The Extensions of Man* (London: Routledge & Kegan Paul, 1964), p. 315.
139 Connor, 'Modern Auditory I', p. 207; Connor, 'Michel Serres's', p. 159.
140 Tr. Connor in 'Michel Serres's', p. 161.
141 Quoted in Kittler, *Gramophone, Film, Typewriter*, p. 30.
142 Beckett, *Complete Dramatic Works*, pp. 218–19.
143 McLuhan, *Understanding Media*, p. 267.
144 Knowlson in Beckett, *Theatrical Notebooks* III, p. xviii.
145 Beckett, *Complete Dramatic Works*, p. 218.
146 Ibid., p. 388.
147 Ibid.
148 Ibid., p. 387.

149 Several critics have observed that the location is recognisably Dublin. See, for instance, Audrey McMullan, 'Samuel Beckett's *Cette fois*: Between Time(s) and Space(s)', *French Studies* 44 (1990), 424–39 (430).

150 Beckett, *Complete Dramatic Works*, p. 390.

151 Ibid., pp. 389, 390.

152 Ibid., p. 390. Beckett himself famously insisted that he could remember life in the womb. Anthony Cronin cites Beckett saying, at the age of sixty-four: '"Even before the foetus can draw breath, it is in a state of bareness and of pain. I have a clear memory of my own foetal existence. It was an existence where no voice, no possible movement could free me from the agony and darkness I was subjected to."' Beckett had also told Peggy Guggenheim 'that he had, in her words, "retained a terrible memory of life in his mother's womb. He was constantly suffering from this and had awful crises, when he felt he was suffocating".' Cronin, *Samuel Beckett*, p. 2.

153 Paul Lawley, 'Stages of Identity: From *Krapp's Last Tape* to *Play*', in Pilling (ed.), *The Cambridge Companion to Samuel Beckett*, pp. 88–105 (p. 88).

154 James Knowlson and John Pilling, *Frescoes of the Skull: The Later Prose and Drama of Samuel Beckett* (London: Calder, 1979), pp. 219–20 (p. 219).

155 Beckerman, 'Beckett and the Act of Listening', p. 160.

156 Antoni Libera, 'Structure and Pattern in "That Time"', *Journal of Beckett Studies* 6 (1980), 81–9; S. E. Gontarski '"Making Yourself All Up Again": The Composition of Samuel Beckett's *That Time*', *Modern Drama* 23 (1980), 112–20.

157 McMullan, *Theatre on Trial*, pp. 48–9.

158 Connor, *Dumbstruck*, p. 7.

159 McMullan, 'Samuel Beckett's *Cette fois*', 426.

160 Walter Asmus, 'Rehearsal Notes for the German Premiere of Beckett's "That Time" and "Footfalls"', in Gontarski (ed.), *On Beckett: Essays and Criticism*, pp. 335–49 (p. 348).

161 Don DeLillo, *The Body Artist* (London: Picador, 2002), p. 48.

162 Ibid., pp. 60–1.

163 Connor, *Dumbstruck*, p. 36.

164 Ibid.

165 Beckett, *Complete Dramatic Works*, p. 388.

166 Ibid., p. 395.

167 Beckett, *Proust*, p. 58.

168 As Clov says in Endgame: 'We too were bonny – once. It's a rare thing not to have been bonny – once.' *Complete Dramatic Works*, p. 113.

169 Ibid., p. 390.

4 SKIN DEEP

1 All of these texts are reproduced in Beckett, *The Complete Short Prose*. Le *Dépeupleur*, the French version of the novella, was famously abandoned by Beckett in 1966, published in fragments, then subsequently unabandoned and

completed in 1970, when Beckett added a final, fifteenth section to the four-teen preceding ones. The novella was first translated into English in 1971, and exists, at present, in three different English language versions: the original and identical British and American editions, both published in 1972 by John Calder and Grove Press respectively; a version published in issue 96 of the *Evergreen Review* in 1973, which for its part was published as a Dell paperback in the same year, and finally the most recent version, published in *Samuel Beckett: The Complete Short Prose 1929–1989*, edited by S. E. Gontarski, which contains features of both of the previous English language versions. See S. E. Gontarski, 'Refiguring, Revising, and Reprinting *The Lost Ones*', *Journal of Beckett Studies* 4 (1995), 99–101.

2 S. E. Gontarski, 'Introduction', in Samuel Beckett, *The Complete Short Prose 1929–1989* (New York: Grove Press), 1995, p. xv. The quote is from Beckett's personal notebooks, which also contain the manuscripts of the two texts, reprinted in Richard Admussen, *The Samuel Beckett Manuscripts: A Study* (Boston: G. K. Hall, 1979), p. 22.

3 Leslie Hill, *Beckett's Fiction in Different Words* (Cambridge: Cambridge University Press, 1990), pp. 149–50.

4 Beckett, *Complete Short Prose*, p. 204.

5 Ibid.

6 For an account of the mathematical errors and inaccuracies in *The Lost Ones*, see Enoch Brater, 'Mis-takes, Mathematical and Otherwise, in *The Lost Ones*', *Modern Fiction Studies* 29 (1983), 93–109. See, also, Gontarski, 'Refiguring, Revising, and Reprinting *The Lost Ones*'.

7 For examples of an allegorical reading, see Peter Murphy, 'The Nature of Allegory in The Lost Ones, or the Quincunx Realistically Considered', *Journal of Beckett Studies* 7 (1982), 71–88; Antoni Libera, 'The Lost Ones: A Myth of Human History and Destiny', in Beja, Gontarski and Astier (eds.), *Samuel Beckett: Humanistic Perspectives*, pp. 145–56 and Lance St John Butler, *Samuel Beckett and the Meaning of Being: A Study in Ontological Parable* (London: Macmillan, 1993). For an account of *The Lost Ones* as a parable of the authorial process, see Eric P. Levy, 'Looking for Beckett's Lost Ones', *Mosaic* 12 (1979), 163–70. For a discussion of entropy and the novella, see Sylvie Henning, *Beckett's Critical Complicity: Carnival, Contestation, and Tradition* (Lexington, KY: University Press of Kentucky, 1988), pp. 159–95. For a reading, finally, of the novella as an example of '(self-dismantling) cybernetic fiction', see David Porush, 'Beckett's Deconstruction of the Machine in *The Lost Ones*', *L'Esprit Créateur* 26 (1986), 87–98.

8 Beckett finished *Comment c'est*, the French version of *How It Is*, in 1960. The thirteen *Texts for Nothing* are reprinted in Beckett, *The Complete Short Prose*, pp. 100–54.

9 Beckett, *Complete Short Prose*, p. 211. John Pilling refers to the style of Beckett's prose in this group of works as a 'notational technique'. John Pilling, *Samuel Beckett* (London: Routledge & Kegan Paul, 1976), p. 50.

10 This move is already anticipated in the search for dark, confined spaces that characterised the four novellas and the Trilogy, and that is present as early in Beckett's work as *Murphy*, namely in Murphy's fascination with the garret and the padded cells of the Magdalen Mental Mercyseat.
11 Beckett, *Complete Short Prose*, p. 214.
12 Henning, *Beckett's Critical Complicity*, p. 180.
13 Beckett, *Complete Short Prose*, p. 214.
14 Henning, *Beckett's Critical Complicity*, p. 187.
15 Beckett, *Complete Short Prose*, p. 193.
16 Ibid., p. 194. The narrator adds, 'nails fallen white over'. Ibid., p. 195.
17 Ibid., p. 182.
18 Ibid., p. 177.
19 Ibid., p. 184.
20 Ibid., p. 193.
21 Ibid., pp. 170, 176.
22 Ibid., p. 204.
23 Ibid., p. 202.
24 Ibid.
25 Ibid., p. 210.
26 Eric P. Levy, *Beckett and the Voice of Species: A Study of the Prose Fiction* (Totowa, NJ: Barnes & Noble, 1980), p. 97. This notion would be supported by the narrator's reference to the three different zones of the cylinder, 'invisible to the eye of flesh'. Beckett, *Complete Short Prose*, p. 216.
27 As Sylvie Henning points out, 'every climber's moves are made by feel [au jugé]'. *Beckett's Critical Complicity*, p. 187.
28 Beckett, *Complete Short Prose*, p. 202.
29 Ibid., pp. 219–20.
30 Anzieu, *Skin Ego*, p. 103.
31 Beckett, *Complete Short Prose*, p. 209.
32 Ibid., p. 173.
33 Ibid., p. 171.
34 The narrator says, for instance, '[l]eft hand clinging to right shoulder ball, right more faint loose fist on ground till fingers tighten as though to squeeze'; 'Loose clench any length then crush down most womanly straining knuckles five seconds then back lax any length, all right, now down while fingers loose.' Ibid., pp. 174, 178.
35 Ibid., p. 210.
36 Anzieu, *Skin Ego*, p. 15.
37 Beckett, *Complete Short Prose*, p. 223.
38 Ibid., pp. 211, 221.
39 Ibid., p. 211.
40 Ibid., p. 215.
41 Ibid., p. 222.
42 Ashley Montagu, *Touching: The Human Significance of the Skin*, 3rd edn. (New York: Harper & Row, 1986), p. 5. Both the brain and the skin develop from the ectoderm. See Anzieu, *Skin Ego*, p. 9.

43 Beckett, *Complete Short Prose*, p. 194.
44 Anzieu, *Skin Ego*, p. 17.
45 Beckett, *Complete Short Prose*, p. 220.
46 Ibid., p. 195.
47 Connor, *The Book of Skin*, p. 53. Billie Whitelaw has said of her work with Beckett: 'Each play I do, I'm left with a legacy or scar. Now, perhaps I'm being silly, perhaps I shouldn't do that, but I feel that the shape my body makes is just as important as the sound that comes out of my mouth.' Quoted in Kalb, *Beckett in Performance* (Cambridge: Cambridge University Press, 1989), p. 236.
48 Alphonse de Lamartine, *Méditations poétiques: choix de poèmes*, ed. Suzette Jacrès (Paris: Larousse, 1968), p. 28. The line is from the poem 'L'isolement' and in Vivian Mercier's translation reads 'You miss a single being and the whole world is unpeopled.' Vivian Mercier, *Beckett/Beckett* (New York: Oxford University Press, 1977), p. 226.
49 Beckett, *Complete Short Prose*, p. 202. The narrator speculates: 'From time immemorial rumour has it or better still the notion is abroad that there exists a way out.' Ibid., p. 206. As Anne Fabre-Luce puts it, in *The Lost Ones*, 'no one is alone, but everyone is hopelessly solitary.' See Anne Fabre-Luce, 'The Lost Ones', tr. Larysa Mykyta and Mark Schumacher, in Graver and Federman (eds.), *Samuel Beckett: The Critical Heritage*, pp. 313–15 (p. 315).
50 Beckett, *Complete Short Prose*, p. 220.
51 Ibid., p. 213. Beckett, with his knowledge of Italian language and literature, may have been aware of Marinetti's essay 'Tactilism', from 1924. Marinetti writes: 'Tactilism . . . must avoid not only collaboration with the plastic arts, but also morbid erotomania. Its purpose must be, simply, to achieve tactile harmonies and to contribute indirectly toward the perfection of a spiritual communication between human beings, through the epidermis.' F. T. Marinetti, 'Tactilism', in *Let's Murder the Moonshine: Selected Writings*, ed. R. W. Flint, tr. R. W. Flint and Arthur A. Coppotelli (Los Angeles: Sun & Moon Classics, 1991), pp. 117–20 (p. 119). Both Marinetti and Beckett have at least three things in common: a suspicion of received notions of vision, an interest in the tactile and in surfaces more generally, and a desire for radical stylistic experimentation, for instance in the rethinking of punctuation. There are, needless to say, endless differences between the two. For Marinetti's view on questions of style, see the 'Technical Manifesto of Futurist Literature', in *Let's Murder the Moonshine*, pp. 92–7.
52 Beckett, *Complete Short Prose*, p. 222.
53 Don Ihde, *Sense and Significance* (Pittsburgh: Duquesne University Press, 1973), p. 99.
54 Tr. Steven Connor in 'Michel Serres's', p. 97.
55 Ihde, *Sense and Significance*, p. 99.
56 For an empirical example of how the tactile can at times collapse the distinction between subject and object, see Don Ihde, *Sense and Significance*, 96–7. There is also a biological explanation to the manner in which the tactile collapses boundaries between the inside and the outside. According to Stanney *et al.*, 'the sensations of the skin adapt with exposure to a stimuli

[sic]. More specifically, the effect of a sensation decreases in sensitivity to a continued stimulus, may disappear completely even though the stimulus is still present, and varies by receptor type.' Whereas phasic receptors adapt quickly, tonic ones are slow to adapt and have an 'afterimage that persists even once the stimulus is removed'. It is as if the skin itself had a short-term memory and a long-term one, as much of Beckett's writing seems to suggest. Stanney and others go on to add that the sensation of touch also depends upon the '[s]urface characteristics of the stimulus'. Soft surfaces are, somewhat surprisingly, more easily felt after initial contact, whereas in order to feel hard surfaces, 'active pressure must be maintained'. Kay M. Stanney, Ronald R. Mourant and Robert S. Kennedy, 'Human Factors Issues in Virtual Environments: A Review of the Literature', *Presence* 7 (1998), 327–51 (337). It should be added, however, as Jean-François Lyotard remarks in the case of vision, that 'even the subtlest explanation of the physico-chemical phenomena that "accompany" vision cannot account for the very fact of seeing.' Jean-François Lyotard, *Phenomenology*, tr. Brian Beakley (Albany: State University of New York Press, 1991), p. 88. In other words, the explanation of the structure of perception forms a poor substitute for the *understanding* of perception. Our need for tactile interaction can also be explained through the burden of selfhood and the manner in which touch at least in part dissolves our sense of separation from the world. For a philo-sophical account of the burden of individual subjectivity, see Jonathan Dollimore, 'Death and the Self', in Porter (ed.), *Rewriting the Self*, pp. 249–61.

57 Sartre, *Being and Nothingness*, p. 418.
58 Beckett, *Complete Short Prose*, p. 221.
59 Ibid., pp. 203–4.
60 Susan D. Brienza, 'The Lost Ones', *Journal of Modern Literature* 6 (1977), 148–68 (150).
61 Walter J. Ong, *The Presence of the Word: Some Prolegomena for Cultural and Religious History* (New Haven and London: Yale University Press, 1967), p. 139.
62 Dollimore, 'Death and the Self', p. 256.
63 Beckett, *Complete Short Prose*, p. 203.
64 Amongst these critics are Steven Connor, *Repetition, Theory and Text*, pp. 104–12; Susan Brienza, 'The Lost Ones' and David Porush, 'Beckett's Deconstruction', 92–6.
65 Connor, *Repetition, Theory and Text*, pp. 107.
66 Machine language, Porush explains, 'is a code which does not permit ambiguity' but rather evokes 'images of positive logic, technical efficiency and computer-like order'. Porush, 'Beckett's Deconstruction', 94.
67 Beckett, *Complete Short Prose*, pp. 202, 203, 205, 206, 206, 204. David Porush also makes this point and says, in addition, that 'Not a single statement or specification or datum is left to stand without some creeping conditional or vagueness or, as statisticians say, "fudging".' Porush, 'Beckett's Deconstruction', 95.

68 Hill, *Beckett's Fiction*, p. 153; Beckett, *Complete Short Prose*, pp. 204, 206, 212, 214.

69 Porush, 'Beckett's Deconstruction', 94; Beckett, *Complete Short Prose*, p. 221.

70 Beckett, *Complete Short Prose*, pp. 220, 203, 220.

71 Ibid., pp. 222, 208.

72 Ibid., pp. 204, 212, 211, 207; Connor, *Repetition, Theory and Text*, p. 109.

73 Beckett, *Complete Short Prose*, p. 220; Connor, *Repetition, Theory and Text*, p. 107.

74 Beckett, *Complete Dramatic Works*, pp. 215, 220, 213; Connor, *Repetition, Theory and Text*, p. 106.

75 Beckett, *Complete Short Prose*, p. 202.

76 Gontarski, 'Introduction', p. xv.

77 Hill, *Beckett's Fiction*, p. 149.

78 Enoch Brater acknowledges that, although Beckett had 'initially told his English publisher' that a misprint had occurred in the measurements of the cylinder in the English version of the text, 'and that the fault was entirely his own, he let it stand'. Brater, *Drama in the Text*, p. 104. Beckett, in other words, chose not to correct the faulty mathematics.

79 Beckett, *Complete Dramatic Works*, pp. 169, 172.

80 Ibid., pp. 173, 176.

81 Ibid., p. 177.

82 Simon Critchley, *Very Little . . . Almost Nothing: Death, Philosophy, Literature* (London and New York: Routledge, 1997), p. 27.

5 COME AND GO

1 Beckett, *Trilogy*, p. 82.

2 Michael Benson, 'Moving Bodies in Hardy and Beckett', *Essays in Criticism* 34 (1984), 229–43 (237).

3 John Pilling, 'Beckett: "That's not moving, that's moving"', in Elizabeth Masten (ed.), *The Timeless and the Temporal: Writings in Honour of John Chalker by Friends and Colleagues* (Queen Mary and Westfield College, University of London: Department of English, 1993), pp. 393–403 (p. 393).

4 Robin Lee, 'The Fictional Topography of Samuel Beckett', in Gabriel Josipovici (ed.), *The Modern English Novel: The Reader, the Writer and the Work* (London: Open Books, 1976), pp. 206–24 (p. 216).

5 Enoch Brater, 'Light, Sound, Movement, and Action in Beckett's *Rockaby*', *Modern Drama* 25 (1982), 342–8 (346).

6 Ibid., 348.

7 Beckett, *Complete Dramatic Works*, p. 434.

8 Steven Connor, 'Slow Going', *Yearbook of English Studies* 30 (2000), 153–65 (155).

9 Connor, 'Slow Going', 155, 153. Connor adds, 'Beckett's work allows, even seems to require, some acknowledgement of this slow going. But it does not

see round the question of its own slowness, is not in charge of the meaning of
its slowness.' Ibid., 154.

10 When Beckett viewed *Quadrat II* for the first time, he famously exclaimed
that it took place 'ten thousand years later!'. Knowlson, *Damned to Fame*,
p. 674.

11 Lee, 'Fictional Topography', p. 209.

12 Ibid. Lee writes: 'The disruption of the novelistic use of place amounts, in
practice, to a disruption of the novelistic presentation of meaning.' Ibid.,
p. 211.

13 Janet Menzies, 'Beckett's Bicycles', *Journal of Beckett Studies* 6 (1980), 97–105
(97–8).

14 Beckett, *Watt*, p. 28.

15 In ancient Greek culture, walking and standing were regarded as 'expressions
of character'. It was, for instance, considered 'manly' to walk with long
strides, whereas taking short steps was the sign of effeminacy. To move
steadily signified being well bred, and 'the word *orthos*, or "upright", carried
the implications of male rectitude'. Richard Sennett, *Flesh and Stone: The
Body and the City in Western Civilization* (London: Faber and Faber, 1994),
pp. 49–50. See also Jan Bremmer, 'Walking, Standing, and Sitting in Ancient
Greek Culture', in Jan Bremmer and Herman Roodenburg (eds.), *A Cultural
History of Gesture: From Antiquity to the Present Day* (Cambridge: Polity,
1993), pp. 15–35. Mauss draws attention to the following aspects of walking
across different cultures: 'breathing, rhythm of the walk, swinging of the fists,
the elbows, progression with the trunk in advance of the body or by advancing
either side of the body alternately (we have got accustomed to moving all the
body forward at once). Feet turned in or out. Extension of the leg.' Marcel
Mauss, 'Body Techniques', in *Sociology and Psychology: Essays*, tr. Ben Brewster
(London, Boston and Henley: Routledge & Kegan Paul, 1979), pp. 95–123
(p. 114).

16 In the novel *Mercier and Camier*, walking is referred to as 'that indescribable
process not unconnected with . . . legs'. Beckett, *Mercier and Camier* (London: Picador, 1988), p. 88. Watt's humorous gait clearly constitutes a marked
way of walking, but as Marcel Mauss pointed out as early as 1934, there is no
such thing as a 'natural way' for the adult, rather the idiosyncrasies of body
techniques consist of a combination of biological, psychological and social
elements. Mauss writes, 'to take ourselves, the fact that we wear shoes to walk
transforms the positions of our feet.' Mauss, 'Body Techniques', p. 102.
Given the amount of attention dedicated to boots in Beckett's writing, one
can only suspect that Beckett must have pondered over a similar point.

17 Merleau-Ponty, *Phenomenology of Perception*, p. 139.

18 Daniel C. Dennett, 'Intentionality', in *Cambridge Dictionary of Philosophy*
(Cambridge: Cambridge University Press, 1995), p. 381.

19 The term itself was coined in the Middle Ages by the Scholastics, and 'revived
by the nineteenth-century philosopher and psychologist Franz Brentano, who
claimed that intentionality defines the distinction between the mental and the

physical; all and only mental phenomena exhibit intentionality.' Dennett, 'Intentionality', p. 381. Edmund Husserl, in turn, was Brentano's student. The definition of intentionality continues to be a contentious issue.

20 Hubert L. Dreyfus, 'The Current Relevance of Merleau-Ponty's Phenomenology of Embodiment', *The Electronic Journal of Analytic Philosophy* 4 (1996), http://ejap.louisiana.edu. One of the most influential medieval theories of intentionality was Aquinas's, who based his ideas on Aristotle's views of thought and perception: 'According to Aristotle, in thought and perception the mind takes on the form of the thing perceived, without receiving its matter. When I think about or perceive a horse, my mind receives the form of horse.' Aquinas took on board Aristotle's view, but stressed that the representation differed from the real horse in that it had only intentional existence. Tim Crane, 'Intentionality', *Routledge Dictionary of Philosophy* (London and New York: Routledge, 1998), pp. 816–21 (p. 817). The idea of representation has been essential to theories of intentionality, and it is this precondition that Merleau-Ponty's version of intentionality abolishes.

21 Dreyfus, 'The Current Relevance'.

22 Langer, *Merleau-Ponty's Phenomenology*, p. 83.

23 Dreyfus, 'The Current Relevance'.

24 In his fascination with slowness and fatigue rather than speed and energy, Beckett is writing against two of the major tropes of modernity. For a discussion of energy and fatigue and their relation to embodiment and the science of work, see Anson Rabinbach's *The Human Motor: Energy, Fatigue, and the Origins of Modernity* (Berkeley: University of California Press, 1992).

25 Gilles Deleuze, 'The Exhausted', tr. Christian Kerslake, *Parallax: A Journal of Metadiscursive Theory and Cultural Practices* 3 (1996), 113–35 (114).

26 Samuel Beckett, *More Pricks Than Kicks* (London: Calder, 1993), p. 39.

27 Hill, *Beckett's Fiction*, p. 61.

28 Julie Campbell, 'Pilgrim's Progress/Regress/Stasis: Some Thoughts on the Treatment of the Quest in Bunyan's *Pilgrim's Progress* and Beckett's *Mercier and Camier*', *Comparative Literature Studies* 30 (1993), 137–52 (142). *Mercier et Camier* was the first novel Beckett wrote in French, in 1946. The novel, however, was not published until 1970, because the publisher, Pierre Bordas, who initially gave Beckett a contract for 'a French edition of the translation of *Murphy* and a general contract for all future work in French and English (including translations)', and who even gave Beckett an advance for the manuscript of *Mercier and Camier* in January 1947, backed off after the bad sales figures for *Murphy*. See Knowlson, *Damned to Fame*, p. 362. Beckett began the English translation of the novel in 1970. *Mercier and Camier* appeared in English in 1974.

29 Angela Moorjani, 'A Cryptanalysis of Beckett's *Molloy*', in Joseph H. Smith (ed.), *The World of Samuel Beckett*, Psychiatry and the Humanities XXII (Baltimore and London: Johns Hopkins University Press, 1991), pp. 53–75.

30 Lee, 'The Fictional Topography', p. 216.

31 In 1946, when visiting his mother, Beckett noticed that her hands were beginning to shake: 'as she put sugar in her tea or replaced the spoon in her saucer,
   it tinkled against the side of the cup'. Knowlson, *Damned to Fame*, p. 343.
32 Beckett, *Trilogy*, p. 9.
33 Lee, 'The Fictional Topography', p. 215.
34 See, for instance, J. C. C. Mays, 'Irish Beckett: A Borderline Instance', in S. E.
   Wilmer (ed.), *Beckett in Dublin* (Dublin: Lilliput Press, 1992), pp. 133–46.
   Eoin O'Brien's rather wonderful *The Beckett Country* (London: Black Cat
   Press and Faber, 1986) offers a photographic reading of Beckett's work.
   Eagleton, in turn, mentions Beckett's 'starved landscapes' that reveal how to
   be stripped of one's own culture makes one a 'citizen of the world'. Terry
   Eagleton, *Heathcliff and the Great Hunger: Studies in Irish Culture* (London
   and New York: Verso, 1995), pp. 281–2.
35 Beckett, *Trilogy*, p. 15.
36 Ibid., p. 216. Of his time spent on the coast, Molloy remarks: 'But perhaps I
   am thinking of another stay, at an earlier time, for this will be my last, my last
   but one, or two, there is never a last, by the sea.' He adds, 'But perhaps I am
   merging two times in one, and two women, one coming towards me, shyly,
   urged on by the cries and laughter of her companions, and the other going
   away from me, unhesitatingly.' Ibid., p. 69.
37 Beckett, *Complete Short Prose*, p. 102.
38 Beckett, *Trilogy*, p. 21.
39 See Ian Hacking, '*Automatisme Ambulatoire*: Fugue, Hysteria, and Gender at
   the Turn of the Century', *Modernism/Modernity* 3 (1996), 31–43.
40 Ibid., 31; A. Pitres, *Leçons cliniques sur l'hystérie et l'hypnotisme faites à
   l'hôpital Saint-André à Bordeaux*, vol. II (Paris: Doin, 1891), p. 268.
41 Hacking, '*Automatisme Ambulatoire*', 33–4.
42 Ibid., 32.
43 Louis Aragon and André Breton, 'The Fiftieth Anniversary of Hysteria', tr.
   Samuel Beckett, in André Breton, *What Is Surrealism? Selected Writings*, ed.
   Franklin Rosemont (London: Pluto Press, 1978), pp. 320–1 (p. 321).
44 André Breton and Louis Aragon, 'Introduction to the Possessions', tr. Samuel
   Beckett, in André Breton, *What Is Surrealism?*, pp. 50–1 (p. 51).
45 Hal Foster, *Compulsive Beauty* (Cambridge, MA and London: MIT Press,
   1993), p. 97.
46 Hacking, '*Automatisme Ambulatoire*', 41. For a full account of the topic, see
   Ian Hacking, *Mad Travellers: Reflections on the Reality of Transient Mental
   Illnesses* (London: Free Association Books, 1999).
47 Beckett, *Trilogy*, p. 17.
48 Numerous suggestions about the relationship between the two parts of the
   novel have been proposed, such as the idea of Moran being an earlier version
   of Molloy. However, far from being Moran's future, 'Molloy clearly already
   exists for him.' Connor, *Repetition, Theory and Text*, p. 57. John Fletcher, in
   his essay 'Interpreting *Molloy*', on the other hand, has suggested that Molloy
   and Moran are one another's Jungian opposites. See John Fletcher,

'Interpreting *Molloy*', in Melvin Friedman (ed.), *Samuel Beckett Now: Critical Approaches to the Novels, Poetry and Plays*, 2nd edn. (Chicago and London: University of Chicago Press, 1975), pp. 157–70. Each reading in which the novel is treated as a story of merging identities, however, leaves important facts unaccounted for, since there are as many differences in the two stories as there are points of overlap. The narrator, in this way, seems both to suggest that we are dealing with one and the same character as well as simultaneously to imply that the mere possibility of the two being thought of as one is absurd. It is as if there were an insistence in the novel upon a parallel between the two stories, but no principles by which to measure the significance of this parallel. Connor, *Repetition, Theory and Text*, p. 59. The relationship between the two stories becomes, as Leslie Hill has pointed out, one 'not so much of merging identities as of aporetic doubling'. The repetition splits the structure of the novel into two non-identical parts, nonetheless refusing the uniqueness of any event or instance and thus ultimately refusing the narratives their self-identity. Furthermore, since Beckett in no way overtly foregrounds his repetitions, the reader will not accredit the first occurrence of an event, object or character as the founding moment of a central motif. Because of the structure of the narratives, both of which start at the end and thus take the form on an analepsis or narrative flashback, any 'founding moment' or 'origin' of a given motif would, in any case, be impossible to trace at the first reading. Hill, *Beckett's Fiction*, p. 68.

49 Beckett, *Trilogy*, p. 26. Molloy goes in search of his mother, while Moran, compelled by Youdi, is in search of Molloy. Molloy, however, seems barely to remember his mother; he has, in any case, forgotten her name and address. As Duerfahrd has pointed out, the very image of Molloy's mother, 'forgetful and bedridden', is representative of the decay of the journey's telos. See Lance Duerfahrd, 'Beckett's Circulation: Molloy's Dereliction', *Proceedings of the Twenty-First Annual Meeting of the Semiotic Society of America* (1996), 144–50 (145–6). Moran, for his part, rapidly forgets the instructions Youdi's messenger Gaber has given him, and is even uncertain whom he is looking for, as '[t]he fact was that there were three, no, four Molloys. He that inhabited me, my caricature of same, Gaber's and the man of flesh and blood somewhere awaiting me . . . I will . . . add a fifth Molloy, that of Youdi.' Beckett, *Trilogy*, p. 106.

50 Beckett, *Trilogy*, p. 11.

51 Ibid., p. 78. The allusion to Descartes is obvious here. In the Third Part of his *Discourse on Method*, Descartes advises the traveller who becomes lost in a forest to keep walking in a straight line, instead of 'turning this way and that', for by proceeding straight forward, the traveller will at least find his way out of the forest. René Descartes, *Discourse on Method*, in *The Philosophical Writings of Descartes*, vol. I, tr. J. Cottingham, R. Stoothoff and D. Murdoch (Cambridge: Cambridge University Press, 1985), p. 123. Beckett's narrator may also be making a sly reference to the Cartesian circle, Descartes's circular discussion of certainty in relation to sensory perception and the existence of

God, for, if we have certainty about our clear and distinct perceptions of reality through the existence of God, as Descartes claimed, then how, in the first place, do we have knowledge of God's existence? If the answer is through our clear and distinct perceptions, the argument becomes circular.

52 The same is true of the room that Molloy occupies in Lousse's house: 'Whereas the room, I saw the room but darkly, at each fresh inspection it seemed changed . . . and in the big frosted window the door was no longer inscribed, but had slightly shifted to the right, or to the left, I forget, so that there now appeared within its frame a panel of white wall, on which I succeeded in casting faint shadows when I moved.' Beckett, *Trilogy*, p. 42.

53 Ibid., p. 20.

54 Ibid., p. 63.

55 Beckett, *Complete Short Prose*, p. 156. Beckett wrote *From an Abandoned Work* between 1954 and 1955.

56 Duerfahrd adds 'upright and vertical' to the list of attributes that *Molloy* obliterates. Duerfahrd, 'Beckett's Circulation', 146. Whilst these principles, as we shall see, are gradually abandoned in the course of the Trilogy, the prominent oscillation between the vertical and the horizontal plays an important part in the novel.

57 Ibid., p. 146.

58 This can also be read as a plot device, namely as a manifestation of the dynamics between what Barthes in *S/Z* names the proairetic and the hermeneutic codes, the former forwarding the narrative, the latter holding it back. See Roland Barthes, *S/Z*, tr. Richard Miller (New York: Farrar, Straus, and Giroux, 1974).

59 Beckett, *Trilogy*, p. 74.

60 Georges Bataille, *Essential Writings*, ed. Michael Richardson (London: Sage, 1998), p. 15. Note also the insistence in Beckett on mud, most prominent in *How It Is*, but also strongly present in *Molloy*, as in several other prose works, particularly the short ones. Mud is not absent from the drama either, as can be evidenced in Estragon's words: 'All my lousy life I've crawled about in the mud! And you talk to me about scenery!' Beckett, *Complete Dramatic Works*, p. 57. In one of his letters to Alan Schneider, of 27 December 1955, Beckett even mentions having himself retreated to his 'hole in the Marne mud'. Harmon, *No Author Better Served*, p. 6. Sand is another recurring motif of disrupting matter in Beckett's work, often likened to the characters themselves, as in the case of Watt.

61 Bataille, *Essential Writings*, p. 15.

62 Beckett, *Complete Short Prose*, p. 33.

63 Theodor W. Adorno, *Negative Dialectics*, tr. E. B. Ashton (London: Routledge, 1990), p. 369.

64 Beckett, *Trilogy*, p. 82.

65 Ibid., p. 35.

66 Ibid., p. 33.

67 Ibid., p. 76.
68 Ibid., p. 47.
69 Ibid., p. 32.
70 Ibid., p. 24.
71 In *Time and Free Will*, Bergson argued that time was, in essence, pure duration, a stream of experience. The same, he added, was true of movement, which was irreducible to the mathematical measure of its trajectory. Bergson summarised his views on movement thus: 'Two elements in motion: (1) the space traversed, which is homogenous and divisible; (2) the act of traversing, indivisible and real only for consciousness.' Henri Bergson, *Time and Free Will: An Essay on the Immediate Data of Consciousness*, tr. F. L. Pogson (London: George Allen, 1912), p. 110. Beckett's early interest in Bergson's ideas is evidenced not only in *Proust*, where Beckett focuses on the latter's interest in time and memory, but also in a Trinity College Modern Languages Society performance of 1931. Beckett and his friend Georges Pelorson compressed Corneille's tragedy *Le Cid* and named the burlesque *Le Kid*, after Charlie Chaplin's film; Beckett also took part in the production as an actor. In a letter to Thomas MacGreevy, Beckett referred to the play as a fusion of Corneille and Bergson. Knowlson, *Damned to Fame*, pp. 123–4, 727n.15. Unfortunately, the script of *Le Kid* has not been recovered.
72 Beckett, *Trilogy*, p. 166.
73 What we have is a 'man in bed, writing about himself in bed writing, and proposing to track himself to his own death, so that his last word may be about his last word – better, may *be* his last word'. Kenner, *Samuel Beckett*, p. 79.
74 Steven Connor writes, 'postmodernity sees its image, or rather does not, in the imperceptible, in the nanoengineered processor based on a single molecule. Samuel Beckett participates in this miniaturization; instead of epics and monuments (*A la recherche du temps perdu, Finnegans Wake*), Beckett scaled down.' Connor, 'Slow Going', 155.
75 Beckett, *Trilogy*, p. 171. Clumsiness, Steven Connor has remarked, 'speaks of the infiltration of falling in human action'. Connor, 'Shifting Ground'.
76 Beckett, *Trilogy*, p. 170. As Blanchot observes, Malone's stick and pencil enlarge 'the circle of his immobility'. Maurice Blanchot, 'The Unnamable', tr. Richard Howard, in Garver and Federman (eds.), *Samuel Beckett: The Critical Heritage*, pp. 116–21 (p. 118).
77 Beckett, *Trilogy*, p. 176.
78 Ibid., p. 171.
79 Ibid., p. 206.
80 Steven Connor, 'The Shakes: Conditions of Tremor', *The Senses and Society* 3 (2008), 205–20 (210).
81 Ibid., 210.
82 Ibid., 211.
83 Beckett, *Trilogy*, p. 225.
84 Connor, 'The Shakes', 210.

85 Sigmund Freud, 'Beyond the Pleasure Principle', in *On Metapsychology: The Theory of Psychoanalysis*, Penguin Freud Library, vol. II (London: Penguin, 1991), pp. 269–337 (p. 311).

86 Knowlson, *Damned to Fame*, pp. 29, 710n.146. We know from Beckett's 'Psychology Notes', held at Trinity College Dublin, that he read Freud's essay 'The Anatomy of the Mental Personality', and was also familiar with Freudian theory through his reading of Ernest Jones's *Treatment of the Neuroses: Psychotherapy from Rest Cure to Psychoanalysis*, which dates from 1920, and his *Papers on Psycho-Analysis*, from 1923. In his notes, taken in the 1930s, Beckett refers to Ernest Jones as 'Erogenous Jones' and as 'Freudchen'. Samuel Beckett, 1930s, 'Psychology Notes', TCD MS 10971/8, Manuscripts Department, Trinity College Library Dublin.

87 Freud, 'Beyond the Pleasure Principle', p. 311.

88 Ibid., p. 312.

89 Beckett, *Trilogy*, p. 165.

90 Freud, 'Beyond the Pleasure Principle', p. 313.

91 As Molloy in the first part of the Trilogy asserts, 'in me there have always been two fools, among others, one asking nothing better than to stay where he is and the other imagining that life might be slightly less horrible a little further on'. Beckett, *Trilogy*, p. 46.

92 Connor, 'The Shakes', 212.

93 The importance of shaking can be seen, for instance, in the cylinder works, in which 'all vibrates, ground, wall, vault, bodies, ashen or leaden or between the two'. Beckett, *Complete Dramatic Works*, p. 183. In his notebooks for the Schiller production of *Krapp's Last Tape*, Beckett inserted the words 'Schauder u. Traum', 'shudder and dream' with a felt-tipped pen. The words, '1st shudder' and 'Second Shudder X' also appear. Beckett, *Theatrical Notebooks* III, pp. 154, 213, 228. Shaking also figures in *Film*, for when O reaches the stairway, we see him 'motionless at foot of stairs, right hand on banister, body shaken by panting'. Beckett, *Complete Dramatic Works*, p. 326. In Beckett's late play *Catastrophe* (French version 1982; English translation 1984), A (assistant) comments on the fact that P (protagonist) is 'shivering' after she removes his gown. Beckett, *Complete Dramatic Works*, p. 458. Until the end of the play, this will constitute P's only movement, apart from the ones imposed upon him by A. Beckett even used similar imagery in writing about his own life. He wrote to his cousin, John Beckett, in 1975, that he had been listening to Schubert's *Winterreise*, 'shivering through the grim journey again'. Knowlson, *Damned to Fame*, p. 626.

94 In *Proust*, Beckett refers to 'our smug will to live'. Beckett, *Proust*, p. 15. There is also much mention in Beckett of the beating of the heart. When Vladimir and Estragon are looking for Pozzo's missing watch, Estragon hears a sound, which turns out to be not the 'half-hunter' but Pozzo's heart. Pozzo himself makes mention of the 'pit-a-pat' rhythm his heart makes when he smokes 'two pipes one on top of the other'. Beckett, *Complete Dramatic Works*, pp. 45, 28.

95 Connor, 'The Shakes', 212.
96 Beckett, *Trilogy*, p. 223.
97 Ibid., p. 226.
98 Bataille, *Essential Writings*, p. 15.
99 This, however, is at times done reluctantly, if not regretfully. While Beckett parts company with the humanist tradition, it is, nonetheless, a tradition he is steeped in.
100 Connor, 'Shifting Ground'.
101 Chapter 6 of *Murphy*, which focuses on Murphy's mind, is an obvious example of Cartesian parody in the novel, and it may also contain an intertextual reference to Descartes's Sixth Meditation, in which the philosopher addresses the mind–body problem. At the end of the novel, all forms of dualism are dismantled, for 'the body, mind and soul of Murphy were freely distributed over the floor of the saloon' where Cooper is drinking. Beckett, *Murphy*, p. 154.
102 Georges Bataille, 'Base Materialism and Gnosticism', tr. Allan Stoekl, in *The Bataille Reader*, ed. Fred Botting and Scott Wilson (Oxford: Blackwell, 1997), pp. 160–4 (p. 163).
103 Ibid., p. 164.
104 Adorno, *Negative Dialectics*, p. 369.
105 Andrew Gibson, *Towards a Postmodern Theory of Narrative* (Edinburgh: Edinburgh University Press, 1996), p. 261.
106 Julia Kristeva, *Powers of Horror: An Essay on Abjection*, tr. Leon S. Roudiez (New York: Columbia University Press, 1982), p. 4.
107 Ibid., p. 3.
108 Beckett, *Trilogy*, p. 279. Amongst the different bodily fluids in the novel the unnamable mentions the possibility of 'liquefied brain'. Beckett, *Trilogy*, p. 269. Yoshiki Tajiri has recently argued that the permeable male body of *The Unnamable* problematises gender boundaries by being governed by 'uncontrollable flows'. Tajiri, *Beckett and the Prosthetic Body*, p. 38.
109 Beckett, *Trilogy*, p. 275.
110 Blanchot, 'The Unnamable', p. 118.
111 Beckett, *Trilogy*, p. 269.
112 Christopher Ricks, *Beckett's Dying Words* (Oxford: Oxford University Press, 1995), p. 147.
113 Gibson, *Towards a Postmodern*, p. 263.
114 Ibid., p. 271.
115 Ibid., pp. 267, 271.
116 Ibid., p. 262.
117 James Gordon Finlayson, 'Adorno: Modern Art, Metaphysics and Radical Evil', *Modernsim/Modernity* 10 (2003), 71–95 (81).
118 By 'wonder', I am referring, of course, to Aristotle, who in the *Metaphysics* (Book A), draws a connection between the philosopher and the 'lover of myth . . . for the myth is composed of wonders', and 'wondering' is the origin of all philosophising (982b). This view is further elaborated in the

Poetics, where it is the presence of 'the wonderful' or 'the marvellous' in tragedy which prompts the audience to trace out the logical, causal and temporal connectedness of the plot, leading to a form of cognitive understanding which has an ontological status of the same sort as philosophical comprehension. The wonderful, in other words, marks the turning-point of the complex plot, triggering the moment at which ignorance gives way to knowledge. In Adorno's negative aesthetics, wonder is replaced by horror.

119 In his essay on *Endgame*, Adorno describes a middle-aged man taking a nap with a cloth on his face, as Hamm does in the play. He goes on to write: 'The cloth makes him unrecognizable. This run-of-the-mill image, hardly unfamiliar even optically, becomes a sign only for the gaze that is aware of the face's loss of identity, of the possibility that its shrouded state is that of a dead man, of how repulsive the physical suffering is that already places the living man among corpses by reducing him to his body.' Theodor W. Adorno, 'Trying to Understand Endgame', in *Notes to Literature*, vol. I, ed. Rolf Tiedemann, tr. Shierry Weber Nicholsen, European Perspectives (New York: Columbia University Press, 1991), pp. 241–75 (p. 255).

120 Beckett, *Trilogy*, p. 267.

121 Ibid., p. 279.

122 The importance of art lies partly in the fact that, under excessive rationalisation, we are under the threat of losing anything that stands for us as other (because it has become contained and is hence no longer experienced as foreign). The horror of modern art, which evades rationalisation, reproduces in us the shuddering that we are at risk of losing.

123 Finlayson, 'Adorno: Modern Art', 80. The centrality of art for Adorno stems precisely from its continuing ability to arouse shudder: 'modern art survives its assimilation to the functional totality ... by becoming difficult, introverted, dissonant, shocking.' Finlayson, 'Adorno: Modern Art', 81.

124 This recurring quotation in Beckett criticism originates in Lawrence Harvey's book. Harvey, who conducted a number of conversations with Beckett between 1961 and 1962 and between 1964 and 1965, recounts the following one: ' "Being," according to Beckett, has been excluded from writing in the past. The attempt to expand the sphere of literature to include it, which means eliminating the artificial forms and techniques that hide and violate it, is the adventure of modern art. Someday someone will find an adequate form, a "syntax of weakness".' Harvey, *Samuel Beckett*, p. 249.

125 See, for instance, Adorno's 'Trying to Understand Endgame'. Adorno also discusses Beckett's work in *Aesthetic Theory*.

126 Beckett, *Trilogy*, p. 352.

127 *The Unnamable* has often been read as a novel that deals with a nightmarish state of life after death. A. Alvarez, for instance, writes: 'Beckett's pessimism was too profound to allow him to believe that death would be an end or even a relief. The voices continue beyond the grave, into the limbo, the "pit", where the Unnamable is fixed.' Alvarez, *Beckett*, p. 70. Where *Malone Dies* appeared to end with the narrator's final extinction, in other words, *The*

Unnamable, in this reading, takes off from the state of affairs that thereby follows. The rotating characters (for Malone is not unique) and recurrent references to questing and sticks are, in this view, but remnants of the unnamable's distant memories or alternatively instances of fellow-dead stuck in limbo. Another way of approaching the novel, however, would be to reverse this paradigm. What if one were to understand the unnamable as trapped in a life in which it imagines itself dead (rather than in a ghostly death in which it imagines itself alive), as victims of Cotard's syndrome do. More accurately even, the oscillations within the logic of the novel flicker between subjectivity and its loss. On 3 December 2006, Peter Fifield presented a paper at the University of Northampton entitled, 'Death *is* an Event in Life: Cotard's Syndrome and Samuel Beckett'.

128 Adorno, *Aesthetic Theory*, p. 245.

129 Ibid., pp. 245–6.

130 Adding to the horror of the novel is the fact that *The Unnamable* appears to provide us with a sufficient number of clues to tie together the loose ends of the Trilogy. We have a reference to writing, to 'the manual aspect of that bitter folly', just as we did in *Molloy* and *Malone Dies*. Beckett, *Trilogy*, p. 276. The unnamable mentions crawling, sticks and a forest, and makes reference to several characters from previous Beckett works. We have enough, in other words, to make us believe that the Trilogy does have a logic or code that can be cracked. But cracking the code finally amounts to acknowledging its vacuous nature. We are not faced with a system, even an outrageously new or alternative one.

131 Significantly, Jacques Derrida has used similar imagery in his discussion of Beckett's language. For Derrida, Beckett is a writer whose texts 'make the limits of our language tremble'. Jacques Derrida, *Acts of Literature*, ed. Derek Attridge (London and New York: Routledge, 1992), p. 60.

132 Beckett to Duckworth. Colin Duckworth, '*Godot*: Genesis and Coposition', in Ruby Cohn (ed.), *Beckett: Waiting for Godot*, Casebook Series (London: Macmillan, 1987), pp. 81–6 (p. 81).

133 Blin took on *En attendant Godot* after numerous other directors had turned it down.

134 I am referring to the religious references in the play. The Lord Chamberlain, whom Beckett once referred to as Lord Chamberpot, and who was 'the official censor and licensee of plays for the theatre', wanted twelve passages of the play omitted. Knowlson, *Damned to Fame*, pp. 411–12.

135 G. S. Fraser, 'Waiting for Godot', in Garver and Federman (eds.), *Samuel Beckett: Critical Heritage*, pp. 97–104 (p. 99).

136 The latest readings have been political in orientation, amongst the most prominent being Declan Kiberd's postcolonial interpretation of Beckett's *oeuvre*. See Declan Kiberd, *Inventing Ireland* (London, Jonathan Cape, 1995).

137 Walter D. Asmus, 'Beckett Directs Godot', *Theatre Quarterly* 5 (1975), 19–26 (23).

138 Vivian Mercier, 'The Uneventful Event', *Irish Times* (18 February 1956), p. 6.
139 Beckett, *Complete Dramatic Works*, pp. 20, 44.
140 Ibid., pp. 51, 61.
141 Ibid., p. 60; Samuel Beckett, *The Theatrical Notebooks of Samuel Beckett*, vol. I, *Waiting for Godot*, ed. Dougald McMillan and James Knowlson (London: Faber and Faber, 1993), p. 95.
142 This is also true of Beckett's other pseudocouples, such as Mercier and Camier, Hamm and Clov, Nagg and Nell and Winnie and Willie.
143 McMillan and Knowlson in Beckett, *Theatrical Notebooks* I, p. 87.
144 Beckett, *Complete Dramatic Works*, p. 11.
145 Beckett had, however, by this time, directed several of his plays. Amongst them figured *Endgame*, *Krapp's Last Tape* and *Happy Days*, all of which he directed at the Schiller-Theater. Asmus, 'Beckett Directs', p. 19.
146 A facsimile of one of the two copies of the German-language translation of *Godot* Beckett used when directing the play at the Schiller-Theater has been published as Samuel Beckett, *Warten auf Godot*, tr. Elmar Tophoven (Frankfurt am Main: Suhrkamp, 2006). It is a facsimile of RUL MS 1482, and includes Beckett's handwritten corrections to the printed text. The importance of physical movement in Beckett's drama is by no means restricted to *Godot*. In the opening stage directions of *Endgame*, for instance, twenty-six lines are dedicated to Clov's movements on stage, and specific mention is made of his '[s]tiff, staggering walk'. On the first page of *Krapp's Last Tape*, Krapp's walk is described as '*laborious*'. Much attention is also given to his other movements, such as '*fumbling*' and '*stooping*'. Beckett, *Complete Dramatic Works*, pp. 92, 215, 215, 216. It is significant that in the infamous 'jurisdiction' of his plays, Beckett was habitually more concerned with controlling the physical aspects of his drama, such as 'the details of light, sound, decor and pacing' than the actual meaning or interpretation of the work. Connor, *Repetition, Theory and Text*, p. 116.
147 Beckett, *Theatrical Notebooks* I, p. 185.
148 Beckett, *Complete Dramatic Works*, pp. 53, 54.
149 Ibid., p. 81.
150 Ibid., p. 12.
151 McMillan and Knowlson in Beckett, *Theatrical Notebooks* I, p. 87.
152 Beckett, *Complete Dramatic Works*, p. 87.
153 Beckett, *Theatrical Notebooks* I, p. 65.
154 Ibid.
155 Ibid.
156 Beckett, *Complete Dramatic Works*, p. 19.
157 McMillan and Knowlson in Beckett, *Theatrical Notebooks* I, p. 88.
158 Beckett, *Complete Dramatic Works*, p. 38.
159 Ibid., p. 44.
160 Jean Martin, 'Creating Godot', in Wilmer (ed.), *Beckett in Dublin*, pp. 25–32 (p. 29).
161 Ibid., p. 29.

162 Ibid.

163 Beckett, *Complete Dramatic Works*, p. 33.

164 Asmus, 'Beckett Directs Godot', p. 21.

165 Bennett, *Complete Dramatic Works*, p. 33.

166 Knowlson, *Damned to Fame*, p. 65.

167 Ibid., p. 217.

168 Samuel Beckett, 1930s, 'Germany, Europe, and the French Revolution. Rabelais', TCD MS 10969, Manuscripts Department, Trinity College Library Dublin.

169 Quoted in Matthijs Engelberts, Everett Frost and Jane Maxwell (eds.), *Notes Diverse Holo: Catalogues of Beckett's Reading Notes and Other Manuscripts at Trinity College Dublin, with Supporting Essays* (Amsterdam: Rodopi, 2006), p. 96.

170 Mikhail Bakhtin, *Rabelais and His World*, tr. Hélène Iswolsky (Bloomington: Indiana University Press, 1984), p. 320.

171 Ibid., p. 317.

172 Ibid., pp. 370–1.

173 Beckett, *Complete Dramatic Works*, p. 56.

174 Ibid., p. 30.

175 Ibid., pp. 26, 62.

176 Ibid., p. 57.

177 A particularly significant orifice in Bakhtin's analysis is the gaping mouth with tongue and teeth, which, of course, brings to mind Beckett's *Not I* (1972).

178 Beckett, *Complete Dramatic Works*, p. 307.

179 The makeup artist was Jocelyn Herbert. Billie Whitelaw's comments are from a television interview conducted for Süddeutscher Rundfunk in 1988 by Walter Asmus, but the thirty-minute interview has never been broadcast in its entirety. The interview was produced to accompany *3 Beckett Stücke*, namely *He Joe*, *Footfalls* and *Rockaby*, but only the plays were transmitted on 9 March 1990. In 1988, three minutes of the interview were broadcast in a programme entitled *Kulturszene*. I am deeply indebted to Stephan Spering at Südwestrundfunk for enabling me to view the full thirty-minute interview.

180 Bakhtin, *Rabelais*, p. 318.

181 Beckett, *Complete Dramatic Works*, p. 68. Malone uses the following figure of speech: 'It is there the demon lurks, like the gonococcus in the folds of the prostate.' Beckett, *Trilogy*, p. 181.

182 Bakhtin, *Rabelais*, p. 370.

183 Beckett, *Complete Dramatic Works*, p. 14. One of the most striking examples of hyperbole occurs in *Malone Dies*: 'All strains towards the nearest deeps, and notably my feet, which even in the ordinary way are so much further from me than all the rest, from my head I mean, for that is where I am fled, my feet are leagues away. And to call them in, to be cleaned for example, would I think take me over a month, exclusive of the time required to locate them. Strange, I don't feel my feet any more, my feet feel nothing any more,

and a mercy it is. And yet I feel they are beyond the range of the most powerful telescope.' Of his backside, Malone says, 'my arse for example, which can hardly be accused of being the end of anything, if my arse suddenly started to shit at the present moment, which God forbid, I firmly believe the lumps would fall out in Australia'. Beckett, *Trilogy*, p. 215.

184 Beckett, *Complete Dramatic Works*, pp. 26, 27. Bakhtin writes: 'The grotesque is interested only in protruding eyes ... Moreover, the bulging eyes manifest a purely bodily tension.' Bakhtin, *Rabelais*, pp. 316–7.

185 Bakhtin, *Rabelais*, p. 322.

186 Beckett, *Complete Dramatic Works*, pp. 22, 26.

187 Ibid., p. 51.

188 Ibid., p. 83.

189 Bakhtin, *Rabelais*, p. 281.

190 Ibid., p. 281.

191 Terry Eagleton, *Sweet Violence: The Idea of the Tragic* (Oxford: Blackwell, 2003), p. 67.

192 Ibid.

193 Ibid., p. 65.

194 Ibid., p. 65–6.

195 Simon Critchley, 'Comedy and Finitude: Displacing the Tragic-Heroic Paradigm in Philosophy and Psychoanalysis', *Constellations* 6 (1999), 108–22 (117).

196 Ibid., p. 119. We are not far from Adorno's observation that in *Endgame*, 'forlorn particulars ... mock the conceptual, a layer composed of minimal utensils, ... lameness, blindness, and the distasteful bodily functions.' Adorno, 'Trying to Understand Endgame', p. 525.

197 Elin Diamond, '"THE SOCIETY OF MY LIKES": Beckett's Political Imaginary', *Samuel Beckett Today/Aujourd'hui* 11 (2001), 383–8 (384).

198 Beckett, *Complete Dramatic Works*, p. 25.

199 Diamond, '"SOCIETY OF MY LIKES"', 382.

200 Beckett, *Complete Dramatic Works*, p. 25.

6 SEEING GHOSTS

1 Hugh Kenner, *The Mechanic Muse* (New York: Oxford University Press, 1987), p. 96.

2 Beckett, *Complete Short Prose*, p. 74.

3 Ezra Pound, *Machine Art and Other Writings: The Lost Thought of the Italian Years*, ed. Maria Luisa Ardizzone (Durham, NC: Duke University Press, 1966), p. 77.

4 See, for instance, Tim Armstrong's fine *Modernism, Technology and the Body: A Cultural Study* (Cambridge: Cambridge University Press, 1998).

5 Sigmund Freud, 'Civilization and Its Discontents', *Civilization, Society and Religion*, Penguin Freud Library, vol. XII, ed. Albert Dickson (Harmondsworth: Penguin, 1991), pp. 243–340 (p. 279).

6 Ibid., p. 280.
7 For a discussion of what Hal Foster has called 'the double logic of the prosthesis', see *Prosthetic Gods* (Cambridge MA and London: MIT Press, 2004),
  p. 113.
8 Laura Danius, *The Senses of Modernism*, p. 19.
9 Ibid.
10 Marta Braun, *Picturing Time: The Work of Etienne-Jules Marey (1830–1904)*
   (Chicago: University of Chicago Press, 1992), p. 43.
11 Ibid., p. 57.
12 Lisa Cartwright, *Screening the Body: Tracing Medicine's Visual Culture*
   (Minneapolis: University of Minnesota Press, 1995), p. 107.
13 Thomas Mann, *The Magic Mountain*, tr. H. T. Lowe-Porter (London, 1999),
   p. 217.
14 Ibid. p. 218.
15 I have used John E. Woods' translation of this quotation, because it delivers
   the mood of the original passage more forcefully than Lowe-Porter's version.
   Thomas Mann, *The Magic Mountain*, tr. John E. Woods (New York, 1995),
   pp. 215–16.
16 Crary, *Techniques of the Observer*, p. 98. Beckett himself refers to afterimages
   in *Murphy* and *Watt*.
17 Ibid., pp. 104–5.
18 Samuel Beckett, 1930s, 'Psychology Notes', TCD MS 10971/7/11, Manuscripts
   Department, Trinity College Library Dublin.
19 Ibid.
20 Ibid., TCD MS 10971/7/12. In an entry made on 3 January 1937 in his
   'German Diaries', Beckett speculates over the complexities of visual
   experience: 'When I take off my glasses and bring my face as close to the
   mirror as my nose permits, then I see myself in my right eye, or alternatively
   my reflection's left eye, half profile left, and inversely. If I squint to the left
   I am full face in left eye, and inversely. But to be full face at once in the
   mirror + in my eye, that seems an optical impossibility. But it is not
   necessary after all to take off my glasses. By keeping them I see myself 3
   times at once, in the mirror, in my glasses and in my eyes.' Samuel Beckett,
   'German Diaries', 3/1/1937, quoted in Nixon, 'Samuel Beckett's "Film
   Vidéo-Cassette projet"'.
21 Beckett, *Complete Short Prose*, p. 118.
22 Beckett, *Complete Dramatic Works*, p. 411.
23 Ruby Cohn, *A Beckett Canon* (Ann Arbor: University of Michigan Press,
   2005), p. 338.
24 Michael Billington, 'First Night', *Guardian* (18 April 1977), 8.
25 Virginia Woolf, 'Street Haunting: A London Adventure', *The Death of the
   Moth and Other Essays* (London: Hogath Press, 1943, pp. 19–29 (p. 21).
26 Ibid. p. 24.
27 Tim Armstrong, *Modernism: A Cultural History*, Themes in Twentieth-
   Century Literature and Culture (Cambridge: Polity, 2005), p. 113.

28 Albright, *Beckett and Aesthetics*, p. 136.
29 Eckhart Voigts-Virchow, 'Exhausted Cameras – Beckett in the TV-Zoo', in Jennifer Jeffers (ed.), *Samuel Beckett: A Casebook* (New York and London: Garland, 1998), pp. 225–49 (pp. 229–30).
30 Süddeutscher Rundfunk is now called Südwestrundfunk Stuttgart.
31 Beckett, *Complete Dramatic Works*, p. 409.
32 Eric Prieto, 'Caves: Technology and the Total Artwork in Reich's *The Cave* and Beckett's *Ghost Trio*', *Mosaic: A Journal for the Interdisciplinary Study of Literature* 35 (2002), 197–231 (207).
33 James Knowlson, '*Ghost Trio/Geister Trio*', in Brater (ed.), *Beckett at 80/ Beckett in Context*, pp. 193–207 (p. 198).
34 Beckett, *Complete Dramatic Works*, pp. 408, 409.
35 Kalb, 'The Mediated Quixote', p. 140.
36 Ibid.
37 This information is from an unpublished manuscript by Reinhart Müller-Freienfels, 'Samuel Beckett: "We do it to have fun together" (Erinnerungen an Beckett in Stuttgart)', Südwestrundfunk Historical Archives, Stuttgart. I am indebted to Dr Jörg Hucklenbroich, who kindly granted me access to this material. Warm thanks are also due to Stephan Spering for his generous help and assistance at SWR.
38 Eckhart Voigts-Virchow, 'Face Values: Beckett Inc., The Camera Plays and Cultural Liminity', *Journal of Beckett Studies* 10 (2002), 119–35 (125). This point, however, is not entirely accurate, for as James Knowlson has observed, on occasion, V either 'makes mistakes and gets the order wrong or she exercises uncertain control over [F]'. Knowlson, 'Ghost Trio/Geister Trio', p. 198. Knowlson's essay offers a meticulous mapping of the BBC and SDR productions of the play.
39 Prieto, 'Caves', 207.
40 Knowlson, *Damned to Fame*, p. 621; Beckett, *Complete Dramatic Works*, p. 408.
41 Beckett, *Complete Dramatic Works*, p. 408.
42 Albright, *Beckett and Aesthetics*, p. 134.
43 Prieto, 'Caves', 209.
44 Beckett, *Proust*, pp. 26–7.
45 Samuel Beckett, 1970s, 'Notes on Tryst', RUL MS 1519/3, Beckett International Foundation, University of Reading.
46 Merleau-Ponty, *Phenomenology of Perception*, p. 203.
47 Beckett, *Complete Dramatic Works*, p. 417. Beckett wanted Klaus Herm for . . . *nur noch Gewölk . . .*, the SDR version of the play, for Herm had also played the role of F in *Geistertrio*. Beckett wrote to Müller-Freienfels, in a letter dated 13 December 1976, that although it was not made explicit, 'the man in ". . . but the clouds . . ." is the same as in <u>Ghost Trio</u>, in another (later) situation, and it would be a great pity if we could not have the same actor for the two parts'. Beckett, 'Letter to Reinhart Müller-Freienfels, 13 December 1976', SWR MS 20/11351, Südwestrundfunk Historical Archives, Stuttgart (1976).

48 Jonathan Kalb, *Beckett in Performance*, pp. 114–15.

49 Beckett, *Complete Dramatic Works*, p. 420.

50 William Butler Yeats, *The Major Works*, ed. Edward Larrissy, Oxford World's Classics (Oxford: Oxford University Press, 2001), pp. 95–6.

51 Knowlson, 'Ghost Trio/Geister Trio', p. 201.

52 Chris Ackerley and Marcel Fernandes, '"By Christ! He Did Die": Medical Misadventures in the Works of Samuel Beckett' (2006). Warm thanks are due to the authors for providing me with a copy of this hitherto unpublished glossary.

53 Knowlson, *Damned to Fame*, p. 166.

54 Ibid., p. 167.

55 Beckett, *Complete Short Prose*, p. 33.

56 Beckett, *Watt*, p. 100.

57 Samuel Beckett, 1930s, 'Whoroscope Notebook', RUL MS 3000, Beckett International Foundation, University of Reading.

58 The X-ray photograph of Bertha Röntgen's hand triggered a craze amongst New York women of fashion, who thereafter had their jewellery-adorned hands X-rayed, in order to prove that beauty was not only skin-deep, but resided in bone structure. See Stanley Joel Reiser, *Medicine and the Reign of Technology* (New York: Cambridge University Press, 1978), p. 61. Young women gave these pictures to their fiancés, while married women, in turn, gave X-ray pictures of their hands to relatives. Cartwright, *Tracing Medicine's Visual Culture*, p. 115. These X-rays acquired a cultural status similar to present-day ultrasound scans of expectant mothers, given to relatives and often displayed in the house.

59 Samuel Beckett, 1935, 'To Thomas MacGreevy, 9/1/1935', TCD MS 10402, Manuscripts Department, Trinity College Library Dublin.

60 Beckett, *Proust*, p. 57.

61 Hugh Culik, 'Mindful of the Body: Medical Allusions in Beckett's *Murphy*', *Eire Ireland* 14 (1977), 84–101 (85).

62 Culik observes that John Benjamin Murphy (1857–1916), for instance, invented 'the "Murphy Button", which is used to connect the separated ends of severed intestine; a "Murphy Method" for suturing arteries; a "Murphy Sign" for detecting gall bladder infection; and a "Murphy Treatment" for tuberculosis, consisting of injecting nitrogen gas into the pleural cavity to collapse the lung – essentially an anaerobic treatment'. W. Gill Wylie and Howard Atwood Kelly, for their part, were both famous gynaecologists, while 'Cooper's name suggests Sir Astley Paston Cooper whose name now graces a hernia, a bit of fascia, and a chronic cystic disease of the breast.' Finally, Rosie Dew's name brings to mind Harold Robert Dew, after whom a 'diagnostic sign of a diaphragmatic hydatid abscess' is named. Culik, 'Mindful of the Body', 91–3.

63 Beckett, *Nohow On*, pp. 42, 46.

64 See Adam Piette, 'Beckett, Early Neuropsychology and Memory Loss: Beckett's Reading of Clarapède, Janet and Korsakoff', *Samuel Beckett Today/ Aujourd'hui* 2 (1993), 41–8.

65 Marita Sturken and Lisa Cartwright, *Practices of Looking: An Introduction to Visual Culture* (Oxford: Oxford University Press, 2001), p. 301.

66 Beckett, *Trilogy*, p. 267.

67 Beckett, *Nohow On*, p. 101. The quotation is from *Worstward Ho*.

68 Sturken and Cartwright, *Practices of Looking*, p. 300.

69 Bojana Kunst, 'The Digital Body: History of Body Visibility', in Nina Czegledy (ed.), *Digitized Bodies: Virtual Spectacles* (Budapest: Ludwig Museum, 2001), pp. 13–27 (p. 22).

70 Stanley Joel Reiser, 'Technology and the Use of the Senses in Twentieth-Century Medicine', in W. F. Bynum and Roy Porter (eds.), *Medicine and the Five Senses* (Cambridge: Cambridge University Press, 1993), pp. 262–73 (p. 270).

71 Sarah Kember, 'Medicine's New Vision?', in Martin Lister (ed.), *The Photographic Image in Digital Culture* (New York and London: Routledge, 1995), pp. 95–114 (p. 100).

72 Roy Porter, *The Greatest Benefit to Mankind: A Medical History of Humanity from Antiquity to the Present* (London: Fontana, 1999), p. 610.

73 Kember, 'Medicine's New Vision?', p. 100.

74 Kunst, 'The Digital Body', p. 22.

75 Reiser, 'Technology and the Use of the Senses', p. 271.

76 Beckett, *Nohow On*, pp. 101–2.

77 *Nacht und Träume* was first broadcast on German television on 19 May 1983. John Pilling, *A Samuel Beckett Chronology* (Basingstoke: Palgrave Macmillan, 2006), p. 221.

78 Samuel Beckett, 1982, 'To Reinhart Müller-Freienfels, 5/8/82, Paris', Südwestrundfunk Historical Archives, Stuttgart.

79 Virtual bodies, after all, have no gender. However, we now know, from Beckett's correspondence, that the hands were large female hands: 'I think no choice but female for the helping hands. Large but female. As more conceivably male than male conceivably female.' Beckett, 'To Reinhart Müller-Freienfels, 5/8/82, Paris', Südwestrundfunk Historical Archives, Stuttgart.

80 Beckett, *Complete Dramatic Works*, p. 446.

81 See James Monaco, *How to Read a Film* (New York: Oxford University Press, 2000), p. 198.

82 Enoch Brater, 'Toward a Poetics of Television Technology: Beckett's *Nacht und Träume* and *Quad*', *Modern Drama* 28 (1985), 48–54 (50–1).

83 The Global Village production was made over a period of eight months, and released in 1988. It is based on Stan Gontarski's original stage direction of the English-language première of the revised text of *What Where* at the Magic Theater, San Francisco, in September 1986. The play formed part of a bill entitled *The Beckett Vision: Rough for Theatre I, The Old Tune, Ohio Impromptu, What Where*. Gontarski's direction of *What Where* was later filmed by John Reilly.

84 Beckett makes this observation in a documentary film called *Waiting for Beckett*, prod. and dir. John Reilly and Melissa Shaw-Smith (Warwick, NY: Global Village, 1994).
85 Cohn, *The Beckett Canon*, pp. 378–9.
86 Samuel Beckett, *Theatrical Notebooks*, vol. IV, *The Shorter Plays*, ed. S. E. Gontarski (London: Faber and Faber, 1999), p. 425. The entire process of revising *What Where* appeared to be a 'Process of elimination'. Beckett, *Theatrical Notebooks* IV, p. 429.
87 Samuel Beckett, 1984, 'To Reinhart Müller-Freienfels, 13/3/84, Paris', SWR MS 20/27587, Südwestrundfunk Historical Archives, Stuttgart.
88 Samuel Beckett, 1984, 'To Reinhart Müller-Freienfels, 5/3/84, Paris', SWR MS 29/720, Südwestrunkfunk Historical Archives, Stuttgart. I am grateful to Angela Moorjani for suggesting this translation.
89 Beckett also makes this clear in his original stage directions for the play, from 1983, where 'Players as alike as possible. Same long grey gown. Same long grey hair.' Beckett, *Complete Dramatic Works*, p. 269.
90 Samuel Beckett, 1984, 'To Reinhart Müller-Freienfels, 1/1/84, Paris', SWR MS 20/27587, Südwestrunkfunk Historical Archives, Stuttgart.
91 Beckett, *Theatrical Notebooks* IV, pp. 428, 429. When the production team in Stuttgart asked Beckett whether the play could be produced with a single actor, Beckett replied, 'One actor will only confuse, unless one can be made up as four. We need resemblance, not identity.' Quoted in Enoch Brater, *Beyond Minimalism: Beckett's Late Style in the Theatre* (New York: Oxford University Press, 1987), p. 62. For Ruby Cohn, Bam, Bem, Bim and Bom, in fact, function as 'avatars of the same figure, whom V calls into being'. Cohn, *The Beckett Canon*, p. 377.
92 Sturken and Cartwright, *Practices of Looking*, p. 304. In actuality, the methods used were very simple. Beckett's cameraman at SDR, Jim Lewis, described the procedure in the following manner: 'I cut a small hole, an aperture, in a piece of cardboard, and placed each cardboard in front of each camera. We used four cameras at the same time and we lined the aperture up to fit the particular face. We had to cut the opening to fit the face, the physiognomy of each face, because they weren't that much alike . . . Then we did makeup, rounding out the head, getting rid of the hair, the ears, darkening the outline to recede into black, hooded the faces. It looked like a science-fiction sort of thing.' Quoted in Brater, *Beyond Minimalism*, p. 161.
93 Sturken and Cartwright, *Practices of Looking*, p. 304. For the English stage première of the play, Beckett 'suggested . . . a hologram of the distorted face of Bam', as Stan Gontarski points out in Beckett, *Theatrical Notebooks* IV, p. 451.
94 Brater, *Beyond Minimalism*, p. 153.
95 Charles Lyons, 'Beckett's Fundamental Theatre: The Plays from *Not I* to *What Where*', in James Acheson and Kateryna Artur (eds.), *Beckett's Later Fiction and Drama: Texts for Company* (Basingstoke: Macmillan, 1987), pp. 80–97 (p. 95).

96 Samuel Beckett, 1984, 'To Reinhart Müller-Freienfels, 1/1/84, Paris', SWR MS 20/27587, Südwestrundfunk Historical Archives, Stuttgart.
97 Beckett, *Complete Dramatic Works*, pp. 273, 275.
98 Albright, *Beckett and Aesthetics*, p. 69.
99 Kenner, *The Mechanical Muse*, p. 100.
100 Samuel Beckett, 1984, 'To Reinhart Müller-Freienfels, 13/3/84, Paris', SWR MS 20/27587, Südwestrundfunk Historical Archives, Stuttgart.
101 Beckett, *Theatrical Notebooks* IV, p. 433.
102 Ibid, p. 443.
103 Gontarski in Beckett, *Theatrical Notebooks* IV, p. 453.
104 Sarah Kember, 'Surveillance, Technology and Crime', in Martin Lister (ed.), *The Photographic Image in Digital Culture* (London and New York: Routledge, 1995), pp. 115–26 (p. 117).
105 Kember, 'Medicine's New Vision?', p. 96.
106 Michel Foucault, *Discipline and Punish: The Birth of the Prison*, tr. Alan Sheridan (Harmondsworth: Penguin, 1977), p. 200. For an analysis of surveillance culture in Beckett's *Molloy*, see Anthony Uhlmann, *Beckett and Poststructuralism* (Cambridge: Cambridge University Press, 1999), pp. 40–57.
107 Kenner, *Mechanical Muse*, p. 103.
108 Beckett, *Complete Dramatic Works*, p. 307.
109 Samuel Beckett, 1975–6, 'Long Observation of the Ray', RUL MS 2909/3, Beckett International Foundation, University of Reading.
110 Lyons, 'Beckett's Fundamental Theatre', p. 96.
111 Jean-François Lyotard, 'Can Thought Go On without a Body?', in *The Inhuman: Reflections on Time*, tr. Geoffrey Bennington and Rachel Bowlby (Stanford: Stanford University Press, 1991), pp. 8–23 (p. 17).
112 Kember, 'Medicine's New Vision?', p. 109.
113 Don Ihde, *Bodies in Technology*, Electronic Mediations, vol. V (Minneapolis: University of Minnesota Press, 2002), p. 15.
114 Sturken and Cartwright, *Practices of Looking*, p. 301.
115 Ibid., p. 302.
116 Lyotard, 'Can Thought Go On without a Body?', p. 22.

Works cited

Acheson, James, 'Beckett and the Heresy of Love', in Linda Ben-Zvi (ed.), *Women in Beckett: Performance and Critical Perspectives* (Urbana and Chicago: University of Illinois Press, 1992), pp. 68–80.

Acheson, James and Kateryna Arthur (eds.), *Beckett's Later Fiction and Drama: Texts for Company* (Basingstoke: Macmillan, 1987).

Ackerley, C. J. and S. E. Gontarski (eds.), *The Faber Companion to Samuel Beckett: A Reader's Guide to His Works, Life, and Thought* (London: Faber and Faber, 2006).

Ackerley, Chris and Marcel Fernandes, '"By Christ! He Did Die": Medical Misadventures in the Works of Samuel Beckett', unpublished paper (2006).

Admussen, Richard, *The Samuel Beckett Manuscripts: A Study* (Boston: G. K. Hall, 1979).

Adorno, Theodor W., *Negative Dialectics*, tr. E. B. Ashton (London: Routledge, 1990).

'Trying to Understand Endgame', in *Notes to Literature*, vol. I, ed. Rolf Tiedemann, tr. Shierry Weber Nicholsen, European Perspectives (New York: Columbia University Press, 1991), pp. 241–75.

Aesthetic Theory, ed. Gretel Adorno and Rolf Tiedemann, tr. Robert Hullot-Kentor, Athlone Contemporary European Thinkers (London: Athlone, 1997).

Albright, Daniel, *Beckett and Aesthetics* (Cambridge: Cambridge University Press, 2003).

All That Fall, radio play, by Samuel Beckett, dir. Donald McWhinnie (BBC Third Programme, 13 January 1957).

Alpaugh, David, '*Embers* and the Sea: Beckettian Intimations of Mortality', *Modern Drama* XVI (1973), 317–28.

Alvarez, A, *Beckett*, 2nd edn, Fontana Modern Masters (London: Fontana, 1992).

Anzieu, Didier, *Skin Ego*, tr. Chris Turner (New Haven and London: Yale University Press, 1989).

Aragon, Louis and André Breton, 'The Fiftieth Anniversary of Hysteria', tr. Samuel Beckett, in André Breton, *What Is Surrealism? Selected Writings*, ed. Franklin Rosemont (London: Pluto Press, 1978). pp. 320–1.

Aristotle, *The Works of Aristotle*, tr. Daniel Ross (Oxford: Clarendon, 1972).

De Anima (On the Soul), tr. Hugh Lawson-Tancred (London: Penguin, 1986).

The Poetics of Aristotle, tr. Stephen Halliwell (Chapel Hill: University of North Carolina Press, 1987).

Armstrong, Tim, *Modernism, Technology and the Body: A Cultural Study* (Cambridge: Cambridge University Press, 1998).

Modernism: A Cultural History, Themes in Twentieth-Century Literature and Culture (Cambridge: Polity, 2005).

Arnheim, Rudolf, *Radio: An Art of Sound*, tr. Margaret Ludvig and Herbert Read (New York: Da Capo Press, 1972).

Asmus, Walter D., 'Beckett Directs Godot', *Theatre Quarterly* V (1975), 19–26.

'Rehearsal Notes for the German Premiere of Beckett's "That Time" and "Footfalls"', in S. E. Gontarski (ed.), *On Beckett: Essays and Criticism* (New York: Grove Press, 1986), pp. 335–49.

Atik, Anne, *How It Was: A Memoir of Samuel Beckett* (London: Faber and Faber, 2001).

Bair, Deirdre, *Samuel Beckett: A Biography* (London: Vintage, 1990).

Bakhtin, Mikhail, *Rabelais and His World*, tr. Hélène Iswolsky (Bloomington: Indiana University Press, 1984).

Barthes, Roland, *Critical Essays*, tr. Richard Howard (Evanston: Northwestern University Press, 1972).

S/Z, tr. Richard Miller (New York: Farrar, Straus, and Giroux, 1974).

Bataille, Georges, *Story of the Eye*, tr. Joachim Neugroschel (Harmondsworth: Penguin, 1982).

'Base Materialism and Gnosticism', in Fred Botting and Scott Wilson (eds.), *The Bataille Reader*, tr. Allan Stoekl (Oxford: Blackwell, 1997), pp. 160–4.

Essential Writings, ed. Michael Richardson (London: Sage, 1998).

Beck, Alan, 'Point-of-Listening in Radio Plays', *Sound Journal* (1998), www.kent.ac.uk/sdfva/sound-journal/beck981.html.

Beckerman, Bernard, 'Beckett and the Act of Listening', in Enoch Brater (ed.), *Beckett at 80/Beckett in Context* (New York and Oxford: Oxford University Press, 1986), pp. 149–67.

Beckett, Samuel, *Whoroscope* (Paris: The Hours Press, 1930).

'Psychology Notes', TCD MS 10971/7, Manuscripts Department, Trinity College Library Dublin (1930s).

'Whoroscope Notebook', RUL MS 3000, Beckett International Foundation, Reading University Library (1930s).

'Letter to Thomas MacGreevy, 5 January 1930', TCD MS 10402, Manuscripts Department, Trinity College Library Dublin (1930).

'Letter to Thomas MacGreevy, 3 February 1931', TCD MS 10402, Manuscripts Department, Trinity College Library Dublin (1931).

'Letter to Thomas MacGreevy, 18 October 1932', TCD MS 10402, Manuscripts Department, Trinity College Library Dublin (1932).

'Letter to Thomas MacGreevy, 8 September 1934', TCD MS 10402, Manuscripts Department, Trinity College Library Dublin (1934).

'Letter to Thomas MacGreevy [undated]', TCD MS 10402, Trinity College Dublin (1934).

'Letter to Thomas MacGreevy, 9 January 1935', TCD MS 10402, Manuscripts Department, Trinity College Library Dublin (1935).

'Letter to Thomas MacGreevy, 6 February 1936', TCD MS 10402, Trinity College Dublin (1936).

'Germany, Europe, and the French Revolution. Rabelais [undated]', TCD MS 10969, Manuscripts Department, Trinity College Library Dublin (1930s).

'German Diaries', Beckett International Foundation, Reading University Library (1936–7).

'Lettre à Georges Duthuit, 9 mars 1949–10 mars 1949', in S. E. Gontarski and Anthony Uhlmann (eds.), *Beckett after Beckett* (Gainesville: University Press of Florida, 2006), pp. 15–8.

'Krapp's Last Tape', typescript, RUL MS 1659, Beckett International Foundation, Reading University Library (1958).

'Letter to Barbara Bray, 11 March 1959', TCD MS 10948/1/1, Manuscripts Department, Trinity College Library Dublin (1959).

'Cendres', *Lettres nouvelles* 36 (1959), 3–14.

Comment c'est (Paris: Editions de Minuit, 1961).

'Notes for Film/Percipi Notes', RUL MS 1227/7/6/1, Beckett International Foundation, Reading University Library (undated).

Murphy (London: Picador, 1973).

'Long Observation of the Ray', RUL MS 2909/3, Beckett International Foundation, Reading University Library (1975–6).

'Ghost Trio', RUL MS 1519/1, Beckett International Foundation, Reading University Library (1976).

'Notes on Tryst', RUL MS 1519/3, Beckett International Foundation, Reading University Library (1976).

'Letter to Reinhart Müller-Freienfels, 13 December 1976', SWR MS 20/11351, Südwestrundfunk Historical Archives, Stuttgart (1976).

The Beckett Trilogy: Molloy, Malone Dies and The Unnamable (London: Picador, 1979).

Watt (London: John Calder, 1981).

'Letter to Reinhart Müller-Freienfels, 5 August 1982', Südwestrundfunk Historical Archives, Stuttgart (1982).

Disjecta: Miscellaneous Writings and a Dramatic Fragment, ed. Ruby Cohn (London: Calder, 1983).

'Letter to Reinhart Müller-Freienfels, 1 January 1984', SWR MS 20/27587, Südwestrundfunk Historical Archives, Stuttgart (1984).

'Letter to Reinhart Müller-Freienfels, 5 March 1984', SWR MS 29/720, Südwestrundfunk Historical Archives, Stuttgart (1984).

'Letter to Reinhart Müller-Freienfels, 13 March 1984', SWR MS 20/27587, Südwestrundfunk Historical Archives, Stuttgart (1984).

Mercier and Camier (London: Picador, 1988).

The Complete Dramatic Works (London: Faber and Faber, 1990).

Nohow On: Company, Ill Seen Ill Said, Worstward Ho (London: Calder, 1992).

Dream of Fair to Middling Women (Dublin: The Black Cat Press, 1992).

More Pricks Than Kicks (London: Calder, 1993).

Samuel Beckett: The Complete Short Prose 1929–1989, ed. S. E. Gontarski (New York: Grove Press, 1995).

Éleuthéria, tr. Barbara Wright (London and Boston: Faber and Faber, 1996).

How It Is (London: John Calder, 1996).

Proust and Three Dialogues with Georges Duthuit (London: John Calder, 1999).

Warten auf Godot, tr. Elmar Tophoven (Frankfurt am Main: Suhrkamp, 2006).

Beja, Morris, S. E. Gontarski and Pierre Astier (eds.), *Samuel Beckett: Humanistic Perspectives* (Cleveland: Ohio University Press, 1983).

Ben-Zvi, Linda, 'Samuel Beckett's Media Plays', *Modern Drama* 28 (1985), 22–37.

Women in Beckett: Performance and Critical Perspectives (Urbana and Chicago: University of Illinois Press, 1990).

Benson, Michael, 'Moving Bodies in Hardy and Beckett', *Essays in Criticism: A Quarterly Journal of Literary Criticism* 34 (1984), 229–43.

Bergson, Henri, *Time and Free Will: An Essay on the Immediate Data of Consciousness*, tr. F. L. Pogson (London: George Allen, 1912).

Berkeley, George, 'Essay towards a New Theory of Vision', in *A New Theory of Vision and Other Select Philosophical Writings* (London: Dent, 1963), pp. 1–86.

Principles of Human Knowledge and Three Dialogues, ed. Howard Robinson, World's Classics (Oxford and New York: Oxford University Press, 1996).

Bernard, Émile, *Souvenirs sur Paul Cézanne et lettres*, 4th edn. (Paris: La Rénovation Esthétique, 1924).

'From *A Conversation with Cézanne*', in Richard Kendall (ed.), *Cézanne by Himself: Drawings, Paintings, Writings* (London: Macdonald, 1990), pp. 289–93.

Billington, Michael, 'First Night', *Guardian* (18 April 1977), 8.

Blanchot, Maurice, 'The Unnamable', tr. Richard Howard, in Lawrence Graver and Raymond Federman (eds.), *Samuel Beckett: The Critical Heritage* (London and New York: Routledge, 1979), pp. 116–21.

Blanke, Olaf, Theodor Landis, Laurent Spinelli and Margitta Seeck, 'Out-of-body Experience and Autoscopy of Neurological Origin', *Brain* 127 (2004), 243–58.

Borély, Jules, 'From *Cézanne en Aix*', in Richard Kendall (ed.), *Cézanne by Himself: Drawings, Paintings, Writings* (London: Macdonald, 1990), pp. 294–6.

Bourdieu, Pierre, *Distinction: A Social Critique of Taste*, tr. Richard Nice (London: Routledge and Kegan Paul, 1984).

Boxall, Peter, 'Beckett and Homoeroticism', in Lois Oppenheim (ed.), *Palgrave Advances in Samuel Beckett Studies* (Basingstoke: Palgrave Macmillan, 2004), pp. 110–32.

Brater, Enoch, 'Dada, Surrealism, and the Genesis of *Not I*', *Modern Drama* 18 (1975), 49–59.

'The Thinking Eye in Beckett's Film', *Modern Language Quarterly* 36 (1975), 166–76.

'Light, Sound, Movement, and Action in Beckett's *Rockaby*', *Modern Drama* 25 (1982), 342–8.

'Mis-takes, Mathematical and Otherwise, in *The Lost Ones*', *Modern Fiction Studies* 29 (1983), 93–109.

'Toward a Poetics of Television Technology: Beckett's *Nacht und Träume* and *Quad*', *Modern Drama* 28 (1985), 48–54.

(ed.), *Beckett at 80/Beckett in Context* (New York and Oxford: Oxford University Press, 1986).

Beyond Minimalism: Beckett's Late Style in the Theatre (New York: Oxford University Press, 1987).

Why Beckett (London: Thames and Hudson, 1989).

The Drama in the Text: Beckett's Late Fiction (New York and Oxford: Oxford University Press, 1994).

Braun, Marta, *Picturing Time: The Work of Etienne-Jules Marey (1830–1904)* (Chicago: University of Chicago Press, 1992).

Bremmer, Jan and Herman Roodenburg (eds.), *A Cultural History of Gesture: From Antiquity to the Present Day* (Cambridge: Polity, 1993).

Breton, André, *What is Surrealism? Selected Writings*, ed. Franklin Rosemont (London: Pluto Press, 1978).

Breton, André and Louis Aragon, 'Introduction to the Possessions', tr. Samuel Beckett, in André Breton, *What is Surrealism? Selected Writings*, ed. Franklin Rosemont (London: Pluto Press, 1978) pp. 50–1.

Brienza, Susan D, 'The Lost Ones', *Journal of Modern Literature* 6 (1977), 148–68.

Bryden, Mary, *Women in Samuel Beckett's Prose and Drama: Her Own Other* (London: Macmillan, 1993).

(ed.), *Samuel Beckett and Music* (Oxford: Clarendon, 1998).

... *but the clouds* ..., TV play, by Samuel Beckett, dir. Donald McWhinnie and Samuel Beckett, perf. Ronald Pickup and Billie Whitelaw (BBC, 17 April 1977).

Butler, Lance St John, *Samuel Beckett and the Meaning of Being: A Study in Ontological Parable* (London: Macmillan, 1984).

Campbell, Julie, 'Pilgrim's Progress/Regress/Stasis: Some Thoughts on the Treatment of the Quest in Bunyan's *Pilgrim's Progress* and Beckett's *Mercier and Camier*', *Comparative Literature Studies* 30 (1993), 137–52.

Cartwright, Lisa, *Screening the Body: Tracing Medicine's Visual Culture* (Minneapolis: University of Minnesota Press, 1995).

Catanzaro, Mary F., 'The Voice of Absent Love in *Krapp's Last Tape* and *Company*', *Modern Drama* 32 (1989), 401–12.

Cervantes Saavedra, *The Adventures of Don Quixote*, tr. J. M. Cohen (Harmondsworth: Penguin, 1963).

Don Quijote de la Mancha, 2 vols. (Madrid: Ediciones Cátedra, 1989).

Chabert, Pierre, 'Beckett as Director', *Gambit* 7 (1976), 41–63.

'The Body in Beckett's Theatre', *Journal of Beckett Studies* 8 (1982), 23–8.

Cohn, Ruby, *Back to Beckett* (Princeton: Princeton University Press, 1973).

A Beckett Canon (Ann Arbor: University of Michigan Press, 2005).

Connor, Steven, *Samuel Beckett: Repetition, Theory and Text* (Oxford: Blackwell, 1988).

'Over Samuel Beckett's Dead Body', in S. E. Wilmer (ed.), *Beckett in Dublin* (Dublin: Lilliput Press, 1992), pp. 100–8.

'Between Theatre and Theory: Long Observation of the Ray', in John Pilling and Mary Bryden (eds.), *The Ideal Core of the Onion: Reading Beckett Archives* (Reading: Beckett International Foundation, 1992), pp. 79–98.

'The Modern Auditory I', in Roy Porter (ed.), *Rewriting the Self: Histories from the Renaissance to the Present* (London and New York: Routledge, 1997), pp. 203–23.

'Auf schwankendem Boden', in Sabine Folie and Michael Glasmeier (eds.), *Samuel Beckett, Bruce Nauman: Kunsthalle Wien, 4. Februar–30. April 2000*, tr. Wolfgang Astelbauer (Vienna: Die Kunsthalle, 2000), pp. 80–7.

'Shifting Ground', www.stevenconnor.com/beckettnauman/.

Dumbstruck: A Cultural History of Ventriloquism (Oxford: Oxford University Press, 2000).

'Slow Going', *The Yearbook of English Studies* 30 (2000), 153–65.

The Book of Skin (London: Reaktion Books, 2004).

'Michel Serres's *Les Cinq Sens*', in Niran Abbas (ed.), *Mapping Michel Serres* (Ann Arbor: University of Michigan Press, 2005), 153–69.

'The Shakes: Conditions of Tremor', *The Senses and Society* 3 (2008), 205–20.

'Beckett and Sartre: The Nauseous Character of All Flesh', in Ulrika Maude and Matthew Feldman (eds.), *Beckett and Phenomenology* (New York and London: Continuum, in press).

Corominas, J. and J. A. Pascual, *Diccionario Crítico Etimológico Castellano e Hispánico* (Madrid: Editorial Gredos, 1981).

Cousineau, Thomas J., 'The Significance of Repetition in Beckett's *Embers*', *Southern Humanities Review* 19 (1985), 313–21.

Crane, Tim, 'Intentionality', *Routledge Dictionary of Philosophy* (London and New York: Routledge, 1998), pp. 816–21.

Crary, Jonathan, *Techniques of the Observer: On Vision and Modernity in the Nineteenth Century* (Cambridge, MA: MIT Press, 1996).

Cremin, Ann, 'Friend Game', *ARTnews* (May 1985), 82–9.

Critchely, Simon, *Very Little . . . Almost Nothing: Death, Philosophy, Literature* (London and New York: Routledge, 1997).

'Comedy and Finitude: Displacing the Tragic-Heroic Paradigm in Philosophy and Psychoanalysis', *Constellations* 6 (1999), 108–22.

On Humour (London: Routledge, 2002).

Croke, Fionnuala (ed.), *Samuel Beckett: A Passion for Paintings* (Dublin: National Gallery of Ireland, 2006).

Cronin, Anthony, *Samuel Beckett: The Last Modernist* (London: Flamingo, 1997).

Culik, Hugh, 'Mindful of the Body: Medical Allusions in Beckett's *Murphy*', *Eire Ireland* 14 (1977), 84–101.

Danius, Laura, *The Senses of Modernism: Technology, Perception, and Aesthetics* (Ithaca and London: Cornell University Press, 2002).

Davidson, Michael, 'Technologies of Presence: Orality and the Tapevoice of Contemporary Poetics', in Adalaide Morris (ed.), *Sound States: Innovative*

Poetics and Acoustical Technologies (Chapel Hill and London: University of North Carolina Press, 1997), pp. 97–125.

Davies, Paul, 'Three Novels and Four *Nouvelles*: Giving Up the Ghost to Be Born at Last', in John Pilling (ed.), *The Cambridge Companion to Beckett* (Cambridge: Cambridge University Press, 1994), pp. 43–66.

Deleuze, Gilles, 'The Exhausted', tr. Christian Kerslake, *Parallax: A Journal of Metadiscursive Theory and Cultural Practices* 3 (1996), 113–35.

DeLillo, Don, *The Body Artist* (London: Picador, 2002).

Dennett, Daniel C., 'Intentionality', in *Cambridge Dictionary of Philosophy* (Cambridge: Cambridge University Press, 1995), p. 381.

Derrida, Jacques, *Acts of Literature*, ed. Derek Attridge (London and New York: Routledge, 1992).

Descartes, René, *Rules for the Direction of the Mind*, in *The Philosophical Works of Descartes*, vol. I, tr. Elizabeth S. Haldane and G. R. T. Ross (Cambridge: Cambridge University Press, 1975), pp. 1–77.

Discourse on Method, in *The Philosophical Writings of Descartes*, vol. I, tr. J. Cottingham, R. Stoothoff and D. Murdoch (Cambridge: Cambridge University Press, 1985), pp. iii–51.

Principles of Philosophy, tr. Blair Reynolds, Studies in the History of Philosophy 6 (Lewiston, Queenston and Lampeter: Edwin Mellen Press, 1988).

Diamond, Elin, '"THE SOCIETY OF MY LIKES": Beckett's Political Imaginary', *Samuel Beckett Today/Aujourd'hui* 11 (2001), 383–8.

'Feminist Readings of Beckett', in Lois Oppenheim (ed.), *Palgrave Advances in Samuel Beckett Studies* (Basingstoke: Palgrave Macmillan, 2004), pp. 45–67.

Doherty, Gerald, *Theorizing Lawrence: Nine Meditations on Tropological Themes*, Studies in Twentieth-Century British Literature 1 (New York: Peter Lang, 1999).

Dollimore, Jonathan, 'Death and the Self', in Roy Porter (ed.), *Rewriting the Self: Histories from the Renaissance to the Present* (London and New York: Routledge, 1997), pp. 249–61.

Dreyfus, Hubert L., 'The Current Relevance of Merleau-Ponty's Phenomenology of Embodiment', *The Electronic Journal of Analytic Philosophy* 4 (1996), http://ejap.louisiana.edu.

Duckworth, Colin, '*Godot*: Genesis and Composition', in Ruby Cohn (ed.), *Beckett: Waiting for Godot*, Casebook Series (London: Macmillan, 1987), pp. 81–6.

Duerfahrd, Lance, 'Beckett's Circulation: Molloy's Dereliction', *Proceedings of the Twenty-First Annual Meeting of the Semiotic Society of America* (1996), 144–50.

Dyson, Frances, 'When Is the Ear Pierced? The Clashes of Sound, Technology, and Cyberculture', in Mary Anne Moser and Douglas MacLeod (eds.), *Immersed in Technology: Art and Virtual Environments* (Cambridge, MA: MIT Press, 1996), pp. 73–101.

Eagleton, Terry, *Heathcliff and the Great Hunger: Studies in Irish Culture* (London and New York: Verso, 1995).

Sweet Violence: The Idea of the Tragic (Oxford: Blackwell, 2003).

Eh Joe, TV play, by Samuel Beckett, dir. Alan Gibson and Samuel Beckett, perf. Jack MacGowran and Sian Phillips (BBC, 4 July 1966).

Elkins, James, *Pictures of the Body: Pain and Metamorphosis* (Stanford: Stanford University Press, 1999).

Embers, radio play, by Samuel Beckett, dir. Donald McWhinnie (BBC Third Programme, 24 June 1959). Repeated 6 September 1999.

Engelberts, Matthijs, Everett Frost and Jane Maxwell (eds.), *Notes diverse holo: Catalogues of Beckett's Reading Notes and Other Manuscripts at Trinity College Dublin, with Supporting Essays* (Amsterdam: Rodopi, 2006).

Esslin, Martin, 'The Mind as Stage', *Theatre Quarterly* 1 (1971), 5–11.

'Samuel Beckett and the Art of Broadcasting', in Martin Esslin (ed.), *Mediations: Essays on Brecht, Beckett and the Media* (New York: Grove Press, 1982), pp. 125–54.

'Samuel Beckett and the Art of Radio', in S. E. Gontarski (ed.), *On Beckett: Essays and Criticism* (New York: Grove Press, 1986), pp. 360–83.

Fabre-Luce, Anne, 'The Lost Ones', tr. Larysa Mykyta and Mark Schumacher, in Lawrence Graver and Raymond Federman (eds.), *Samuel Beckett: The Critical Heritage* (London and New York: Routledge, 1979), pp. 313–5.

Federman, Raymond, 'Film', in Lawrence Graver and Raymond Federman (eds.), *Samuel Beckett: The Critical Heritage* (London and New York: Routledge, 1979), pp. 275–83.

Feldman, Matthew, *Beckett's Books: A Cultural History of Samuel Beckett's 'Interwar Notes'*, Continuum Literary Studies Series (New York and London: Continuum, 2006).

Feshbach, Sidney, 'Unswamping a Backwater: On Samuel Beckett's *Film*', in Lois Oppenheim (ed.), *Samuel Beckett and the Arts: Music, Visual Arts, and Non-Print Media*, Border Crossings II (New York and London: Garland, 1999), pp. 333–63.

Film, screenplay by Samuel Beckett, dir. Alan Schneider, perf. Buster Keaton (1965, videocassette, Applause, 1999).

Film, screenplay by Samuel Beckett, dir. David R. Clark, perf. Max Wall (UL-AVC, 1979).

Finlayson, James Gordon, 'Adorno: Modern Art, Metaphysics and Radical Evil', *Modernism/Modernity* 10 (2003), 71–95.

Fletcher, John, 'Interpreting Molloy', in Melvin Friedman (ed.), *Samuel Beckett Now: Critical Approaches to the Novels, Poetry and Plays*, 2nd edn. (Chicago and London: University of Chicago Press, 1975), pp. 157–70.

Fletcher, John and John Spurling, *Beckett the Playwright* (New York: Hill and Wang, 1972).

Flynn, Thomas R., 'Foucault and the Eclipse of Vision', in David Michael Levin (ed.), *Modernity and the Hegemony of Vision* (Berkeley: University of California Press, 1993), pp. 273–86.

Foster, Hal, *Prosthetic Gods* (Cambridge, MA and London: MIT Press, 2004).

Foucault, Michel, *Discipline and Punish: The Birth of the Prison*, tr. Alan Sheridan (Harmondsworth: Penguin, 1977).

The Order of Things: An Archaeology of the Human Sciences (London: Routledge, 1986).

Fraser, G. S., 'Waiting for Godot', in Lawrence Graver and Raymond Federman (eds.), *Samuel Beckett: The Critical Heritage* (London and New York: Routledge, 1979), pp. 97–104.

Freud, Sigmund, 'The Anatomy of the Mental Personality', in *New Introductory Lectures on Psychoanalysis*, tr. W. J. H. Sprott (London: Hogarth Press, 1933), pp. 78–106.

'Beyond the Pleasure Principle', in *On Metapsychology: The Theory of Psychoanalysis*, ed. Angela Richards, Penguin Freud Library, vol. II (London: Penguin, 1991), pp. 269–338.

'Civilization and Its Discontents', in *Civilization, Society and Religion*, ed. Albert Dickson, Penguin Freud Library, vol. XII, (Harmondsworth: Penguin, 1991), pp. 243–340.

Frost, Everett C., 'Fundamental Sounds: Recording Samuel Beckett's Radio Plays', *Theatre Journal* 43 (1991), 361–76.

Gallagher, Shaun, 'Body Schema and Intentionality', in José Luis Bermúdez, Anthony Marcel, and Naomi Elian (eds.), *The Body and the Self* (Cambridge, MA: MIT Press, 1995), pp. 225–44.

Geistertrio, TV play, by Samuel Beckett, dir. Samuel Beckett, perf. Klaus Herm and Irmgard Först (SDR, 1 November 1977).

Gespräch Whitelaw-Asmus, TV documentary, dir. Werner Sommer (SDR, 22 July 1988).

Ghost Trio, TV play, by Samuel Beckett, dir. Donald McWhinnie and Samuel Beckett, perf. Ronald Pickup, Billie Whitelaw and Rupert Horder (BBC, 17 April 1977).

Gibson, Andrew, *Towards a Postmodern Theory of Narrative* (Edinburgh: Edinburgh University Press, 1996).

Giddens, Anthony, *The Transformation of Intimacy: Love, Sexuality and Eroticism in Modern Societies* (Cambridge: Polity, 1992).

Gontarski, S. E., '"Making Yourself All Up Again": The Composition of Samuel Beckett's *That Time*', *Modern Drama* 23 (1980), 112–20.

'*Film* and Formal Integrity', in Morris Beja, S. E. Gontarski and Pierre Astier (eds.), *Samuel Beckett: Humanistic Perspectives* (Cleveland: Ohio University Press, 1983), pp. 129–36.

The Intent of Undoing in Samuel Beckett's Dramatic Texts (Bloomington: Indiana University Press, 1985).

(ed.), *On Beckett: Essays and Criticism* (New York: Grove Press, 1986).

'Refiguring, Revising, and Reprinting *The Lost Ones*', *Journal of Beckett Studies* 4 (1995), 99–101.

'Introduction', in S. E. Gontarski (ed.), *Samuel Beckett: The Complete Short Prose 1929–1989* (New York: Grove Press, 1995), pp. xi–xxxii.

(ed.), *The Shorter Plays*, vol. IV of *The Theatrical Notebooks of Samuel Beckett* (London: Faber, 1999).

Gontarski, S. E. and Anthony Uhlmann (eds.), *Beckett after Beckett*, Cross-currents: Comparative Studies in European Literature and Philosophy (Gainesville: University Press of Florida, 2006).

Graver, Lawrence and Raymond Federman (eds.), *Samuel Beckett: The Critical Heritage* (London and New York: Routledge, 1979).

Gregory, Derek, *Geographical Imaginations* (Cambridge, MA and Oxford: Blackwell, 1994).

Gunn, Dan, 'Until the gag is chewed. Samuel Beckett's letters: eloquence and "near speechlessness"', *Times Literary Supplement* (21 April 2007), 13–15.

Guralnick, Elissa S., *Sight Unseen: Beckett, Pinter, Stoppard, and Other Contemporary Dramatists on Radio* (Athens, OH: Ohio University Press, 1996).

Gutting, Gary, *Michel Foucault's Archaeology of Scientific Reason*, Modern European Philosophy (Cambridge: Cambridge University Press, 1989).

Hacking, Ian, '*Automatisme Ambulatoire*: Fugue, Hysteria, and Gender at the Turn of the Century', *Modernism/Modernity* 3 (1996), 31–43.

Mad Travellers: Reflections on the Reality of Transient Mental Illnesses (London: Free Association Books, 1999).

Hale, Jane Alison, *The Broken Window: Beckett's Dramatic Perspective* (West Lafayette, IN: Purdue University Press, 1987).

Hancock, Philip, Bill Hughes, Elizabeth Jagger, Kevin Paterson, Rachel Russell, Emmanuelle Tulle-Winton and Melissa Tyler (eds.), *The Body, Culture and Society* (Buckingham and Philadelphia: Open University Press, 2000).

Harmon, Maurice (ed.), *No Author Better Served: The Correspondence of Samuel Beckett and Alan Schneider* (Cambridge, MA and London: Harvard University Press, 1998).

Harvey, Lawrence, *Samuel Beckett: Poet and Critic* (Princeton: Princeton University Press, 1970).

Hayles, Katharine, 'Voices out of Bodies, Bodies out of Voices: Audiotape and the Production of Subjectivity', in Adalaide Morris (ed.), *Sound States: Innovative Poetics and Acoustical Technologies* (Chapel Hill and London: University of North Carolina Press, 1997), pp. 74–96.

Haynes, John and James Knowlson, *Images of Beckett* (Cambridge: Cambridge University Press, 2003).

Heidegger, Martin, 'The Age of the World Picture', in *The Question Concerning Technology and Other Essays*, tr. William Lovitt (New York: Harper & Row, 1977), pp. 115–54.

'The Question Concerning Technology', in *The Question Concerning Technology and Other Essays*, tr. William Lovitt (New York: Harper & Row, 1977), pp. 3–35.

Henning, Sylvie Debevec, '"Film": A Dialogue between Beckett and Berkeley', *Journal of Beckett Studies* 7 (1982), 89–99.

Beckett's Critical Complicity: Carnival, Contestation, and Tradition (Lexington, KY: University Press of Kentucky, 1988).

Hill, Leslie, *Beckett's Fiction in Different Words* (Cambridge: Cambridge University Press, 1990).

Hull, John, *Touching the Rock: An Experience of Blindness* (London: SPCK Publishing, 1990).

Ihde, Don, *Sense and Significance* (Pittsburgh: Duquesne University Press, 1973).

Listening and Voice (Athens, OH: Ohio University Press, 1976).

Bodies in Technology, Electronic Mediations, vol. V (Minneapolis: University of Minnesota Press, 2002).

Jagger, Elizabeth, 'Consumer Bodies', in Phil Hancock, Bill Hughes, Elizabeth Jagger, Kevin Paterson, Rachel Russell, Emmanuelle Tulle-Winton and Melissa Tyler (eds.), *The Body, Culture and Society* (Buckingham and Philadelphia: Open University Press, 2000), pp. 45–63.

Jay, Martin, *Downcast Eyes: The Denigration of Vision in Twentieth-Century French Thought* (Berkeley: University of California Press, 1993).

Jeffers, Jennifer (ed.), *Samuel Beckett: A Casebook* (New York and London: Garland, 1998).

Johnson, Galen A. 'Phenomenology and Painting: "Cézanne's Doubt"', in Galen A. Johnson (ed.),*The Merleau-Ponty Aesthetics Reader: Philosophy and Painting*, Northwestern University Studies in Phenomenology and Existential Philosophy (Evanston: Northwestern University Press, 1993), pp. 3–13.

'Structures and Painting: "Indirect Language and the Voices of Silence"', in Galen A. Johnson (ed.),*The Merleau-Ponty Aesthetics Reader: Philosophy and Painting*, Northwestern University Studies in Phenomenology and Existential Philosophy (Evanston: Northwestern University Press, 1993), pp. 14–34.

Jonas, Hans, *The Phenomenon of Life: Toward a Philosophical Biology* (New York: Delta, 1966).

Jones, Ernest, *Treatment of the Neuroses: Psychotherapy from Rest Cure to Psychoanalysis* (New York: Schocken Books, 1963).

Papers on Psycho-Analysis (London: Baillière, Tindall and Cox, 1923).

Josipovici, Gabriel, *Touch* (New Haven and London: Yale University Press, 1996).

Joyce, James, *Ulysses* (Harmondsworth: Penguin, 1992).

Kahn, Douglas, 'Introduction: Histories of Sound Once Removed', in Douglas Kahn and Gregory Whitehead (eds.), *Wireless Imagination: Sound, Radio, and the Avant-Garde* (Cambridge, MA: MIT Press, 1992), pp. 1–29.

Kahn, Douglas and Gregory Whitehead (eds.), *Wireless Imagination: Sound, Radio, and the Avant-Garde* (Cambridge, MA: MIT Press, 1992).

Kalb, Jonathan, *Beckett in Performance* (Cambridge: Cambridge University Press, 1989).

'The Mediated Quixote: The Radio and Television Plays', in John Pilling (ed.), *The Cambridge Companion to Samuel Beckett* (Cambridge: Cambridge University Press, 1994), pp. 124–44.

Kember, Sarah, 'Medicine's New Vision?' in Martin Lister (ed.), *The Photographic Image in Digital Culture* (Abingdon: Routledge, 1995), pp. 95–114.

'Surveillance, Technology and Crime', in Martin Lister (ed.), *The Photographic Image in Digital Culture* (Abingdon: Routledge, 1995), pp. 115–126.

Kenner, Hugh, *Samuel Beckett: A Critical Study* (Glasgow: John Calder, 1962).
   The Mechanic Muse (New York: Oxford University Press, 1987).
   A Reader's Guide to Samuel Beckett (London: Thames and Hudson, 1988).
Kern, Stephen, *The Culture of Time and Space 1880–1918* (Cambridge, MA and London: Harvard University Press, 2003).
Kerslake, Christian, 'The Exhausted: Translator's Introduction', *Parallax* 3 (1996), 113–15.
Kiberd, Declan, *Inventing Ireland* (London: Jonathan Cape, 1995).
Kittler, Friedrich A., *Gramophone, Film, Typewriter*, tr. Geoffrey Winthrop-Young and Michael Wutz (Stanford: Stanford University Press, 1999).
Knowlson, James, '*Ghost Trio/Geister Trio*', in Enoch Brater (ed.), *Beckett at 80/Beckett in Context* (New York and Oxford: Oxford University Press, 1986), pp. 193–207.
   (ed.), *The Theatrical Notebooks of Samuel Beckett*, vol. III, *Krapp's Last Tape* (London: Faber and Faber, 1992).
   Damned to Fame: The Life of Samuel Beckett (London: Bloomsbury, 1996).
Knowlson, James and John Pilling, *Frescoes of the Skull: The Later Prose and Drama of Samuel Beckett* (London: Calder, 1979).
Krapp's Last Tape, film, by Samuel Beckett, dir. Atom Egoyan, perf. John Hurt (RTÉ and Channel 4, 2000).
Kristeva, Julia, *Powers of Horror: An Essay on Abjection*, tr. Leon S. Roudiez (New York: Columbia University Press, 1982).
Kunst, Bojana, 'The Digital Body: History of Body Visibility', in Nina Czegledy (ed.), *Digitized Bodies: Virtual Spectacles* (Budapest: Ludwig Museum, 2001), pp. 13–27.
Lakoff, George and Mark Turner, *More Than Cool Reason: A Field Guide to Poetic Metaphor* (Chicago: University of Chicago Press, 1989).
Lamartine, Alphonse de, *Méditations poétiques: choix de poèmes*, ed. Suzette Jacrès (Paris: Larousse, 1968).
Langer, Monika M., *Merleau-Ponty's Phenomenology of Perception: A Guide and Commentary* (London: Macmillan, 1989).
Lawley, Paul, '"Embers"; an interpretation', *Journal of Beckett Studies* 6 (1980), 9–36.
   'Stages of Identity: From *Krapp's Last Tape* to *Play*', in John Pilling (ed.), *The Cambridge Companion to Beckett* (Cambridge: Cambridge University Press, 1994), pp. 88–105.
Lecourt, Édith, 'The Musical Envelope', in Didier Anzieu (ed.), *Psychic Envelopes*, tr. Daphne Briggs (London: Karnac Books, 1990), pp. 211–35.
Lee, Robin, 'The Fictional Topography of Samuel Beckett', in Gabriel Josipovici (ed.), *The Modern English Novel: The Reader, the Writer and the Work* (London: Open Books, 1976), pp. 206–24.
Levin, David M., *The Opening of Vision: Nihilism and the Postmodern Situation* (New York: Routledge, 1988).
Levy, Eric P., 'Looking for Beckett's Lost Ones', *Mosaic* 12 (1979), 163–70.
   Beckett and the Voice of Species: A Study of the Prose Fiction (Totowa, NJ: Barnes & Noble, 1980).

Libera, Antoni, 'Structure and Pattern in "That Time"', *Journal of Beckett Studies* 6 (1980), 81–9.

'The Lost Ones: A Myth of Human History and Destiny', in Morris Beja, S. E. Gontarski and Pierre Astier (eds.), *Samuel Beckett: Humanistic Perspectives* (Cleveland: Ohio University Press, 1983), pp. 145–56.

Lyons, Charles, 'Beckett's Fundamental Theatre: The Plays from *Not I* to *What Where*', in James Acheson and Kateryna Arthur (eds.), *Beckett's Later Fiction and Drama: Texts for Company* (Basingstoke: Macmillan, 1987), pp. 80–97.

Lyotard, Jean-François, *Phenomenology*, tr. Brian Beakley (Albany: State University of New York Press, 1991).

'Can Thought Go On without a Body?', in *The Inhuman: Reflections on Time*, tr. Geoffrey Bennington and Rachel Bowlby (Stanford: Stanford University Press, 1991), pp. 8–23.

Maier, Michael, 'Nacht und Träume. Schubert, Beckett und das Fernsehen', *Acta Musicologica* 68 (1996), 167–86.

'Geistertrio: Beethovens Musik in Samuel Becketts zweitem Fernsehspiel', *Archiv für Musikwissenschaft* 57 (2000), 172–94.

Mann, Thomas, *The Magic Mountain*, tr. John E. Woods (New York: Alfred A. Knopf, 1995).

The Magic Mountain, tr. H. T. Lowe-Porter (London: Vintage, 1999).

Marinetti, F. T., *Let's Murder the Moonshine: Selected Writings*, ed. R. W. Flint, tr. R. W. Flint and Arthur A. Coppotelli (Los Angeles: Sun & Moon Classics, 1991).

'Tactilism', in F. T. Marinetti, *Let's Murder the Moonshine: Selected Writings*, ed. R. W. Flint, tr. R. W. Flint and Arthur A. Coppotelli (Los Angeles: Sun & Moon Classics, 1991), pp. 117–20.

'Technical Manifesto of Futurist Literature', in F. T. Marinetti, *Let's Murder the Moonshine: Selected Writings*, ed. R. W. Flint, tr. R. W. Flint and Arthur A. Coppotelli (Los Angeles: Sun & Moon Classics, 1991), pp. 92–7.

Marinetti, F. T. and Pino Masnata, 'La Radia', in Douglas Kahn and Gregory Whitehead (eds.), *Wireless Imagination: Sound, Radio, and the Avant-Garde* (Cambridge, MA: MIT Press, 1992), pp. 265–8.

Martin, Jean, 'Creating Godot', in S. E. Wilmer (ed.), *Beckett in Dublin* (Dublin: Lilliput Press, 1992), pp. 25–32.

Mason, Rainer Michael (ed.), *Bram van Velde: 1895–1981* (Geneva: Musée RATH, 1996).

Mauss, Marcel, 'Body Techniques', in *Sociology and Psychology: Essays*, tr. Ben Brewster (London, Boston and Henley: Routledge & Kegan Paul, 1979), pp. 95–123.

Mays, J. C. C., 'Irish Beckett: A Borderline Instance', in S. E. Wilmer (ed.), *Beckett in Dublin* (Dublin: Lilliput Press, 1992), pp. 133–46.

McLuhan, Marshall, *Understanding Media: The Extensions of Man* (London: Routledge & Kegan Paul, 1964).

McMillan, Dougald, 'Samuel Beckett and the Visual Arts: The Embarrasment of Allegory', in S. E. Gontarski (ed.), *On Beckett: Essays and Criticism* (New York: Grove Press, 1986), pp. 29–45.

McMillan, Dougald and James Knowlson (eds.), *The Theatrical Notebooks of Samuel Beckett*, vol. I, *Waiting for Godot* (London: Faber and Faber, 1993).

McMullan, Audrey, 'Samuel Beckett's *Cette fois*: Between Time(s) and Space(s)', *French Studies* XLIV (1990), 424–39.

McMullan, Anna, *Theatre on Trial: Samuel Beckett's Later Drama* (New York and London: Routledge, 1993).

McNay, Lois, *Foucault: A Critical Introduction* (Cambridge: Polity, 1994).

McWhinnie, Donald, *The Art of Radio* (London: Faber, 1959).

Menzies, Janet, 'Beckett's Bicycles', *Journal of Beckett Studies* 6 (1980), 97–105.

Mercier, Vivian, 'The Uneventful Event', *Irish Times*, 18 February 1956, p. 6.

Beckett/Beckett (New York: Oxford University Press, 1977).

Merleau-Ponty, Maurice, *The Primacy of Perception, and Other Essays on Phenomenological Psychology, the Philosophy of Art, History and Politics*, ed. James M. Edie (Evanston, IL: Northwestern University Press, 1964).

'The Primacy of Perception and Its Philosophical Consequences', tr. James M. Edie, in *The Primacy of Perception and Other Essays on Phenomenological Psychology, the Philosophy of Art, History and Politics* (Evanston, IL: Northwestern University Press, 1964), pp. 12–42.

Phenomenology of Perception, tr. Colin Smith (London: Routledge, 1992).

'Cezanne's Doubt', tr. Michael B. Smith, in Galen A. Johnson, *The Merleau-Ponty Aesthetics Reader: Philosophy and Painting*, Northwestern University Studies in Phenomenology and Existential Philosophy (Evanston: Northwestern University Press, 1993), pp. 59–75.

'Indirect Language and the Voices of Silence', tr. Michael B. Smith, in Galen A. Johnson, *The Merleau-Ponty Aesthetics Reader: Philosophy and Painting*, Northwestern University Studies in Phenomenology and Existential Philosophy (Evanston: Northwestern University Press, 1993), pp. 76–120.

'Eye and Mind', tr. Michael B. Smith, in Galen A. Johnson, *The Merleau-Ponty Aesthetics Reader: Philosophy and Painting*, Northwestern University Studies in Phenomenology and Existential Philosophy (Evanston: Northwestern University Press, 1993), pp. 121–49.

Mitchell, Timothy, 'The World as Exhibition', *Comparative Studies in Society and History* 31 (1989), 217–36.

Monaco, James, *How to Read a Film* (New York: Oxford University Press, 2000).

Montagu, Ashley, *Touching: The Human Significance of the Skin*, 3rd edn. (New York: Harper & Row, 1986).

Moorjani, Angela, 'A Cryptanalysis of Beckett's *Molloy*', in Joseph H. Smith (ed.), *The World of Samuel Beckett*, Psychiatry and the Humanities 12 (Baltimore and London: Johns Hopkins University Press, 1991), pp. 53–72.

Morris, Adalaide (ed.), *Sound States: Innovative Poetics and Acoustical Technologies* (Chapel Hill and London: University of North Carolina Press, 1997).

Morris, Frances (ed.), *Paris Post-War: Art and Existentialism 1945–55* (London: Tate Gallery, 1993).

Murphy, Peter, 'The Nature of Allegory in The Lost Ones, or the Quincunx Realistically Considered', *Journal of Beckett Studies* 7 (1982), 71–88.

Müller-Freienfels, Reinhart, 'Samuel Beckett: "We Do It to Have Fun Together" (Erinnerungen an Beckett in Stuttgart)', Südwestrundfunk Historical Archives, Stuttgart.

Nacht und Träume, TV play, by Samuel Beckett, dir. Samuel Beckett, perf. Helfrid Foron, Stephan Pritz and Dirk Morgner (SDR, 19 May 1983).

Nixon, Mark, 'Samuel Beckett's "Film Vidéo-Cassette projet"', in Ulrika Maude and David Pattie (eds.), *Beckett on TV*, special issue of *Journal of Beckett Studies* (in press).

Noise, radio programme, by Steven Connor, prod. Tim Dee, five episodes (BBC Radio 3, 24–28 February 1997).

. . . nur noch Gewölk . . ., TV play, by Samuel Beckett, dir. Samuel Beckett, perf. Claus Herm and Cornelia Boje (SDR, 1 November 1977).

O'Brien, Eoin, *The Beckett Country* (London: Black Cat Press and Faber, 1986).

Ong, Walter J., *The Presence of the Word: Some Prolegomena for Cultural and Religious History* (New Haven and London: Yale University Press, 1967).

Oppenheim, Lois (ed.), *Samuel Beckett and the Arts: Music, Visual Arts, and Non-Print Media*, Border Crossings II (New York and London: Garland, 1999).

The Painted Word: Samuel Beckett's Dialogue with Art (Ann Arbor: University of Michigan Press, 2000).

Palgrave Advances in Samuel Beckett Studies (Basingstoke: Palgrave Macmillan, 2004).

Oxford English Dictionary, 2nd edn. 'Record', v., Ia; 'Yield', v., III (Oxford: Oxford University Press, 1989).

Perloff, Marjorie, 'The Silence That Is Not Silence: Acoustic Art in Samuel Beckett's Embers', in Lois Oppenheim (ed.), *Samuel Beckett and the Arts: Music, Visual Arts, and Non-Print Media*, Border Crossings II (New York and London: Garland, 1999), pp. 247–68.

Piette, Adam, 'Beckett, Early Neuropsychology and Memory Loss: Beckett's Reading of Clarapède, Janet and Korsakoff', *Samuel Beckett Today/Aujourd'hui* 2 (1993), 41–8.

Pilling, John, *Samuel Beckett* (London: Routledge & Kegan Paul, 1976).

'Beckett: "That's not moving, that's moving"', in Elizabeth Masten (ed.), *The Timeless and the Temporal: Writings in Honour of John Chalker by Friends and Colleagues* (Queen Mary and Westfield College, University of London: Department of English, 1993), pp. 393–403.

(ed.), *The Cambridge Companion to Samuel Beckett* (Cambridge: Cambridge University Press, 1994).

(ed.), *Beckett's Dream Notebook* (Reading: Beckett International Foundation, 1999).

A Samuel Beckett Chronology, Author Chronologies (Basingstoke: Palgrave Macmillan, 2006).

Pitres, A., *Leçons cliniques sur l'hystérie et l'hypnotisme faites à l'hôpital Saint-André à Bordeaux*, vol. II (Paris: Doin, 1891).

Porter, Roy (ed.), *Rewriting the Self: Histories from the Renaissance to the Present* (London and New York: Routledge, 1997).

The Greatest Benefit to Mankind (London: Fontana, 1999).

Porush, David, 'Technology and Postmodernism: Cybernetic Fiction', *Substance: Current Trends in American Fiction* 27 (1980), 92–100.

'Beckett's Deconstruction of the Machine in The Lost Ones', *L'Esprit Créateur* 26 (1986), 87–98.

Pound, Ezra, *Machine Art and Other Writings: The Lost Thought of the Italian Years*, ed. Maria Luisa Ardizzone (Durham, NC: Duke University Press, 1966).

Pountney, Rosemary, '*EMBERS*: An Interpretation', *Samuel Beckett Today/ Aujourd'hui* 2 (1993), 269–73.

'Beckett and the Camera', *Samuel Beckett Today/Aujourd'hui: The Savage Eye/ L'oeil fauve* 4 (1995), 41–52.

Prieto, Eric, 'Caves: Technology and the Total Artwork in Reich's *The Cave* and Beckett's *Ghost Trio*', *Mosaic: A Journal for the Interdisciplinary Study of Literature* 35 (2002), 197–213.

Prinz, Jessica, 'Resonant Images: Beckett and German Expressionism', in Lois Oppenheim (ed.), *Samuel Beckett and the Arts: Music, Visual Arts, and Non-Print Media*, Border Crossings II (New York and London: Garland, 1999), pp. 153–71.

Quadrat I & II, TV plays, by Samuel Beckett, dir. Samuel Beckett, perf. Helfrid Foron, Jürg Hummel, Claudia Knupfer and Susanne Rehe (SDR, 8 October 1981).

Rabinbach, Anson, *The Human Motor: Energy, Fatigue, and the Origins of Modernity* (Berkeley: University of California Press, 1992).

Rée, Jonathan, *I See a Voice: A Philosophical History of Language, Deafness and the Senses* (London: HarperCollins, 1999).

Reiser, Stanley Joel, *Medicine and the Reign of Technology* (New York: Cambridge University Press, 1978).

'Technology and the Use of the Senses in Twentieth-Century Medicine', in W. F. Bynum and Roy Porter (eds.), *Medicine and the Five Senses* (Cambridge: Cambridge University Press, 1993), pp. 262–73.

Renard, Jules, *The Journals of Jules Renard*, ed. and tr. Louise Bogan and Elizabeth Roget (New York: George Braziller, 1964).

Ricks, Christopher, *Beckett's Dying Words* (Oxford: Oxford University Press, 1995).

Ricoeur, Paul, *The Conflict of Interpretations*, tr. Don Ihde (Evanston, IL: Northwestern University Press, 1974).

Rodaway, Paul, *Sensuous Geographies: Body, Sense and Place* (London and New York: Routledge, 1994).

Russell, Rachel, 'Ethical Bodies', in Phil Hancock, Bill Hughes, Elizabeth Jagger, Kevin Paterson, Rachel Russell, Emmanuelle Tulle-Winton and Melissa Tyler (eds.), *The Body, Culture and Society* (Buckingham and Philadelphia: Open University Press, 2000), pp. 101–16.

Sartre, Jean-Paul, *Being and Nothingness: An Essay on Phenomenological Ontology*, tr. Hazel E. Barnes (London and New York: Routledge, 2007).

Scarry, Elaine, *The Body in Pain: The Making and Unmaking of the World* (New York and Oxford: Oxford University Press, 1985).

Schapiro, Meyer, *Paul Cézanne* (London: Thames and Hudson, 1988).

Schneider, Alan, 'On Directing Film', *Samuel Beckett Today/Aujourd'hui 4: The Savage Eye/L'oeil fauve* (1995), 29–40.

Sennett, Richard, *Flesh and Stone: The Body and the City in Western Civilization* (London: Faber, 1994).

Serres, Michel, *Les Cinq sens* (Paris: Hachette, 1998).

Siccama, Wilma, 'Samuel Beckett's *Film* and the Dynamics of Spectating: Our Look is Turned on Us', *European Journal for Semiotic Studies* 9 (1997), 201–22.

Stanney, Kay M., Ronald R. Mourant and Robert S. Kennedy, 'Human Factors Issues in Virtual Environments: A Review of the Literature', *Presence* 7 (1998), 327–51.

Sturken, Marita and Lisa Cartwright, *Practices of Looking: An Introduction to Visual Culture* (Oxford: Oxford University Press, 2001).

Tajiri, Yoshiki, *Samuel Beckett and the Prosthetic Body: The Organs and Senses in Modernism* (Basingstoke: Palgrave Macmillan, 2007).

The Other Beckett 2, radio programme, by Martin Esslin (BBC Radio 3, 7 September 1999).

Turner, Bryan S., *The Body and Society: Explorations in Social Theory*, 2nd edn (London: Sage, 1996).

Uhlmann, Anthony, *Beckett and Poststructuralism* (Cambridge: Cambridge University Press, 1999).

   Samuel Beckett and the Philosophical Image (Cambridge: Cambridge University Press, 2006).

Van Laan, Thomas F., '*All That Fall* as "a Play for Radio"', *Modern Drama* 28 (1985), 38–47.

Voigts-Virchow, Eckhart, 'Exhausted Cameras – Beckett in the TV-Zoo', in Jennifer Jeffers (ed.), *Samuel Beckett: A Casebook* (New York and London: Garland, 1998), pp. 225–49.

   'Face Values: Beckett Inc., the Camera Plays and Cultural Liminity', *Journal of Beckett Studies* 10 (2002), 119–35.

Waiting for Beckett, documentary film, prod. and dir. John Reilly and Melissa Shaw-Smith (Warwick, NY: Global Village, 1994).

Was Wo, TV play, by Samuel Beckett, dir. Samuel Beckett, perf. Friedhelm Becker, Alfred Querbach, Edwin Dorner and Walter Lagnitz (SDR, 13 April 1986).

Weller, Shane, *Beckett, Literature, and the Ethics of Alterity* (Basingstoke: Palgrave Macmillan, 2006).

   'Phenomenologies of the Nothing: Democritus, Heidegger, Beckett', in Ulrika Maude and Matthew Feldman (eds.), *Beckett and Phenomenology* (New York and London: Continuum, in press).

What Where, film, by Samuel Beckett, dir. S. E. Gontarski and John Reilly, perf. Richard Wagner, Tom Luce, Dave Peichert and Morgan Upton (Warwick, NY: Global Village, 1988).

Wilcher, Robert, ' "Out of the Dark": Beckett's Texts for Radio', in James Acheson and Kateryna Arthur (eds.), *Beckett's Later Fiction and Drama: Texts for Company* (Basingstoke: Macmillan, 1987), pp. 1–17.

Wilmer, S. E. (ed.), *Beckett in Dublin* (Dublin: Lilliput Press, 1992).

Wood, Rupert, 'An Endgame of Aesthetics: Beckett as Essayist', in John Pilling (ed.), *The Cambridge Companion to Beckett* (Cambridge: Cambridge University Press, 1994), pp. 1–16.

Woolf, Virginia. 'Street Haunting: A London Adventure', *The Death of the Moth and Other Essays* (London: Hogarth Press, 1943), pp. 19–29.

'On Being Ill', *Selected Essays*, ed. David Bradshaw, Oxford World's Classics (Oxford: Oxford University Press, 2008), pp. 101–10.

Worth, Katharine, 'Beckett and the Radio Medium', in *British Radio Drama*, ed. John Drakakis (Cambridge: Cambridge University Press, 1981), pp. 191–217.

Yeats, William Butler, *The Major Works*, ed. Edward Larrissy (Oxford: Oxford University Press, 2001).

Zilliacus, Clas, *Beckett and Broadcasting: A Study of the Works of Samuel Beckett for and in Radio and Television*, Acta Academiae Aboensis, Ser. A, Humanoira 51: 2 (Åbo, Finland: Åbo Akademi, 1976).

'All That Fall and Radio Language', in Lois Oppenheim (ed.), *Samuel Beckett and the Arts: Music, Visual Arts, and Non-Print Media*, Border Crossings II (New York and London: Garland, 1999), pp. 295–310.

Index

Lightning Source UK Ltd.
Milton Keynes UK
03 December 2010

163841UK00001B/31/P